HIGHLAND PARK

Borough of Homes

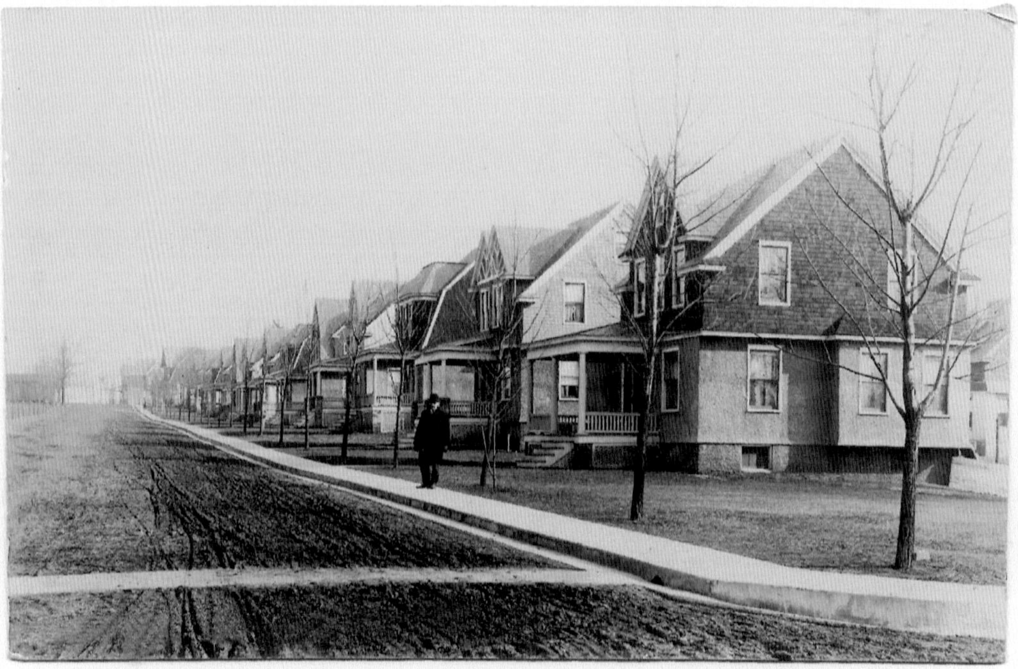

Watson Whittlesey's Livingston Manor, 1906. This postcard was created to promote Whittlesey's new development on Highland Park's north side. The photograph shows the first group of houses constructed in 1906 on Grant Avenue.

THE MAKING OF AMERICA

HIGHLAND PARK

Borough of Homes

JEANNE KOLVA AND JOANNE PISCIOTTA
FOR THE HIGHLAND PARK HISTORICAL SOCIETY

ARCADIA PUBLISHING

ISBN 978-0-7385-2472-6

Published by Arcadia Publishing
Charleston, South Carolina

Printed in the United States of America

Library of Congress Catalog Card Number: 2005923396

For all general information contact Arcadia Publishing at:
Telephone 843-853-2070
Fax 843-853-0044
E-mail sales@arcadiapublishing.com
For customer service and orders:
Toll-Free 1-888-313-2665

Visit us on the Internet at www.arcadiapublishing.com

CONTENTS

ACKNOWLEDGMENTS

It has been a pleasure working on this manuscript and I would like to offer at least one million thanks to my family and friends for their support. This is a wonderful town and I am proud to serve as borough historian. While Joanne and I tried to include everything in this text, we realize that there are still missing pieces and therefore, the work of this historian presumably will be never ending. I dedicate this book to my dears, the three Rice members of my family—Geno, Dan, and Becky.

—Jeanne Kolva

My paternal relatives were among the first Italian-Americans in town. Originally from Sicily, they lived in New Orleans, Albany, and Boston before moving to New Jersey in the early part of the twentieth century. Frank and Flora, my grandparents, and their four sons and one daughter settled on Karsey Street, a very rural and undeveloped area of Highland Park, when my father Ted, or "Sal," was only a baby. Later four more sons were born to the couple.

The siblings grew up, left home, returned, and married. An older child, Carl, Highland Park's building inspector, was caught up in the town's political wars of the 1950s. My father, Ted, became the first college graduate in the family. A younger child, Frank, became a medical doctor. Richard, the youngest and a World War II veteran, published a twenty-two page rhymed poem depicting his youth on Karsey Street during the 1920s.

Masons by trade, my relatives built a number of homes on the street to accommodate their expanding extended family. At one time there were six Pisciotta owned homes on Karsey Street. Eventually our family homes spread onto other nearby streets.

Spanning several generations, these relatives were eyewitnesses to and, in some cases, actors in the many events discussed in this book. My Uncle Joe glided across the floor of the dance hall in Forest Park after its establishment across the street. Uncle Frank and his friend Felix Farenga stole rides on the merry-go-round. Later, Uncle Richie played among the park's ruins.

I too lived my earliest years on Karsey Street. I attended both Irving and Lafayette Schools, as did my father a generation earlier. Along with my cousins

Ginger and Flora Muhleisen and my brother Teddy, I played in the woods of the Peach Orchard. Over the years I saw great changes in the southeast section of Highland Park. I saw acres of wooded land become acres of apartment complexes. I saw the paving of streets and the establishment of house-to-house mail delivery.

Although living in town my entire life, there was much about Highland Park's history I did not know. Researching this book unearthed many interesting town facts and brought me closer to my own family history as well. It was a very emotional experience.

Today all the members of Frank and Flora's original family are deceased and their grandchildren and great-grandchildren are scattered throughout the United States. It is to these original Karsey Street relatives, and especially to the memory of Mary Myers Pisciotta and Theodore Pisciotta, my parents, that I dedicate this book.

—Joanne Pisciotta

INTRODUCTION

The pictorial history published in 1999, *Images of America: Highland Park, New Jersey*, was a fine tribute to our community but was confined by what had been photographed, drawn, or printed in the past. The text supported the images. However, the written word can reveal many more facts about this town's past, especially those that have not been recorded as pictures, but recorded as earlier texts. The co-authors of the 1999 pictorial, Jeanne Kolva and Joanne Pisciotta, found it necessary to write a second book about Highland Park, and a proposal was accepted by Arcadia to include this town in their Making of America series. After Ms. Kolva compiled information from newspapers on microfilm and Ms. Pisciotta read through numerous volumes of Borough Council minutes, the writing tasks were divided into two parts. Ms. Kolva wrote about the earliest inhabitants, the Lenape up to those living in the 1910s, and Ms. Pisciotta wrote about the town from 1920 to the present day.

This volume includes previously unknown facts about important people such as the Reverend Caughey, A.J. Gebhardt, Robert Wood Johnson Jr., and Chrissie Bartle, who resided and worked here. Research revealed that our colonial past was defined by a few large farmsteads, a mill, and a ferry tavern. The pattern of development begun in the nineteenth century continued until it resulted in the borough of homes we know and love today. Our relationship with the city of New Brunswick across the Raritan River is acknowledged, but the focus is on our separate growth within the boundaries established in 1905, the year the Borough of Highland Park was born. How appropriate that this volume is to be printed in the borough's centennial year. Documenting the borough has also revealed how much of our town's heritage is no longer visible due to the demolition of many of our earliest buildings by fire and bulldozer. Politics shaped much of the town's growth throughout the twentieth century and the town weathered many of that century's catastrophes with aplomb.

This book is also a tribute to those who wrote about, photographed, and gathered information about specific elements of the town, making it more accessible to the present authors. To those earlier historians, especially the myriad of anonymous newspaper reporters who did not even know that this was to be their role, we owe our gratitude.

Chapter One

SEVENTEENTH AND EIGHTEENTH CENTURIES

The history of the nation is only the history of its villages writ large.
—Woodrow Wilson, 1895

Upon hearing the descriptive name "Highland Park" for the compact borough in Middlesex County, New Jersey, relativity must be kept in mind because the town is situated on land that is only 60 to 120 feet above sea level on the eastern bank of the Raritan River. However, it stands across the wide, tidal river and a broad flood plain from the city of New Brunswick, whose downtown is at an even lower elevation. Highland Park's mature street trees also form a park-like green canopy over the houses and streets below, but the densely built and maturing suburban town no longer resembles the undeveloped woodlands it was like when it received its descriptive name in the second half of the nineteenth century.

The borough does not have a unique name. It is also the name of towns in several other states, most famously Highland Park, Illinois, as well as numerous local parks throughout the country. Nevertheless, the Borough of Highland Park, New Jersey covers a little under two square miles of land situated in the broad Piedmont Uplands section of the Piedmont physiographic zone that covers much of eastern New Jersey. The underlying Brunswick formation of red shale and sandstone dates from the Triassic era of 180 to 150 million years ago. The Raritan River cuts across this formation creating a boundary between the Piedmont Uplands and the Coastal Plain physiographic zone to the south. After the retreat of the great Wisconsin glacier from the last ice age, New Jersey's land, like much of the United States eastern seaboard, became covered with the great Eastern Deciduous forests. The town's geography plays but a little role in its history, which was written largely by the successive waves of inhabitants that have settled upon this relatively high and park-like land.

Although the Lenape lived for more than 7,000 years in the region that would later include the land within Highland Park's boundaries, the indigenous people left little permanent record. Woodland Indians never developed a system of writing and few of their material remains have been unearthed even close to the Highland Park vicinity. Herbert C. Kraft, the authoritative author of *The Lenape-Delaware Indian Heritage*, wrote that the central New Jersey Lenape who lived along the Raritan River were speakers of the Munsee dialect of the Algonquinn family of languages. "Lenape" has been variously translated to mean "common person," "men of the same nation," and "real person." Archeological advances within the last fifty years have revealed evidence that Paleo-Indians first entered the area approximately 12,000 years ago. It was a colder climate then and animals, including mastodons and caribou, were plentiful. Fluted points used for hunting have been discovered in New Jersey.

Later periods brought people sustained by small game hunting, fishing, and the gathering of nuts, berries, and wild roots. Technology including cooking pots and storage containers indicated that the hunter/gatherers became horticulturists. A ceramic bowl from the late Archaic period was found nearby along the Raritan River in South Amboy. There is also physical evidence of more complex nomadic lives during the Late Woodland Period that included the use of bows and arrows, canoes for traveling, and beads for trade.

Archeologists reasonably have concluded that Highland Park's hard and rocky soil was too great an obstacle for the Lenape's agricultural methods, which did not incorporate metal farm tools or work animals. The late Woodland period was the era of the Lenapes' first encounters with European explorers.

Historians rely on Europeans' reports for written information about the Lenape; however, many of these writing are prejudiced, short, and faulty. There are no known accounts from the Lenapes' point-of-view. In 1609, Henry Hudson was a casual observer of the Lenape on his third trip up the river that would later bear his name. Another observer, Van Tienhoven of New Netherlands, wrote on March 4, 1650,

> The district inhabited by a nation called the Raritangs is situated on a fresh water river that flows through the center of the lowland which the Indians cultivated. It is the handsomest and pleasantest country that man can behold and furnished the Indians with abundance of maize, beans, pumpkins and other fruits. This district was abandoned by the natives for two reasons: the first and principal is that finding themselves unable to resist the southern Indians [Shawnese] they migrated further inland; the second, because the country is flooded every spring frequently spoiling and destroying their supplies of maize which were stored in holes underground.

New Jersey's early Dutch settlers described the new land in letters and remonstrances. In 1649, Dutchman Adriaen Van Der Donck shared his impressions of the New World land he had lived upon since 1641: "the land is fertile and capable of being entirely cultivated by an abundance of people, were it judiciously divided according to circumstances." It would be only in a few short years that the land on the eastern bank of the Raritan River would begin to be so judiciously divided and cultivated.

In 1664, the English took over New Jersey's land from the Dutch. Richard P. McCormick, in *New Jersey from Colony to State*, outlines this early history. James Duke of York executed deeds of lease and release for part of his American territory. With the signing of these deeds on June 23 and 24, 1664, the separate history of New Jersey as a colony began when Lord John Berkeley, Baron of Stratton; and Sir George Carteret of Saltrum were given full ownership of the land. Berkeley's portion was in the west and Carteret's in the east. They assumed that their new roles as proprietors came with the power to appoint the public officials, create courts, make laws, create towns, and establish militias. However, unbeknownst to Berkeley and Carteret, the Duke of York had sent a governor, Colonel Richard Nicholls, to administer the New Jersey lands. Nicholls had already proceeded to parcel out the land in large tracts to groups of owners.

In 1664, John Bailey, Daniel Denton, and Luke Watson, a group from Jamaica, Long Island calling themselves "the associates," purchased from the Lenape a region that extended north from the Raritan River to the Passaic River and extended thirty miles west of the Hudson River. They paid twenty fathoms of cloth, two coats, two guns, two kettles, ten barrels of lead, twenty handfuls of gunpowder, and four hundred fathoms of white wampum. The associates established the community of Elizabethtown. These early settlers' land claims were soon rectified after Colonel Philip Carteret, Sir George Carteret's cousin, was sent to the colony to become East Jersey's first governor. The southern section of the associates' large claim was granted to a company of New Englanders in December 1666. In a short time, these grantees established the towns of Woodbridge and Piscataway. Farmsteads were established on lands fashioned into lots from 60 to 150 acres in size.

A document now known as the Concessions and Agreements of 1665 was drawn up as a provisional constitution. It called for a form of self-government in which two freeholders from each town were elected to an assembly on the first of January each year. A general assembly was then formed from the elected men, the governor, and a council of appointees. The Concessions and Agreements also contained what appeared to be a fair system of land distribution; however, the early settlers did not own their land outright, but were required to pay annual rents that were to be first due in 1670. This system often was the cause of conflict between the tenders of the land who wanted to be landholders and the remote governors and administrators who maintained possession of it. By 1672 many inhabitants still had not paid their rents, resulting in administrative upheavals. John Whitehead summed up this confusing state of affairs: "To the soil of New Jersey there were four great sources of title: first through the Indian; then through the Dutch; thirdly those from governor Nicholls; and lastly those from the Lord Proprietors."

East and West Jersey formally separated in July 1676. In 1679, "New Piscataqua" in East Jersey hosted its first assembly meeting. One year later a power struggle erupted between the governor of New York, Sir Edmond Andros, and Philip Carteret. This struggle and the death of Sir George Carteret in 1681 led to an undermining of Carteret's authority. By 1682 a new group of twenty-four proprietors, twenty of whom were members of the Society of Friends, including William Penn, bought East Jersey.

Middlesex County was first incorporated by the General Assembly under the government of the proprietors in 1682. In that year George Drake, a dissident Baptist and owner of land in the southwest part of Highland Park, became a deputy to the Assembly from Piscataway. Drake also served as an overseer of the highways and justice of the town court. In New Jersey as a colony and as a state, Francis Bazley Lee stated that in nearly all the East Jersey towns, political elevation was based upon strict adherence to the teachings of a particular religious society. This strictness was in accordance with the spirit of the age—religious enthusiasm that had swept over England and Scotland. To the province of East Jersey, the settlers brought a strong spirit of political and religious independence. Whether they came from Massachusetts, the Connecticut Valley, from the shore communities of Long Island, or from the Calvinistic centers of England and Scotland, they were filled with that mighty purpose to create in the new land a government where political righteousness should guide the course of the state. From 1687 to 1692, the local officers governed East Jersey.

Highland Park's first settlers of record were Henry Greenland and his wife Mary. They were given 420 acres by the Piscataway founders in 1675, including 300 acres along present-day River Road, near the Amtrak railroad bridge and Johnson Park. This land is situated along the Raritan River at the point it becomes far too shallow to allow ocean-going vessels further upstream. It is due to another traveling diarist Jasper Danckaerts that we know that Greenland opened and operated an "Ordinary or Tavern at the place of crossing the river, which they call the falls." Danckaerts recounted in his Journal of 1679 that he stayed at Greenlands and that "close by Mr. Greenland's was a dwelling of some Indians who were of service to Mr. Greenland in many things."

Danckaerts returned to the New Brunswick area one year later and mentioned meeting several Indian guides and seeing several Indian houses.

Henry Greenland was quite the local celebrity. He was a doctor, captain of the Piscataway militia, and a county court judge. According to William H. Benedict, noted New Brunswick historian, it was at Greenland's house that the commissioners met to try to agree on a line between East and West Jersey. Greenland lived on the frontier of this still natural region. He and most of the early settlers including George Drake had come from the Piscataqua region of the Massachusetts Bay Colony. The name "Piscataway" references a New England group of Native Americans. After 1681, Benjamin Dunn was owner of the land to the south and east of the main road. George Drake's lands encompassed 194 acres on the southwest side of the future borough described in 1925 as land "from Greenland's beginning at the brook and extending down to Benjamin Dunn's, now the Crowell's place in part, and covering about all of the built-on portions of Highland Park." Crowell's Road marks today's eastern border between Highland Park and Edison. By 1683, the Greenlands and their grown children, Frances and Henry Jr., moved thirteen miles up the Assunpink Trail to the Millstone River, upstream of Stony Brook, then still part of Piscataway, but now in Princeton Township.

The early settlement history of Highland Park's land is found in Piscataway Township records, although the earliest extant deeds date only from the late 1700s. For at least a century, isolated farmsteads were established in the fertile Raritan River valley. Long lots with narrow river frontage and long upland extensions were established giving the maximum number of settlers access to the river for livestock, water power, and transportation while maintaining the higher and drier areas for cultivation. Eighteenth century census data included in Thomas F. Gordon's 1834 *Gazetteer of the State of New Jersey* indicates that the population of Middlesex County in 1737 was 4,764 people: 4,261 whites and 503 slaves and other "Negroes." There was a population increase of 2,800 by 1745. In 1790, there were 14,638 whites and 1,318 slaves for a total of 15,956 county residents.

The relatively small land mass that would eventually become Highland Park was divided into large parcels of hundreds of acres owned over the centuries by a very small number of people including Philip French, Benjamin Dunn, Benjamin Fitzrandolph, William Edgar, George Farmar, and the Merrell and Van Horn families. Covering only two square miles, Highland Park could only accommodate a very small number of farmsteads. One was advertised for sale in the *New York Gazette* in 1731:

> The plantation now in the Tenure & Occupation of Myndert Lefever, containing one Hundred and five Acres of good choice

> Land, great parts of it improved, and within Fence, and the rest well timbered. There is on it a good Dwelling House, a Barn, and an Orchard. It lyes in Piscattaway Township, on the road that leads from Perth Amboy to New Brunswick, about one half mile from Inian's Ferry.

In the 1740s the Merrells farmed the area at the crossroads of the Upper and Mill Roads, near today's intersection of Montgomery Street and North Fifth and Raritan Avenues. There is a good possibility that it was the same farm advertised one decade earlier. It is difficult to decipher exactly where these farm boundaries were because early surveyors used ephemeral markers such as tree stumps, clumps of trees, and neighboring lands to describe property boundaries. Early Piscataway Township tax ratable records indicated that the Merrell farm consisted of 100 acres. In 1778, the family was taxed for their ownership of one slave, two horses, and six pigs. The smaller section of the "Lucas House" in the twentieth century was most likely the Merrell farmhouse constructed in the early colonial period. Its small size, narrow leaded window panes, and side wall chimney identify it as a colonial era dwelling. Unfortunately, this house was demolished in the 1950s to make way for the public library, one decade before the historic preservation movement got its start in the United States.

The next owners of Greenland's Highland Park land just north of Mill Brook constructed a mill and dammed up the brook in 1694. It remained a noted feature on eighteenth and nineteenth century maps. As the proprietorship changed hands, so too did the name of the mill. On the "New mapp of East and West Jarsey" dated 1706, a building is depicted in close proximity to the Mill Brook and is labeled "Vincents." This referred to Vincent Runyon, who lived there from 1691 to 1706. On a 1745 drawing titled "A Map of the Road Trenton to Amboy," a house at the Mill Brook is labeled "Matthew's Mill." (*See p. 65.*) Doctor Mercer's name appears next to a house on the 1766 "Map of the Division line between the Counties of Middlesex and Somerset." In 1777 "Bray's Mill" is noted. Additional information about the history of the mill outlined below was compiled by Richard L. Porter of the Rutgers Center for Public Archaeology in 1992.

In 1787, Peter and Hendrick Probasco placed a notice in the June 12 edition of the *Brunswick Gazette* offering the gristmill formerly owned by William Mercer for sale. The mill was described as having two run of stones and doing both merchant and custom work. Peter Probasco was operating the millwork and living in a dwelling on the property. Three years later, a 1790 map of French's patent shows the mill under new proprietorship. It has become "Stryker's Mill." New Brunswick merchant John Bray became owner once again in 1791 as Probasco transferred one half share of the Grist Mill property. The deed included the mill pond, mill race, the "waste race," and the "tumbling dam." Eventually Bray became the full owner and in 1808, Bray shared ownership with his brother-in-law Jacob Snyder. Snyder became the full owner and after his death in 1815 left the property to his children. The inventory included with the will noted a gristmill, copper shop, and a "New House." Reuben Marthis of New Brunswick became the next owner in 1815 and successfully ran the mill until 1835. In 1827, a brief ad in the October 3 edition of the *New Brunswick Times* reveals his ownership strategy.

> GRAIN & MEAL WANTED—Wanted to purchase at my Mills opposite New Brunswick, RYE and INDIAN CORN—Also Rye and Corn MEAL ground fine for distilling—for which the highest price *in Cash* will be paid. For those crossing the Brunswick Bridge with the above articles, *the toll will be paid by me.*—Rueben Marthes.

In 1835, Marthis was sued for overdue mortgage payments and the mill and distillery were sold at a public auction. Bought by a member of the Snyder family, the dam was rebuilt. By 1850 the building had become "T. Garrison's Grist mill" as noted on Ortley's "Map of Middlesex County." Through other owners, the mill, distillery, and cider works continued operating into the late 1860s or early 1870s. Now, however, there is no remaining evidence of the dam or the mill buildings at the brook, which runs freely into the Raritan River.

Early roads through New Jersey were enlarged versions of the original Lenape trails. In 1880, C.D. Deshler wrote about the early aboriginal roads of New Jersey:

> The Indians were natural engineers. If their path crossed a stream, it was either at the easiest and safest fording place or above the point which was most likely to interruption from freshets; if they traversed a swamp, it was at the precise spot where permanent solid ground was to be found; if they crossed a range of hills, it was by an easy grade and where the height and breadth were least formidable.

New Jersey comprises a transitional land where Pennsylvania and the states further south meet New York and the New England states to the north. The colonists' widened paths facilitated trade and communications between these two diverse regions. One of the oldest roads in the state, the road through Highland Park, forded the Raritan River at the point near the position of today's railroad bridge. It was an enlarged version of the Lenape's Assunpink Trail from Raritan Bay to the Delaware River. Parts of Madison Avenue, Montgomery Street, and Woodbridge Avenue (Route 514) now barely trace its original path when it was the only road through town. J. Terhune wrote about this early road in the 1855 New Brunswick City Directory:

> In 1676, the Governor and council adopted some general regulations for the opening of roads. The only road that had been laid out by the Europeans in New Jersey was that connecting the City of New Amsterdam [now New York City] with the settlement on the Delaware. This road followed the "old road" as now termed from Elizabeth Town Point to Woodbridge, through Bonhamtown and Piscatawaytown [in today's Edison] to the ford of "the river" just above the present railroad viaduct landing on the west side. This road was little more than a footpath and intended only to accommodate a man and horse.

Water travel was important to the early development of New Jersey. Despite the Assunpink Trail's significance as an overland route, New Jersey's colonists remained reliant on water transportation for most long distance travel and haulage. Early settlements such as New Brunswick were determined by their location bordering navigable waterways. Nevertheless, from 1705 to 1713, county road supervisors laid out over thirty roads connecting outlying communities with larger town centers. Many of the road and bridge right-of-ways established during this time remain intact.

Even at low tide, crossing the Raritan River created very wet travelers. In 1685 John Inian, a New Yorker who became a large landholder in New Brunswick, established ferry service between New Brunswick and Highland Park at a place in the Raritan River several hundred feet downstream from the fording place at Greenland's inn. Eighteenth century maps indicate that Inian constructed a new shortcut directly to his ferry landing that veered southward off the main road approximately at today's Fifth Avenue. Inian's pathway was largely but not completely incorporated into Raritan Avenue after 1806. Noted New Brunswick historian John P. Wall discovered a petition dated April 19, 1686 in which John Inian "set forth that he has been at considerable expense to accommodate the country, in making out a road to the falls from his house upon the Raritan and has furnished himself with all accommodation with boats, canoes, etc., fitting for ferrying over the Raritan River all travelling with horses and cattle." He asked that the commissioners set the rates for his ferry, which apparently was already operating. Inian and his wife Mary were given official proprietary rights for the rest of their lives in 1697. They also were given five shillings every year to transport, at no charge, all postmen and town officials, beginning on February 5, 1697.

John Inian died in 1699 and Mary followed him to the grave one year later. Cornelius Longvelt was heir. Unlike the mill, the ferry continued to be known as that of its first owners, although other operators took it over during the century before the first bridge was constructed. The rights to operate Inian's Ferry were conveyed from Thomas and Anne Farmar to Phillip French, a merchant in New York who soon became a Highland Park landowner, in 1732.

In the tidal river, the ferry was not always reliable. Traveling from New Brunswick in 1744, Dr. Alexander Hamilton quipped in his travel journal, "Friday, June 15. A little before 6 in the morning I forded Raretin River, the tide being low and the skeow aground so that I could not ferry it over." He was traveling to Perth Amboy. On the return trip in September, the ferry was in operation for his passage back to New Brunswick. Passing through Piscataway, he noted that the "Country here is pleasant and levell, intermixed with skirts of woods and meadow ground, the road in generall good but stonny in some places." Another eighteenth century journal keeper, the Reverend Manasseh Cutler, noted in the 1780s that "the Raritan is a beautiful river, but the water is very shoal. The ferryman told me that in dry seasons it had been forded where the boat passed. Ferriage, 1 shilling 6 pence."

Both local and long-distance travelers used the ferry to cross the Raritan River. It also facilitated regularly scheduled stagecoaches. The first stagecoach lines were established in the early part of the eighteenth century. A stagecoach "fitted up with benches and covered over, so that passengers could sit easy and dry" ran between New Brunswick and Trenton as early as 1732. It was advertised in *The American Weekly Mercury*. The trip took five days over roads that were little more than wide footpaths. Travel time decreased as the decades progressed. On April 25, 1765 *The Pennsylvania Gazette* printed this announcement:

> This is to inform the public, that a Stage will be performed from Powles's Hook opposite New York, to Philadelphia, in the following manner, viz. Mr. John Mersereau's waggon sets off from Powles's Hook every Wednesday and Saturday mornings, is met at the New Blazing Star, at twelve o'clock on the same day, by Mr. William Richard's waggon, which proceeds immediately to New Brunswick; from Brunswick Mr. John Downey's waggon proceeds to Trenton, on every Monday and Thursday mornings; and from Trenton Mr. John Barnhill's waggon proceeds to Philadelphia, on every Tuesday

> and Friday. The waggon sets off from Philadelphia on every Monday and Thursday for Trenton, from Trenton to New Brunswick on every Tuesday and Friday, from Brunswick to the New Blazing Star, and from thence to Powles's Hook on every Wednesday and Saturday; so the conveyance of passengers and goods will be performed from New York to Philadelphia, and from Philadelphia to New York, in three days at farthest. All persons that are pleased to encourage this necessary undertaking, may depend on civil treatment, a faithful performance of the several stages, and good accommodation at all the taverns they put up at. —John Mesereau, John Downey, William Richards, John Barnhill.
>
> *n.b.* From the first of May passengers may be conveyed from Philadelphia to New York for Four Shillings per stage, which will be Twelve Shillings to York; and in the winter season Five Shillings per stage, which will be Fifteen Shillings.

The post also was transported through Highland Park territory. In 1775, riders set off from Newark at 8:00 a.m. on Mondays and Thursdays and went through Elizabethtown, Woodbridge, Bonhamtown, Piscatawaytown, and Brunswick before reaching Princeton and ultimately, Philadelphia. The return mail to Newark was carried on Wednesdays and Saturdays. For this reason, Woodbridge Avenue was known for many decades as the "Old Post Road."

One of the establishments where travelers could find temporary lodging and residents could congregate was the Ferry House tavern situated on the Piscataway side of the Raritan River. The ferry house is depicted standing just to the south of Inian's road at its junction with the riverbank on a 1766 map drawn by Azariah Dunham titled "A map of the Division Line between the Counties of Middlesex and Somerset." (*See p. 67.*) Additional documentation about Highland Park's earliest tavern has been found in a collection of tavern license petitions at the State Archives in Trenton. The first petition, dated 1760, is a request to the honorable justices of the peace that Francis Holman receive a license to operate his Piscataway tavern near the ferry. Assenting neighbors signed the petition. The signatures included those of Ephraim Randolph, Benjamin Stelle, A. Dunham, Benjamin Dunn, Richard Merrell, and Jonathon Fitzrandolph. Evidently, Holman was the tavernkeeper for two more years. In 1763 a group of "sundry inhabitants of the Township of Piscataway" thought it necessary "that a public house should be continued at Brunswick Ferry where Francis Holman lately dwelt." Because Lawrence DeCamp had rented that house and farm, the petition signers did "recommend him as a person qualified for that service and pray that he may have License granted him for that end."

The next tavernkeeper was Isaac Egbertson. He received licenses for several years and was well regarded by his neighbors:

> To the Honorable Bench of Judges & Justices, of the Court of Quarter Sessions held at the City of Perth Amboy in the County of Middlesex on Tuesday the 19th day of July 1768, Whereas Isaac Egbertsen Tavernkeeper at the ferry house Opposite the City of New Brunswick in the County aforementioned Hath for several years last past obtained a License from said court to sell and Retail Strong Liquors by small measure and to keep a house of publick entertainment for gentlemen, strangers and Others; and whereas the said Isaac Egbertsen and family have behaved themselves discreetly and well to all gentlemen and others that was pleased to favor him with their Custom therefore we the subscribers do Humbly Request that it may please the Honourable Bench aforementioned Grant a License to the said Isaac Egbertsen for the Like use aforementioned during the ensuing Year Which will very much oblige Gentlemen Your most Humble Servants—Samuel Sharp, Wilhelmus Lupardus, J. Dunn, Thomas Goodfellow, Benjamin Dunn, Richard Merrell, Samuel Johnson, Hugh Dunn.

The following year, 1769, Jacob Weiser became the licensee. From 1770 to 1772, Martin Neefees held the license and from 1773 to 1775, John Voorheis was the tavernkeeper. There is a break in the recordkeeping for the years of the Revolutionary War.

In 1908, noted New Brunswick historian John P. Wall wrote an essay titled "New Brunswick in the Critical Period of the Revolution." The small role that Highland Park played is here excerpted in part from Wall's essay. On December 1, 1776 General George Washington wrote to the president of the congress that "the enemy appeared in several parties on the heights opposite Brunswick, and were advancing in a large body towards the crossing place." With too few troops to stop them, the British army under Lord Cornwallis "took the fort opposite Brunswick, plunged into the Raritan river, and seized the town." Washington retreated to Trenton. During the British occupation, local farmers were compelled to deliver goods into their hands. Barns were torn down to supply timber for the construction of a temporary bridge over the Raritan. As many as 6,000 Hessian soldiers with many cannons were stationed in redoubts on the bluffs both to the north and south sides flanking the road and bridge. An earthwork fort located atop the bluff that overlooks the river where the YM-YWHA currently is situated became the station for the 28th regiment of Hessians. The 35th regiment of the Hessians manned another fort on the bluff above River Road between today's Walter and Harrison Avenues.

The numerous troops covered the countryside and occupied all available farmsteads. General Washington, stationed in Pennsylvania, was kept well informed of events taking place in New Jersey due to a network of patriot intelligence agents. The warfare caused great civil disturbances, with neighbors often supporting opposing sides. The British Army's occupation of New Brunswick lasted for seven months until they evacuated from the city on June 22, 1777 in front of Washington's advancing troops.

By 1783, a traveler, Johann David Schoepf, noted that "in Brunswick the royal barracks still stand, for which there are no soldiers, and an English church remains for which there is no congregation. This section of Jersey suffered the most during the war, from the troops of both parties." After the war of independence was over, life returned to normal and new names on the petitions for the Ferry House tavern licenses showed a change of landownership in Piscataway Township. For example, Philip French's extensive acreage on the Highland Park side of the Raritan River "between the river, Inian's ferry, Richard Merrill's, and Benjamin Dunn's" was sold at a sheriff's sale in 1784 to Ann Van Horne. The resumption of tavernkeepers requesting a Ferry House tavern license took place in 1781. It was on the behalf of Matthew Sleght. In 1783 William Rider was the tavernkeeper. The next was William Carlisle in 1784. By 1787, Joshua Mercereau was the tavernkeeper and licensee. (*See p. 66.*) No other petitions after 1788 were in the state archives.

Throughout the eighteenth century, taverns were strictly regulated. Rates were set twice a year at the Spring and Fall Sessions of the Justices of the Peace for everything from cost of meals and drinks of various kinds to oats and hay for the horses. For example, in 1764 the cost of a breakfast was set at nine pence and a quart of lime punch cost one shilling and four pence. The most expensive drink was Madeira wine at two shillings and three pence per pint. A quart of oats cost two pence. Tavernkeepers were given notice "By Order of the Court" that "the above mentioned Liquors and Oats, when called for, are to be delivered in full Measure, to Travellers and Sober People." The penalty for noncompliance was a stiff fine of twenty shillings a day.

The ferry house is depicted on a 1790 map of New Brunswick and on a 1795 drawing of the new Albany Street Bridge by Thomas Russell, but it is not known how many more years after 1795 the tavern continued to operate. It is presumed that the Albany Street Bridge changed the transportation habits of the colonialists by eliminating what seemed to have been frequent long waits for the tides, boats, and ferrymen to align for favorable river crossings. The bridge also allowed Piscataway residents and travelers an express way into New Brunswick to sample the offerings of the city's taverns. In 1797, William Priest, another traveling diarist wrote,

> We dined at New Brunswick, where there is a wooden bridge, with stone piers, thrown over a broad and rapid river. Our landlord informed us, several Englishmen assured him, "It was very like Westminster Bridge." Though my conscience would not permit me, exactly to chime with my countrymen, it is but justice to acknowledge, that when the infant state of the country is considered, it is a work of equal magnitude, boldly designed, and neatly executed.

According to a May 18, 1872 *New Brunswick Daily Times* article, the first Albany Street Bridge, constructed of wood planks on stone piers, first began as an idea put forth before the New Jersey Legislature on November 17, 1790 and recorded on paper as an act "To Build a Toll-Bridge over the River Raritan, at the City of New Brunswick." The preamble stated:

> James Parker and others, proprietors of the bank and water lots, houses, and wharves on the River Raritan, and of the lands adjacent thereto, in the City of New Brunswick, in the County of Somerset, and Peter Probasco, Dinah Probasco, and Hendrick Bargu, representatives of the late John Probasco, who died seized of the lands opposite thereto, have made an application to the Legislature of this State for a law to enable them to build a toll-bridge over the River Raritan.

New Brunswick historian William Benedict wrote that approval was forthcoming. Commissioners were named to choose the site of the bridge, raise money from subscribers, and construct the bridge. The site at the foot of Albany Street was set in 1791. The construction financing was controlled by the commissioners in agreement with the City of New Brunswick elected officials, who acted as monitors for the state legislature. Initially, the tolls that would be charged were stipulated to be one-fifth of the ferry toll and foot traffic was supposed to be free. The money was also deposited into an account that was part of the state treasury rather than an account controlled by the commissioners. Due to these constrictions, investors did not anticipate great profits and the bridge commissioners had a difficult time raising necessary capital to complete construction. It did not help matters when in the early phase of construction the bridge was determined to be constructed so poorly that it was dismantled and rebuilt. The proposed toll was subsequently raised to equal that of the ferry toll. This change facilitated investment, although the dividends for the investors were not very favorable compared to other business deals of the same period.

In 1794 the new set of bridge plans drawn up by Mr. Newton was accepted. He called for fourteen- by twelve-foot stone piers to be built on foundations of pine logs. According to Dr. Henry Baldwin in 1889, "the stone for the piers was freighted by James Ross of Bonhampton and brought from Blackwell's Island in the East River near New York City on two sloops owned by him and called the *Favorite* and the *Victory*." In June of 1795, a smaller footbridge used by the workmen was washed downstream by floodwaters, but the newly constructed stone piers stood firm. The skilled masons from New York, Mr. Gosman and Mr. Russel, received praise for their fine workmanship. By October 28, 1795 the bridge was completed enough to support some traffic. The Bridge Commissioners hired John Vandeventer to be the toll collector for $150 per year and gave him the use of the tollhouse. A *New Jersey Chronicle* article from November 16, 1795 stated that the bridge "was so far completed as to render it possible for carriages to use it." The article described the bridge:

> being about three hundred feet and thirty yards; its width sufficient for carriages to pass each other exclusive of a convenient footwalk. The woodwork of this lofty structure rests upon thirteen large and lofty pillars, including two abutments, which for strength and elegance we are warranted in claiming far exceeds anything of its kind in America. A draw is placed over the deepest water for permitting vessels to pass and repass. No workmen were killed during its construction.

A surviving toll sheet indicates that the cost of crossing depended on the size and elegance of the vehicle or animal. A single horse pulling a cart only paid one shilling. A horse and chaise were charged 1 shilling and one pence while a two-horse wagon or sleigh was charged 1 shilling and 6 pence. The riders in a four-horse wagon, coach, or sleigh needed to pay 2 shillings and 9 pence to cross the bridge. A man could cross for 2 pence and if he pushed a wheelbarrow, he would need to pay one pence more. Hogs and sheep were charged the same, one pence for each animal. Cattle cost two and a half pence and a man and a horse paid 5 pence. Entries in the New Brunswick Bridge Company's "Weekly Book for the Toll Received" show the large number of stagecoach lines paying to use the new bridge. Records included payments from the Federal Line, the Mail Stage, the Stage Industry, the Stage Dispatch, the Mail Pilot, Captain William Jones Stages, and Vernon's Stages.

In the *Traveller's Directory: The Main Road from Philadelphia to Washington* published in 1802, S.S. Moore and T.W. Jones observed, "the Bridge across the Rariton, is one of the most elegant and expensive in the United States; it is built of wood, nine hundred and fifty feet long, opposite Albany Street; the piers are of hewn stone." The bridge became a permanent connection for the inhabitants on both sides of the Raritan River where once an impermanent connection operated. The Albany Street Bridge became one of the most important elements contributing to the development of Highland Park in the following two centuries.

Chapter Two

1800 TO 1868

The wheel is a dial by which can be reckoned the degree of progress of every civilization.
—J. Elfreth Watkins, 1892

With the construction of the "Brunswick Bridge" in 1795, the century-old ferry service between Highland Park and New Brunswick ended. Wheeled vehicles, pedestrians, and livestock could cross the toll bridge for approximately the same cost, only now much faster and without the limitations caused by low tides, ferries in midstream, and delayed ferrymen. In his 1892 book *The Camden and Amboy Railroad*, J. Elfreth Watkins mentions that during the Revolutionary War, miserable conditions hampered the transportation of cannons and continental troops over the roads. With the war over and regular commerce on the upswing, the need for road improvements became paramount. On March 3, 1806, the State of New Jersey authorized the construction of the Essex and Middlesex Turnpike. This new roadway began where Inian's original shortcut met up with the main road (at today's Sixth Avenue) extending it northeasterly for six miles in a virtually straight path to Metuchen. The new Turnpike created the triangular intersection of Woodbridge and Raritan Avenues that is still in existence. After a survey established the path, the roadbed was graded, smoothed, and coated with gravel. The new road was beautifully rendered in ink on Henry Plum's "Map of the Turnpike Road from New Brunswick to Judge Lawrence's in Newark" drawn in September of 1806.

In the 1810s, the addition of convenient connections from turnpike stages to steamboats rejuvenated interest in the water routes from the Raritan River at New Brunswick to New York. For many years, steamboats remained a favorite way to travel longer distances for many passengers.

According to Piscataway Township tax ratable records, in 1808 Jacob Probasco owned eight cattle and 160 acres of land between the Mill Brook, River Road, and the Middlesex and Essex Turnpike on the east bank of the Raritan River. One year later, Probasco conveyed his tract to John Henry Livingston (1746–1825), the new professor of theology and president of Queen's College. This land transaction on October 19, 1809 marked the beginning of the long-standing relationship between the institution that would become Rutgers University and the town that would become Highland Park. It also marked the beginning of this specific tract of land being called "Livingston Manor," a name it has retained to the present. Not much is known about the first owner of the Livingston Homestead property or the type of dwelling most likely built by Probasco in the late 1700s upon it. According to Alexander Gunn's 1829 biography of Livingston:

> Soon after his arrival in New Jersey, he wrote a few lines to his friend Isaac L. Kip, Esq. of New York, which begins thus: "Many cares and arrangements, inseparable from a new habitation, have engrossed my attention since I came to this place, and prevented me from dropping a line to you. The new part of my dwelling is yet under the hands of the carpenters, and the old requires much alteration and amendments, to render it comfortable for the approaching winter."
>
> He was under the necessity of purchasing the place that was now undergoing repairs and alterations, to put it in a comfortable state; and to pay for it, he had depended upon the sale of some property he had in New York. More than a year elapsed, however, before he could effect a satisfactory sale of this property, and meanwhile, his situation was an anxious one.

Dr. Livingston was an influential theologian. He united two factions of the Dutch church in America at the time. He and his wife Hannah owned the Highland Park land until conveying it to Richard Lupardus in November 1818. Dr. Livingston also owned a house and property in New Brunswick. The prominent thoroughfare, Livingston Avenue, commemorates his early nineteenth century residency there. The next Livingston family owners around 1843 constructed the large house currently situated on the ancestral Livingston land in Highland Park.

The new century of the young republic also brought progressive social ideas. On February 15, 1804, New Jersey adopted "An Act for the Gradual Abolition of Slavery." This law freed all African-American children born on or after July 4, 1804, after serving an apprenticeship to their mother's owner for twenty-one years if female and twenty-five years if male. Thomas F. Gordon's 1834 *Gazetteer of New Jersey* notes that the "vice of slavery was early introduced into the state and took deep root, particularly in East Jersey." Over 12,000 slaves resided statewide in New Jersey in 1800. After the law was passed, the next census in 1810 showed the number of slaves reduced to 10,851 and then in 1820 to 7,557. The act was amended further and by 1830 there were 23,157 people living in Middlesex County with the statistical breakdown of 10,543 free white males, 10,487 free white females, 309 slaves, 904 free black males, and 914 free black females. The townships were not listed with individual totals. An ad in the April 18, 1816 *New Brunswick Times* indicates that slaves were present in Highland Park. It reads, "George Farmer offers $50 reward for Elisha, a negro man, who ran away from his place, Belle Vue, opposite New Brunswick, on March 27." The 1830 census data indicted that fifty-four male slaves lived in the County of Middlesex.

The 1830s saw the rise of activities along the underground railroad's route through Highland Park, which most likely followed the path of the newly installed railroad line from Highland Park to Newark. The following is an excerpt from Wilbur Siebert's account first published in 1898:

> Just east of New Brunswick, the conductors sometimes met with opposition in attempting to cross the Raritan River on their way to Jersey City. To avoid such interruption the conductors arranged with Cornelius Cornell, who lived on the outskirts of New Brunswick, and presumably, near the river, to notify them when there were slave-catchers or spies at the regular crossing. When the way was clear at the Raritan the company pursued its course to Rahway; here another relay of horses was obtained and the journey continued to Jersey City.

An elegant, two-story, Federal style farmhouse was constructed overlooking the Raritan River and the marshy area known as "the Meadows" on the south side of town in the 1820s. A detailed article written when it was in the process of demolition in March 1927 stated that many early owners of the 100-year-old house included Herman Edgar, John Hicks, James Stout, and James Bishop. In 1830, the residents would have had a first hand look at the damage caused by a combination of high tide and a storm from the east, which drove the Raritan River waters onto the Meadows leaving a large quantity of mackerel, which were collected and salted. In December of 1830 another heavy eastern wind interacted with a high tide, which took away much of the Meadow's vegetation.

James Bishop ran a fleet of boats to South America in the rubber trade. Bishop was affiliated with Christopher Meyer of the Meyer Rubber Company. Both James Donaldson senior and junior later owned the house and land down to the Raritan. Donaldson Park was so named to honor them. Donaldson farm was a poultry farm, one of the largest in the county, and it was here that Rutgers College students would come to study farming methods in the late nineteenth century. After the poultry plant was given up, the farmhouse was demolished and the farm was converted into building lots named Riverview Terrace.

According to historian William H. Benedict, in 1824 dignitaries in New Brunswick extended an invitation to Revolutionary War hero General Lafayette. He accepted and on September 23 left New York. He and his party were met in Bonhamtown the next day by the first squadron of Horse Artillery, who accompanied him through Highland Park. At the bridge, the Military Artillery made a salute by cannon in front of 8,000 people who traveled from near and far to see the famous man. This was one of many such celebrations shared by Highland Park and New Brunswick on or around the Albany Street Bridge.

The *New Brunswick Times* of June 20 and 21, 1835 recorded the harrowing account of a devastating tornado that swept through that city and the surrounding countryside the evening of Friday, June 19 beginning at 5:00 p.m.

Having made such parts of the city through which it passed a complete wreck, it crossed the river and struck the woods, uprooting some of the largest trees, twisting off the bodies of others, and throwing several fifty yards from the places where they stood. In one place it appears to have played for some time, in a circle, tearing up the grass and leaving the earth bare of any vegetation. It then passed over the farm of James T. Dunn, threatening the house but changing its direction and going instead a few paces to the rear, razing the barn and all the outbuildings and dashing in a few of the window casements of the dwelling. A lad named Jerome Finch was hurt, but not dangerously, by a falling tree. Now striking the woods, the tornado passed on to the house of Joel Randolph, tearing off the gable end of the roof and considerably injuring the barn. It again took to the woods in a northeasterly course until near Piscatawaytown, where its course turned east.

Professor Lewis Beck happened to be on a steamship in the Raritan River heading for New Brunswick when the tornado passed over the city. His eyewitness account was recorded in a newspaper article and included a keen personification: "soon a tremendous rush of wind passed through the city and in a moment the dense column, which had been an object of so much wonder and dread, stood on the opposite bank of the river, as it were, rallying for another desolating march." The article ended with this nota bene: "Carpenters and masons will find steady employment in our city for some time."

In the late 1820s, discussions were taking place throughout the country about the new transportation technology of the "iron horse" and the hopes of being able to import this English invention into the United States. In 1828, the cornerstone of the Baltimore and Ohio Railroad was laid and two years later, the first railroad for New Jersey, the Camden and Amboy Railroad and Transportation Company, was authorized by an act of the state legislature. The route of this railroad was through southern Middlesex County. The New Brunswick area received rail service several years later. Thomas Gordon reported in his 1834 *Gazetteer*:

> The New Jersey Rail-Road and Transportation Company was incorporated by the act of 7th March 1832 with a capital of $750,000 and the privilege to double it, and divided into shares of $50 each; with power to make a rail-road not more than 66 feet wide, with as many tracks as they may deem proper, from such point in the city of New Brunswick, as which shall be agreed upon by them and the corporation of that city, through or near the villages of Rahway and Woodbridge, within half a mile of the market house, in Elizabethtown, and through Newark.

The railroad from Newark was constructed in 1836 and for two years its terminus was on the Highland Park side of the Raritan River. An 1873 publication, *New Brunswick and Its Industries*, contained this account of the first train:

> On January 2, 1836, a new locomotive, the "New Brunswick," attached to thirteen cars, decorated with banners bearing the names of the counties, cities, and villages along the road, and United States and State flags, came down at the rate of fifteen miles an hour from Newark, freighted with guests from all along the line, to East New Brunswick. Here the visitors were received by Alderman Zabriskie, who conducted them in carriages over the Albany Street Bridge to the Court House, where had been prepared a sumptuous collation; the feast was accompanied by the inevitable toasts and speeches. On January 4, regular trains, three each way, commenced running from Rahway to Newark, fifty cents fare. Trains had to stop across the river, as there was at that time no railroad bridge. The depot stood on the right as the train came in, on the little knoll now covered with cedars, and omnibus coaches ran thence to the City Hotel, via the Albany Street Bridge, at the low charge of six and a quarter cents.

Rail passengers continuing their journeys to New Brunswick and beyond had to make their way down a steep flight of steps from the tracks, proceed along River Road, and cross the Raritan River on the Albany Street Bridge.

The end of the line on the eastern bank of the Raritan River was called East New Brunswick, which became the standard name of the area. Interestingly, the land along the railroad tracks continued to be defined as East New Brunswick well into the early twentieth century. This name distinguished the lands on both sides of the transportation corridor as a separate region in contrast to the elevated residential areas, which were called "Highland Park" more and more often after the 1870s.

In 1836 a hotel was constructed overlooking the Raritan just to the south of the railroad tracks. It was advertised in the local papers as an ideal summer retreat. However, it is not known how long the hotel operated or when it was demolished. In 1838 itinerant artist J.H. Bufford stayed at the hotel long enough to finish a drawing "from nature and on stone" that was published as a large lithographic print titled "View from Railroad Hotel at East New Brunswick."

Bufford's 1838 lithograph illustrates the newly constructed, wooden, double decker long truss railroad bridge designed by Thomas Hassard that carried railroad traffic on its upper chord and highway traffic below. The drawing does not depict the controversy that surrounded the $57,532 railroad bridge during its construction, which commenced in 1836 and was completed by November of 1837. With the possibility of having two nearby pedestrian bridges, the directors of a newly merged transportation company declared on May 4, 1838, "Whereas the Albany Street bridge of this Company is in a condition to require frequent repairs and the lower story of the railroad's viaduct will afford a convenient means of crossing, herefore the Bridge Co. can use and collect the same tolls as on the Albany Street Bridge, and in return shall tend the draw [over the newly built Delaware and Raritan Canal] and keep the lower story of the railroad bridge in repair." This arrangement led to further decay of the Albany Street Bridge, which over the first three decades of its operation turned out to be a poor investment for its shareholders. Repairs were expensive and often delayed to the point that the bridge suffered from a significant loss of structural integrity. After the railroad bridge opened, the Albany Street Bridge was allowed to deteriorate until it was declared a nuisance by a Middlesex County grand jury in September of 1848. By April 1849, the bridge—constructed in 1795 and hailed as a magnificent structure by early travelers—was dismantled.

Although pedestrian and vehicular traffic could cross the Raritan on the lower level of the double decker railroad bridge, it was an arduous and frightful passage with trains lumbering overhead. In May of 1851, a small group of wealthy New Brunswick and Highland Park residents met with the intention of forming a new company to rebuild the Albany Street Bridge. A new corporation was established, the remaining stone piers were assessed, and Philadelphian Daniel Stone drew up architectural plans. The bridge was rebuilt at a cost of $8,500 based on Stone's plans and under his construction management. "Neilson and Miller furnished the timber; Doty and Ford, the plank; H. Richmond furnished the pale brick, and J.H. Newell graded the road up the hill."[1] The rebuilt bridge was completed in April of 1853. In the introduction of the 1855 New Brunswick directory, author J. Terhune stated, "A toll is charged that pays the annual expenses, a handsome dividend to the stockholders, and a surplus for repairs." The lower level of the railroad bridge was closed to pedestrian traffic by an express understanding between the Stockholders of the Albany Street Bridge and the Directors of the Rail Road.

In 1851 two of the new corporate owners of the rebuilt Albany Street Bridge, Robert J. Livingston and Samuel V. Hoffman, each received a lifetime of free passage for themselves and their families and teams. These prominent men were residents along River Road. Livingston resided at the Livingston Homestead constructed *c.* 1843 on the land formerly owned by his uncle, the Reverend John H. Livingston. Hoffman lived on the former Greenland property upon which the Cenacle retreat house currently is situated just to the north of Mill Brook and the railroad tracks.

As recorded in the Middlesex County deed office, on April 7, 1843 Louisa M. Livingston purchased the ninety-six-acre tract on which the Livingston Homestead, a grand two-and-one-half story Greek Revival style house, was constructed. She and her husband Robert James Livingston were New Yorkers and typically used their Highland Park mansion as a summer retreat. Nevertheless, the land remained productive as tenant farmers tended the property. The Livingstons retained the estate until 1891. The substantial house continues as a private residence and was the first of Highland Park's historic houses to be listed in the New Jersey and National Registers of Historic Places.[2]

The other investor in the company that rebuilt the Albany Street Bridge was Highland Park resident Samuel Verplanck Hoffman. According to his October 16, 1880 obituary, S.V. Hoffman was a wealthy attorney from Columbia County in New York. He practiced law from 1825 to 1840. He lived in a brownstone in New York City and spent the summers with his family in New Brunswick, where he owned a county seat. This house at 411 River Road, which was up to 2004 the Sisters of the Cenacle Retreat house, was most likely constructed by Hoffman in the 1840s. It is illustrated in the 1876 *Atlas of Middlesex County* but

[1]For more information about the complicated ownership agreements see William H. Benedict, *New Brunswick in History*, 1925, pp. 58–61.

[2]Stacy E. Spies, Livingston Homestead National Register Nomination, 2001.

was drawn before it received three dormers and the larger wrap-around porch seen today.

Despite the transportation improvements, rural Highland Park did not see a large increase in the number of residential properties in the mid-nineteenth century. A typical advertisement from these early years read:

> A Farm of 104 Acres, Pleasantly situated on the Raritan, and nearly opposite the lower part of New Brunswick, is offered at private sale. The land is of the first quality, consisting of a bottom meadow, arable and a proportion of Woodland. Manure can be conveniently landed within a quarter of a mile of the premises. On the farm is a convenient and comfortable dwelling house containing seven rooms and a kitchen, a good barn, waggon house, &c. &c.—also a variety of choice fruit trees.

This farm most likely covered a large portion of Highland Park's south side. Unfortunately, the farmhouse advertised is long gone. A map of Middlesex County drawn in 1850 by J.W. Otley and J. Keily depicts the Highland Park area with only a dozen scattered mansions and farmsteads. Both the Hoffman and Livingston houses are indicated, as are the farmsteads owned by families with the names of Merrell and Dunn. This suggests that the land continued to retain its rural character. The one new development shown in this map was the first side street that coursed southward from the main road toward the riverbank and J. Bishop's farmstead, today's Cedar Avenue. It would be the sole south side street for only a few years.

In the 1850s, the land along the riverbank south of the main road was part of the extensive Van Horne (sometimes spelled Van Horn) estate. Over time, the Van Hornes sold many smaller parcels. In 1854, owner John Pyatt sold the land along the riverbank to builder William Flagg, who in turn, sold an even smaller plot (about six acres) to Elizabeth Reed and her husband William in 1859. Premises as well as land are mentioned in this later deed conveyance. The house is now known as the Meyer-Rice House and is the daycare facility for the YW-YMHA. The Reeds sold the six-acre estate and premises to Luke C. Coe in 1864 and other owners followed. It was during 1855 to 1865 that parcels of land on the bluff at the riverbank were being developed into an exclusive residential area named in various sources either "Raritan Park" or "Highland Park."

The 1873 booklet *New Brunswick and Its Industries* included an accolade to the mansion on the Highland Park side of the Raritan River, describing it as "one of the most elegant residences to be found in the State." This Italianate mansion near the Albany Street Bridge has a fine silhouette atop the high bluff overlooking the Raritan River and the city of New Brunswick. However, little was recorded about the builder William Flagg. His name and his New Brunswick street address are listed in the 1855 New Brunswick directory and his name appears on the 1868 wall map, indicating that by then he had moved to a house on Raritan Avenue. Evidence of his presence in Highland Park besides the deed record comes from a sentence in *New Brunswick and Its Industries*: "Mr. Coe, buying the large stucco mansion which with several others of the fine residences thereabouts Mr. William Flagg with an enterprise a decade ahead of the town had built, proceeded at considerable expense to beautify the grounds, including the costly terracing which is now a chief feature of the other side of the river as viewed from the west bank."

Although more research is needed to make an identical match, the Meyer-Rice mansion shares similarities with several Italian Villa designs illustrated in books of plans by Philadelphia architect Samuel Sloan. Sloan's designs depict structures with elements found in the mansion, such as the square plan, balanced and symmetrical window arrangements, segmental arch windows with hood moldings, bracketed cornice, a cupola, and the pilasters made from raised stucco. During this time of romantic revival style architecture, Sloan was not the only architect promoting Italian Villa designs. Others included John Notman, Calvert Vaux, and Andrew Jackson Downing.

In the mid-nineteenth century, A.J. Downing advocated for the construction of dwellings with stucco exteriors, not only for the practical purpose of superior heat retention but also for the aesthetic quality that suggested eternal duration. In 1854 Downing wrote, "Outside plastering or stuccoing is generally so little understood in this country and has been so badly by many masons, that there is an unjust prejudice against it, in many parts of the union." Downing's influence on the literate elite and their suburban design and construction was enormous. It seems highly probable that the Meyer-Rice mansion was built with these ideals in mind.

In 1867, Coe sold the house to Wright Robin and in turn, two years later, Wright Robin sold it to Lewis LeGrand Hyatt, president of the New Jersey Rubber Company. By 1877 a new owner, Joseph Fisher, took up occupancy. The owner's name, "J.T. Fisher," is written in the lower right corner detail from an 1880 map of New Brunswick. Fisher was a postmaster of New Brunswick who fell into bankruptcy shortly after buying the mansion.

In 1882, John Christopher Meyer and Kate D. Meyer of New Brunswick bought the house and property at a sheriff's auction. They were the high bidders, offering $10,050. Tragically, Mr. Meyer died at age forty-four only six years later.

In the second half of the nineteenth century the Meyer family's fortune had been amassed from its business of binding cloth to rubber for manufacturing such products as rubber boots. Christopher Meyer was celebrated as the owner of the Meyer Rubber Company in New Brunswick. After his death Kate Meyer continued to live in the house, along with her children and sisters, well into the twentieth century. By the time of the Meyer family occupancy in the 1880s, the Romanesque porch had been constructed.

In the 1920s, the house and grounds were purchased by Meyer's daughter and son-in-law Margaretta M. Rice and her husband James Kearney Rice Jr. According to descendants, three full-time servants also lived in the house: the cook, a waitress, and a chambermaid. They also employed full-time gardeners. The June 15, 1921 *Daily Home News* reported:

> Hundreds of people are stopping daily for a glance at the show place of Highland Park—the home of J. Kearney Rice, Jr. The roses in the old-fashioned garden have been in full bloom for several days and everyone who sees them compliments Mr. and Mrs. Rice upon their excellent arrangement of the flower beds and the designs used by landscape gardeners for beautifying the entire property. It requires the time of three men each day to keep the lawn and flower beds in proper condition.

California photographer and author Margaretta K. Mitchell grew up in the house. Upon her mother Margaretta Rice's death in 1950, J. Kearny Rice became sole owner. He sold the property to David Freeman and Leon Smith on September 14, 1951.

According to the "Personality Profile" in a 1957 *Jewish Journal*, nearby Raritan Avenue resident Adele Brody had the wonderful idea that the unoccupied Rice estate would be perfect for a Jewish Community Center. Funded by the Jewish Community Center of New Brunswick, Highland Park and Vicinity, the estate was purchased in 1955 for $1. Reopened with a new purpose in 1956, the Meyer-Rice mansion became the center for such diverse activities as boxing and wrestling lessons, lectures, dances, and art and music classes. George Segal, who would later receive international acclaim for his realist sculptures, gave art lessons and organized exhibitions of his students' works, which included those of the well-known artist Lucas Samaras. In January 1957, a nursery school on the upper floors opened with eight children whose parents paid $1 per child, per day.

Because the 1873 New Brunswick booklet stated "several residences," William Flagg was surely also the builder of the Stout residence next to the house that would become known as the Meyer-Rice House, as well as the aptly named "Redcliffe" mansion further south on Adelaide Avenue. This red sandstone Gothic Revival house stood on seventeen acres overlooking the Raritan River and City of New Brunswick for a century until it was demolished and replaced with post–World War II garden apartments, originally called the Redcliffe Apartments but now renamed Colonial Gardens. Beginning in 1863, Redcliffe was the home of Abraham V. Schenck (1821–1902) an attorney, New Brunswick mayor, and state senator. By 1919 the estate became the Redcliffe Manor School, a school for well children. From 1923 to 1945, the Redcliffe Boarding House was run by daughters Emily B. and Edith M. Schenck.

William Flagg also left his mark on Highland Park by naming the avenue from which his property and houses were accessed—Adelaide Avenue. The mentioned but unnamed avenue in earlier deeds was now specified as "Adelaide Avenue" in deed conveyances that took place after Flagg's ownership. It remains a mystery whether the name belonged to a relative. Several deeds and an obituary indicate his wife's name was Adaline. By 1873, Adelaide Avenue was gated at its entrance. A map drawn in 1861 by Walling is the first that shows Adelaide Avenue closer to the river and paralleling Cedar Avenue. The 1861 map also depicts several additional houses along River Road between the two bridges. New names appear on the old farmsteads further away from the river along the main road.

During the decade of the 1860s, marked by the Civil War, the area that would soon become known as Highland Park was undergoing additional segmentation and development. Luke C. Coe filed a subdivision map in the Middlesex County Clerk's office on January 25, 1865. It outlined the lots of "Coe's Park" south of the main road, but the streets of the map are not named. The only clue as to where Coe's Park was situated is on the 1868 map. (*See p. 71.*) It has a square indicating Coe's Park about halfway down Cedar Avenue. Coe advertised his plan in the *New Brunswick Fredonian* August 30, 1866 and, according to deed research, several sales of plots took place in the ensuing years to Joseph Cunningham, William Van Sickle, William Flagg, Eliza Kelley, and Mary Perviel, among others. They may have been land speculators only because William Flagg's house at the corner of the main road and Cedar Avenue is the only one depicted on the 1868 map. An article from the January 28, 1870 *Daily Fredonian* noted:

> The changes and improvements recently made and contemplated in that portion of East New Brunswick known as "Coe's Park" bid fair to make that the most desirable locality, contiguous to our City, for the erection of first-class residences. The Messrs. H. and W. Benner,

> in addition to the improvements made by their own new residences and the opening of First and Second Avenues and Benner Street, have just disposed of several lots for the almost immediate erection of residences; and contemplate, with other property-holders in the park, to open Third Avenue and lay out several new streets.

The author of the 1873 publication *New Brunswick and Its Industries* hailed the early suburbanization:

> Across the Albany Street Bridge is now one of the most beautiful suburbs which any small city possesses, and which is yearly improving prepatory to annexation. About the year 1855, the embowered Swiss stone cottage of Dr. Smith, the Italian villa and handsome dwelling of Mr. William Flagg, with Mr. Schenck's, Mr. Hattersley's, Mr. Towle's, and Mr. Pyatt's fine residences, were all East New Brunswick could boast of. About 1865 Mr. Luke C. Coe took up residence there and laid out a park, lots of which he sold on the condition of immediate improvement by building. When he removed, three or four years later, Mr. Benner took up the work and there have been erected many handsome dwellings in the park, while well-made and graded roads have been constructed. We regard the building up of East New Brunswick, and especially of Raritan Park, as not the least of our accomplishments.

Joining the active mills on Mill Brook were several other nineteenth-century manufacturers. In the 1860s, Cedar Avenue led directly to the U.H. Dudley & Company canning factory situated on the inside curve of the Raritan River waterfront. Ironically, its existence is only known because a *Daily Fredonian* article of May 12, 1871 details its destruction by fire. The building was a large 200- by 45-foot, three-story brick and frame cannery. "The building contained considerable machinery used in pressing tin for cans; also a large quantity of canned corn, pears, raspberries and squash; bottled table oil and barrels of oil." An 1876 map of Middlesex County marks its location on the riverbank with a dot and the words "Ruins of old factory." The cannery workers must have had a pleasant walk through Highland Park countryside each day.

An ad for the Highland Park Needle Works, manufacturers of spring knitting needles, appeared in the 1890 New Brunswick City Directory stating that the company was established in 1860. Little is known about this factory except that it was located somewhere on the south side streets, which would situate it off Cedar Avenue. Sharing the same name as the borough, the Needleworks could have officiated the nickname of the borough. The co-owners, Mr. Lydell and Mr. Beekman, donated a bell to the first "Highland Park" school in 1886.

Another early business was a brewery. A three-story frame building was first constructed in 1867 by Martin Klein on land where the Montgomery Street Apartments now are situated. Located in a hollow north of the main road and located just west of Second Avenue, the land had a small stream that emptied into the Raritan River. The brewery made good use of the stream for all its drainage. A fire on July 29, 1873 destroyed the original building. The brewery was rebuilt by 1877. The new owners of the Raritan Brewery, Mr. Becker and Mr. Whitemeyer, kindly delivered a barrel of their bock beer to the editorial offices of the *New Brunswick Daily Times* in May of 1877, which prompted a rave review and the following poem:

Bock, bock, Raritan Bock;
Better than whiskey, or brandy, or hock;
Good for the stomach, the heart and the head,
As light as a feather, as solid as lead;
Not a pain in a hogshead, a drunk in the sea—
A schooner of bock is the schooner for me.

A map generated in 1868 titled "Map from Newark Bay to Washington's Rock" at Rutgers University shows the rural hamlet of Highland Park with thirty-two squares indicating buildings—fifteen to the south of the main road and seventeen to the north. (*See p. 71.*) Most notable are the J.E. Langstaff farmstead, which is the only house in the triangle area; five buildings associated with the railroad; two houses marked R.J. Livingston; and a scattering of new houses along the main road, Raritan Avenue and Adelaide Avenue. The next two decades would see a continuation of this preliminary suburban development, which would eventually result in today's borough of homes.

Chapter Three

1870 TO 1885

Every historian discloses a new horizon.

—George Sand, 1871

It was during the spring of 1870 that the small hamlet of East New Brunswick became part of the newly formed Raritan Township along with other lands in both Piscataway and Woodbridge Townships. At times very confusing, the small hamlet of Piscatawaytown further east along Woodbridge Avenue also became part of Raritan Township. The *Daily Fredonian* of March 10, 1870 proclaimed:

> Thank heavens, we have found something to agree upon at last. We have agreed to differ pretty sharply about depots, schools, etc. but upon the point of controlling and managing our township affairs, I think we are a unit, Democrats and Republicans . . . all are weary of being controlled by the "Claybank Clique" and long for independent vote and action. This feeling has found expression in the idea of a new township with Metuchen for its center. Bonhamtown on the south, Menlo on the east, Oak Tree on the north, and New Durham on the west would be heartily glad to cut loose from Woodbridge and cast their votes in Metuchen. It is believed that Piscatawaytown and East New Brunswick would not seriously object to the change either.

According to Agnes Saunders in her 1937 "Notes on the History of Piscatawaytown," representatives from the various centers met to agree on boundaries and names for the new township. Three names were suggested: Washington, Metuchen, and Raritan, with the last being selected. Several local townsfolk objected to the changes and insisted that East New Brunswick remain a part of Piscataway. The final boundary was decided upon in Trenton and reported in the *Daily Fredonian*:

> During the evening, numberless interviews were had with the Piscataway men, but no arrangement could be effected. They

> insisted on a line turning short to the river this side of the old church, and giving them East New Brunswick. It was understood that Piscatawaytown would strongly object to such a line, and that East New Brunswick would be dissatisfied unless we took them in. So this line was thrown back on Piscataway, taking in half a mile north of the railroad and running straight to the river.

After more wrangling over the boundary, the New Jersey legislature created the Township of Raritan and it included the lands of East New Brunswick. The first election took place on April 16, 1870 with township committeemen Michael Lupardus, Lewis Thomas, and R.B. Crowell selected. The township name remained Raritan until 1954 when voters made a choice in a tight contest between "Edison" and "Nixon." Raritan Township became Edison in honor of the inventor from Menlo Park, Thomas Alva Edison.

Although Luke C. Coe had the idea of developing the land to the south of the main road for stately residential properties, he was followed by a more successful company of developers. Brothers Hiram and Wesley Benner are credited with encouraging the construction of individual houses on their newly created avenues of South First, Second, Third, and Fourth Avenues, and the cross streets of Magnolia, Benner, and Harper Streets beginning in the late 1860s. Hiram Benner's house stood on the east side of First Avenue between Benner and Magnolia Streets. Harper Street was named after William Harper, who was in the oil and lamp business and who constructed the Second Empire style house at the corner of South Second Avenue. Following the pattern in other suburban areas, a grid of streets was marked out and individual lots of less than an acre in size were sold. New landowners found local architects and builders to construct houses from the standardized plans and materials locally available but individualized based on their particular tastes.

Improvements were celebrated in local press accounts. By 1872, Mr. Bradshaw's residence on Benner Street was not only constructed, but also burglarized. East New Brunswick's residents were listed separately in the 1892 New Brunswick City Directory. Bradshaw's neighbors were grocer V.M. Suydam and Peter Van Deventer. Other residents of Highland Park included Joseph Duclos, an architect who lived in the Italianate house on South Adelaide and Raritan Avenues and who commuted to his job at the Architectural Iron Works in Brooklyn. Coal merchant Augustus T. Stout lived next door to L.L. Hyatt, president of the New Jersey Rubber Company. Others included the Reverend James Caughey; George Buttler of Buttler and Johnson sash and blind manufacturers; Silas Hall, the florist who owned a large fifty acre tract with greenhouses and farm buildings on the south side at Benner Street and

Fourth Avenue; and Professor James Garland, a musician, music store owner, and music teacher. Garland and his family lived in the large Italianate house on the corner of South First Avenue and Benner Street.

On September 20, 1875, Professor Garland committed the Highland Park crime of the nineteenth century. The attempted murder of his wife Amanda was detailed without reserve for several days in the *New Brunswick Daily Times*. As his legally separated wife and two daughters were packing their things in preparation to move to an apartment in New Brunswick, Garland unexpectedly returned home from the music store and fired three shots at his wife. Two of the three bullets hit her. She ran outside and collapsed on the front lawn while Garland proceeded to an upstairs bedroom where he shot himself three times, partially slit his throat, and took a hammer to his own skull. Despite his violent attempt at suicide, unconsciousness ultimately saved his life. Neighbors who heard the shots quickly sent for two local doctors. As Dr. English attended to Amanda Garland, the other, Dr. Mulford, attended to the professor. Both Garland, who ultimately spent five years in state prison, and his ex-wife, survived. After her recovery she, along with her children, moved to New Brunswick and continued to run the music store. Garland returned to the New Brunswick area after his prison term. His next attempt at suicide in 1884 was successful.

Other residents of Highland Park in its early stage of development were Reverend James Caughey and his wife Caroline. In 1868 the Caugheys retired to a quiet life in Highland Park after buying premises on Raritan Avenue opposite Cedar Avenue. In the mid 1900s, this large dwelling operated as the Park Towne Manor, but was demolished to make way for the commercial building at 75 Raritan Avenue in the late 1980s. Before his retirement in 1868, Reverend Caughey was a Methodist evangelist who traveled throughout Ireland, England, Scotland, Canada, and on occasion, the United States. His *New Brunswick Daily Times* obituary stated, "as a preacher he was fluent, eloquent, and practical, appealing directly to the sympathies. His style was his own, and his tongue was never silent when pursuing his work of saving souls." Reverend Caughey was given credit by William Booth, the founder of the Salvation Army, for inspiring him to live a devout Christian life after the fifteen-year-old Booth attended several of Caughey's revival meetings in Nottingham, England in 1844.

Caughey and Booth had the opportunity to meet face to face in New Brunswick in 1883 when Booth was on a cross-country tour preaching throughout the United States and Caughey attended the local meeting. Warm embraces and conversation soon followed. They never met again as

Reverend Caughey died on January 30, 1891 at his home in Highland Park. His gravestone in Elmwood Cemetery in New Brunswick reads: "He that winneth souls is wise and he that turneth many to righteousness shall shine as the stars forever. The path of the just is as the shining light that shineth more and more unto the perfect day."

During the early 1870s, street corner discussions took place about making the Albany Street Bridge a toll-free bridge. In March 1872 the area's state assemblyman, Mr. Fisher, appointed five prominent New Brunswick and Highland Park residents to a commission to appraise the value of and purchase the bridge from the bridge's proprietors, which would extinguish all exclusive privileges to a toll bridge over the Raritan. Evidently, negotiations stalled because a new commission made up of three freeholders, none of whom lived in Middlesex County, was established the following year for the same purpose. The proprietors of the New Brunswick Bridge Company did not accept the assessment of $40,000 for the bridge and $6,000 for the franchises. The case went before the court in April of 1874. Concurrently, a different commission was investigating possible locations for an entirely new bridge over the Raritan that would have emanated from any of the streets leading down to New Brunswick's busy wharves. The Middlesex County freeholders decided to keep negotiating to purchase the Albany Street Bridge and in the end bought it for $58,000. The liberation of the bridge was declared at 11:30 a.m. on July 3, 1875. The event was celebrated with a grand parade of dignitaries, and the publication of a poem titled "Free Bridge:"

> The gates are open and the bridge is free;
> They are open for you and they are open for me;
> And when you enter you will no more find
> A man after you, close behind,
> Commanding, Stop! Pay your toll,
> If you value the connection of body and soul,
> Such an argument as that you will no longer find;
> You may pass unmolested and look behind.
> The gates that enclosed you are now open wide,
> And the day of the opening, we'll remember with pride.

Loiterers on the bridge and complaints about them soon followed. The freeholders also had to allocate tax dollars to pay for routine maintenance and repairs. In 1877, new planks of pine from Florida and Georgia were installed and city prisoners became painters, whitewashing the outer railings in 1882.

The drawbridge over the Delaware and Raritan Canal, which was owned and maintained by the Delaware and Raritan Canal Company, continued to cause delays and accidents.

With the free bridge also came an increase in the number of tramps in the vicinity. The following report came from the *New Brunswick Times* on July 14, 1875:

> Mr. Samuel Ballard is the proprietor of an extensive property in East New Brunswick, which is in charge of his brother-in-law, and which is so inviting in appearance as to attract the notice of the numerous "knights of the road" passing by that way. Lately the latter gentleman has been much troubled by tramps, who beg almost piteously for work or bread. Mr. Ballard thought he would test their sincerity and so he provided some loads of stones to have them broken. Every tramp that now comes along is offered a hammer to go to work on the stones at the rate of a dollar a day. To Mr. Ballard's surprise not one has accepted his offer; the stones lie unbroken, and he is free from the pest of feeding lazy tramps.

Other tramps had set up a camp in the woods at the pond formed by the dam at Mill Brook to the north of the railroad tracks. Locomotives stopped here to fill their water tanks, making a convenient but unofficial station stop. The problem with this transient subculture was statewide and the state legislature acted by creating a tramp law in 1876. The condition was defined and the law called for jail time for all tramps. Police officers were warned that if they willfully neglected to arrest a tramp, they would be fined $10. Many articles about the tramp camp in East New Brunswick highlighted their plights. There were fights, robberies, and several deaths. On March 4, 1880, the following article appeared in the *New Brunswick Daily Times*:

> We are reliably informed by a farmer living on the Holman farm, whose dwelling house is near the head of the old mill pond on the north side of the railroad, across the river, that on Sunday last he counted one hundred and twelve tramps in the neighborhood of his house. His wife has constantly within reach, a loaded double-barreled shotgun, which she is obliged to have near for protection.

In the early 1880s, the Pennsylvania Railroad Company started aggressively dismantling any camps found along its tracks. Notwithstanding, the East New Brunswick camp continued to flourish into the early 1900s until the railroad company finally moved the trains' water stop away from Mill Brook pond, then known as Johnson's Pond after the land's purchase by Robert Wood Johnson Sr. in 1900.

Highland Park can attribute its growth after 1875 to the free bridge. The number of residents listed in the East New Brunswick section of the New Brunswick City directories gradually increased during the years between 1875 and 1885. The little hamlet was given its own map, although with many misspelled names, in the 1876 atlas by Everts and Stewart of Philadelphia. In 1882 Highland Park was described by W. Woodford Clayton in his *History of Union and Middlesex Counties* with a brief statement: "Highland Park, as it is called, is a desirable location for suburban residences, and already contains many handsome mansions, with fine grounds, drives, and other accessories."

On August 1, 1877 the following article appeared in the *New Brunswick Daily Times*:

> New Iron Bridge—It is believed to be the purpose of the Pennsylvania Railroad Company to erect a new iron bridge to take the place of the old wooden one at this city. Contractors from various cities have lately visited this place with the view of gaining data on which to base their estimates of the expense. While the bridge is in course of construction trains will be run on a single track.

By November, the Keystone Bridge Company had been selected and work installing signals and switches to lead the trains onto a single track took place in December. Curiosity about the new bridge prompted the New Brunswick mayor to ask for a meeting with the general manager of the Pennsylvania Railroad. In early January 1878, the plans for the new bridge and new piers were circulated among the city officials. On February 13, the pier for the draw over the Delaware and Raritan Canal was nearly completed and the iron for the draw was expected to arrive in a day or two.

Then, on Saturday, March 9, 1878 the fifty-year old wooden bridge was destroyed by flames in less than two hours between 5:30 a.m. and 7:00 a.m. New Brunswick's fire companies were helpless to save the bridge and could only protect the railroad's outbuildings on each riverbank. Newspaper accounts state frankly that this was a very suspicious fire. "It is thought by many that the burning of the bridge was not accidental, but the work of design. The wind was almost a dead calm, but yet the flames seemed to lap the timbers as though they were saturated with kerosene."

By Thursday, March 14, 1878 trains were again crossing the Raritan on a temporary structure that had been constructed by a team of 700 laborers working from dawn to dusk. The workers constructed the wooden trestle to hold new sleepers and iron rails under the supervision of Foreman Mershon of the Keystone Bridge Company. Train traffic continued to operate with passengers debarking on both sides of the Raritan River and again crossing on the Albany Street Bridge to make connections. At 2:15 p.m., Engineer John McVey drove engine number 923 and forty-four cars over the newly constructed railroad bridge. Thousands of people witnessed the event. Thus, in five days, the Pennsylvania Railroad Company had erected a bridge 916 feet in length.[1] In two months by May 4, 1878, the wooden trestle bridge was replaced with an iron under-deck truss bridge that would carry the busy railroad line for the next two decades.

In November 1878, Joseph Schneider became the new owner of the Raritan Brewery. He would own it for twelve years until all of the buildings were destroyed by wind-whipped fire on October 20, 1891. Schneider was a colorful character who continued the earlier brewers' tradition of bringing kegs of beer to the offices of the local newspapers. Not surprisingly, Schneider's beer was also declared the finest in the land. In 1883, the editorial staff of the *New Brunswick Daily Times* toured the brewery and wrote about their visit. The capacity was 3,000 barrels per annum with four kegs making up every barrel. "The machinery now used is all new. The steam boiler is of 25 horsepower capacity, the malt grinding machine, the cooling compartments and apparatus are all first class and of the best material."

The 1870s were an era when members of high society gathered in clubs they formed around shared interests. The Raritan Boat Club built and maintained a floating clubhouse on the Raritan River tethered to the Albany Street Bridge. (*See p. 68.*) Those wealthy enough to own boats avidly supported this club, although it wasn't until the 1890s that the Boat Club became firmly established. In the 1870s, Germans in New Brunswick gathered for singing and formed the German Glee Club Aurora, which would later be named the Aurora Singing Society. This group would eventually purchase property in Highland Park. However, common occurrences also had entertainment value.

An incident on September 4, 1875 received the headline "An Exciting Runaway." Apparently a team of horses attached to an ice wagon became startled in East New Brunswick and crossed the Albany Street Bridge "at a pace that made the structure tremble like an aspen leaf." At the time the horses were crossing the bridge there was the usual evening crowd of people and "were it not for their danger it would have been amusing to see their confusion in scrambling and tumbling about in their exciting efforts to find places of security." Such runaways took place on a regular basis and were

[1]The information about the fire and the new bridge was gathered from articles in the *New Brunswick Daily Times* the week of March 9 to 15, 1878.

often written up in the following day's newspaper. Other newsworthy animal antics included a heifer that was standing on the tracks and killed by the nine o'clock train out of New Brunswick one day in 1879. Several cars of the train derailed, but no serious damage occurred. Nevertheless, all trains were delayed about twenty minutes that morning. In 1884, a large drove of over 3,000 sheep passed through the area along Raritan Avenue on their way to the countryside west of New Brunswick. This is the same year in which three houses had telephones: Joseph J. Bonney, #N.B. 79; Dr. Fairchild-Richards, #N.B. 78; and John C. Meyers, #N.B. 72. With stories such as these, the rural character of Highland Park during this time is very easy to envision.

Due to a rise in the number of dwellings, by 1885 there were enough families with children to support the creation of the Highland Park school district. Before the first one-room school was constructed, the young pupils had to travel to the Piscatawaytown school or cross the bridge into New Brunswick. By 1888, there were at least seventy houses in the little hamlet including three on River Road near the Albany Street Bridge built by the Conovers. Alexander Merchant, Highland Park's most prodigious early twentieth-century architect, drew a map of Highland Park in 1888 as he remembered it many years later. He accurately indicated the position of houses and names of the occupants primarily on the south side streets and along the south side of Raritan Avenue. In the years to come, the large tracts of farmland would continue to be subdivided and houses would sprout where livestock once grazed.

Chapter Four

1885 TO 1905

Journalism is the first draft of history.

—Joaquin Estefania, 1996

It is interesting to note that there were three competing newspapers covering Highland Park in the late nineteenth century. The *Daily Home News* was inaugurated in 1879 as a rival to the established *New Brunswick Daily Times* and the *Daily Fredonian* began publication in 1886. The coverage of these papers varied significantly. For example, on October 12, 1885 the *Daily Times* printed the following article:

> The New School House—A new school house has just been completed in East New Brunswick, known as "Highland Park School District No. 75." Before this was built, the children of that neighborhood were compelled to walk two or three miles to attend school, besides paying for their tuition. County Superintendent Willis received a petition from the residents of that vicinity last summer, asking for a new school house, and now they have a cozy, one story building of the Queen Anne style, 20 by 42 feet. The cost of the building is $3,300.

The *Daily Home News* printed a similar announcement—but six months later on March 22, 1886. The school presumably had a finished-looking exterior to receive the premature announcement by the overeager *Times* reporter long before the interior was ready for its pupils.

During the autumn and winter of 1885–1886, a small number of the children attended public school locally in rooms rented from Dr. Chevalier at 233 Magnolia Street. Hillsborough teacher Chrissie Bartle, "a lady teacher of ability," became Highland Park's first teacher. Architect George K. Parsell designed the first school. He was a New Brunswick based architect who also designed a house on South First Avenue for himself in the 1880s, the Waldron Company factory in Highland Park in 1896, the Highland Park firehouse, and New Brunswick's Free Public Library on Livingston Avenue in 1902, which are only a few of his many local commissions. The school on the corner of South

Second Avenue and Benner Street had a nineteen- by thirty-foot classroom, a ten-foot square recitation room, and two cloakrooms each six by ten feet. The building was surrounded with a large play yard. The masons hired were Van Sickle and Son, and the carpentry was contracted out to Connet and Cathcart.

The school district was bounded by the railroad tracks on the north, Vandeventer's Lane on the east, and the river to the south and west. Vandeventer's lane corresponds approximately to North Tenth Avenue. At first there were only nine students, but by the time the school was complete in March 1886 there were thirty-three pupils ranging in age from five to fifteen years. The boys were in charge of the pot-bellied stove centered in the schoolroom and Miss Bartle, when interviewed in the 1940s, stated that "they were either frozen or roasted out most of the time."[1]

As soon as the building was opened, many of Highland Park's other nascent organizations used the one-room school for meetings. On January 24, 1887, forty-five people met there to discuss several issues including whether the Raritan Township hamlet of Highland Park should become a borough, and also the state of the Albany Street Bridge. There was no consensus about the borough issue; however, everyone was in agreement that the Middlesex County Freeholders should "without delay construct a good and substantial bridge across the Raritan River at the foot of Albany Street, in the place of the present dilapidated structure, that is a menace to the lives of our families."[2] A new bridge became a reality several years later in the early 1890s, but it would take a decade and a half for Highland Park to become an independent borough.

Another group that used the school for its earliest gatherings was the Union Sunday School group. In November 1886, Protestants affiliated with New Brunswick's churches established the Highland Park Union Sunday School for the religious instruction of children. Over 100 people celebrated its one year anniversary in 1887 with a pageant held in what was called a church, but in essence was a converted barn on Magnolia Street owned by Hiram Garretson. The festivities included the children singing, scripture lessons, and addresses by Professor Jacobus and Dr. English. The congregation also created a "chapel fund" and sponsored events to raise money. They were very successful and in only four years had raised several hundred dollars. On February 25, 1890, the *Daily Times* reported that a site had been secured for a new Reformed Church in Highland Park on the northeast corner of Second Avenue and Benner Street. Members of the First Reformed Church in New Brunswick started the church in Highland Park because the city membership was too

[1]All of this information is excerpted from the history of the Highland Park schools written by Superintendent of Schools Samuel J. Shultise in 1940.

[2]*New Brunswick Daily Times*, January 25, 1887.

large for one pastor to minister to properly. A chapel was constructed and the bell was swung into the belfry on April 8, 1890. The elders and deacons were selected in July 1890 and included Hiram Garretson, Nelson Smock, Joshua Dixon, Luther Riddle, Henry Senker, and Andrew Conover. Unfortunately, no illustrations of this chapel have been located and it no longer exists.

The Reformed congregation continued to grow under the pastorate of Reverend A.S. Van Dyke and by 1897, a decision had been made to build a church. The *Daily Times* reported on September 16, 1897 that ground had been broken and that "George B. Rule will do the carpenter work and William H. Hendricks will have charge of the mason work." The young architect Alexander Merchant (1872–1952), who was a member of the congregation, had drawn up the plans. Merchant was born in Glasgow, Scotland on January 7, 1872. His father was a purser on the National Line sailing between Liverpool and New York City. In the late 1870s, Merchant's family settled in Long Island City, Queens, where Alexander received his elementary education. He had no formal secondary education. As a sixteen-year-old in 1888, he began apprenticing to architect D.D. Williamson in New Brunswick where he remained for five years. It is said that around 1893, Merchant began to work in the office of Carrere & Hastings in New York. He stayed with the New York firm until he was granted a license and returned to settle in Highland Park.

The cornerstone for the modest brick, central-tower church with its Gothic Revival windows was laid on October 3, 1897. Construction took one year and the church was dedicated during a three-day celebration beginning on October 3, 1898. In 1904 the congregation was given matching funds to purchase a pipe organ from philanthropist Andrew Carnegie. On September 29, 1904 the *Home News* reported that "the organ, aside from its first class musical qualities, is also very handsome. The case was especially designed by Alexander Merchant, the architect who designed the church and planned the organ to be in consonance with the building." This church remains on South Second Avenue and has received several additions throughout its century of existence.

Until the late 1880s, shoppers had to go into the city of New Brunswick for their necessities. In May of 1888, Charles Ten Broeck constructed Highland Park's first grocery store on Raritan Avenue close to North Second Avenue. Now gone, this store had been Gilbert's Antique shop in the 1970s. The town's first store would soon be joined by a competitor—Gebhardt's, which opened one year later in 1889 on the corner of Raritan and South First Avenues. Both stores became the loci for social gatherings, postal services, and political discussions. For example, in March 1894 petitions requesting a Raritan Township polling place to be located within Highland Park were available at both stores. Unfortunately, Raritan Township officials determined that with only 100 voters in Highland Park, a local polling place would have exceeded the number allowed for the Township voters and would have been illegal. Additionally, the officials cited the fact that the macadam road and railroad ran from Highland Park to the polls in Metuchen, making for round trips of less than one hour for voters.

Highland Park's second store was established in 1889 by G.B. Gebhardt and by 1894, Anthony J. Gebhardt took the reins. He advertised his newly acquired Highland Park Meat Market in the *Daily Times* on November 2, 1894. "I propose to sell the best quality of meats at the lowest prices possible for cash, and respectfully request your patronage. I will make a special effort to give perfect satisfaction and guarantee prompt delivery." It was such a successful business that Gebhardt added a third floor to his building by 1897. On August 24, 1900, the store was struck by lightning and Frank Whitlock, the bookkeeper, sustained a slight shock. The building did not catch fire, but the experience was a startling one for all in the store.

The Gebhardts celebrated the twentieth anniversary of their store in 1909. By then, the small "mom and pop" operation had expanded to include "a large crop of assistants who delivered three wagonloads on weekdays and four on Saturdays." In the days before telephones and with three postal deliveries each day, customers ordered their groceries by sending postcards to the store.

Another business that got its start in the 1880s was Kitchenmeister Florist. This business continued to operate under the same name until 2004, although beginning in the 1990s it was no longer owned by the original family. After first coming to the area from Philadelphia as a gardener in the 1870s, in 1888 Edward Kitchenmeister (1850–1906) bought his homestead on a lane that later would be named North Fifth Avenue. He erected greenhouses, and sold plants and flowers at wholesale and retail prices to achieve his success. A blaze in 1891 was reported in the *Daily Times*: "A fire broke out in the barn of Michael Fox on Fifth Avenue and spread to the premises of Florist Edward Kitchenmeister, reducing his dwelling house, wagon house and barn to ashes. Mr. Kitchenmeister managed to save his horse and one wagon. His greenhouse escaped only because it was too far removed from the flames." A new house was built and the business rebounded. He continued selling bedding plants including geraniums, dahlias, pinks, phlox, heliotrope, and pansies, among others, to many customers until he died of pneumonia in 1906. His wife and children carried on the business for many years at both their florist shop in New Brunswick and at the greenhouses off North Fifth Avenue in the aptly named "Floral Valley."

As more people found the small hamlet a desirable place to live, houses continued to be built, primarily along Raritan Avenue. Two in particular remain little changed from the time they were first built just east of South Second Avenue. The houses at 202 and 204 Raritan Avenue are the best examples of the trend to construct dwellings in the latest style along the main thoroughfare. This prominent house on the corner (#202) is a good example of the Stick style, with its façade elements hinting at the internal structural components. The house was built from plans selected from R.W. Shoppell's book titled "Shoppell's Modern Houses." In 1888, the Burns family resided there. William Burns was an active member of the community, sometimes acting as chair of the early political meetings held at the school. In 1996, the Burns family house was restored by Dr. Jay Zand, an optometrist, who uses the former residence for his business. This adaptive reuse reflects one of the current trends of historic preservation—reusing large Victorian houses for professional offices.

By 1890, the student population of ninety had exceeded the capacity of the one-room school that had been built to accommodate sixty. In order to fit them all in, the students had been divided into two groups, one meeting in the morning and the other group meeting in the afternoon. In March 1890, the school district's trustees asked for citizenry support to construct an additional schoolroom. A bond issue for $2,500 was passed and an additional room was constructed. Leona Bonney was hired as the second teacher and the children, now in two classes, once again attended for a full day. The school was expanded with another room and rearranged one more time in 1897. This addition was designed by the young architect Alexander Merchant, who would become the most prolific architect of the area in the years to come.

During the late nineteenth century the Middlesex County freeholders funded various road projects. In 1891, Raritan Avenue received a covering of macadam—crushed stones coated in tar—from the Albany Street Bridge to the forks of the Piscatawytown and Metuchen Roads at today's Sixth Avenue. By 1895 the entire length to Metuchen had been macadamized. The macadam was twelve feet wide and eight inches thick. Freeholders from other counties traveled to see this highly acclaimed roadway. Bicycle enthusiasts rode on it even in the winter. When the trolley tracks were later laid along Raritan Avenue in 1897, the workmen struggled to uproot the thick pavement.

In 1887, Highland Park residents began to advocate for streetlights. By 1895, the majority of voting residents wanted gas lights because they were less expensive than electric lights. Light commissioners were chosen and the decision to assess property owners to pay for the lights went into effect. On the evening of October 17, 1895 the first gas streetlight was lit and it remained aglow until 2:00 a.m. the next morning. Eleven lights were positioned along Raritan Avenue from the bridge to the fork, primarily at the cross streets. The coming of the light was heartily welcomed by the residents.

The New Brunswick company of Johnson & Johnson was founded in 1886 when the brothers James, Edward, and Robert Johnson first rented an old factory on Neilson Street. After a devastating fire in 1890, the company rebuilt in the city and also established a small presence in Highland Park. Initially the attraction was the rural character of the hamlet. The November 20, 1890 *Daily Fredonian* announced that the "Messrs. Johnson will store their combustible naphtha in a building which will shortly be constructed in an isolated part of Highland Park. The new storage will be on the property owned by Edward Riddle situated on the river road near the railroad track." Several weeks later, the same newspaper announced:

> Johnson and Johnson have completed their new frame building at Highland Park, which will be fully equipped and ready for the manufacture of mustard plasters on a large scale under the exclusive management of William H. Johnson, who is now a citizen of Highland Park. The building is situated in the valley of A.J. Conover's property, where all the refuse of naphtha, benzene, and other materials in use are conveyed to the river with that of the brewery, by the sewer or gully drain, under the building.

The 1892 Sanborn Fire Insurance Company map depicts this factory on land just off Raritan Avenue. The forty- by seventy-five-foot building is labeled as an oil silk factory rather than a mustard plaster factory. The map illustrates the one and one-half-story building with a series of steam pipes connected to several small masonry sheds. The buildings were constructed on the hill just north of the dogleg of North Adelaide Avenue. This site in still rural Highland Park was selected for its drainage and also because of the extreme fire hazard of the stored chemicals, which proved fortuitous with the event of a blaze reported by the *Daily Times* on October 29, 1891:

> The mustard house, a one-story frame building situated near the river road and distant from the Albany Street Bridge about 400 feet, was burned to the ground a few minutes before 5 p.m. yesterday. The fire was the result of contact between gas from naphtha and an inflammable plaster preparation revolving on a reel. The two elements met in friction on the reel and produced an instantaneous and uncontrollable conflagration. . . . The nearby buildings were

> saved by the timely arrival of steamer No. 3 and hose carriage, and Liberty Hose . . . Messrs. Johnson and Johnson will rebuild at once.

And they did rebuild. The new buildings were to be constructed of iron. The mustard and machinery departments were to be separated. Mr. William Henderson, a blacksmith, was awarded the contract. By 1896, Johnson & Johnson had also constructed a two-story factory and two single-story buildings as well as a few smaller storage sheds. The buildings are illustrated on the 1897 Sanborn map of Highland Park. In addition, a two-story frame building on Cedar Avenue a few lots to the south of Raritan Avenue is labeled "Johnson & Johnson Suspensory Bandages Etc."

In 1899, Robert Wood Johnson Sr. purchased the old S.V. Hoffman tract just to the north of the railroad tracks. In January of 1900, a *Daily Times* article reported that this land was named "Red Cross Park" and that the company intended to relocate all its operations to new buildings to be built there. An article in the March 11, 1901 *Daily Times* provides evidence that Johnson & Johnson actually constructed additional buildings just north of the railroad. This article stated that Johnson's mustard house was flooded to a depth of two feet by water spilling over the dam of Johnson's pond. This only makes sense if the mustard house was close to the Mill Brook.

Buildings on River Road at its junction with the Mill Brook are illustrated on the 1907 promotional map for the Livingston Manor Building Lots. Unfortunately, the area of Highland Park that lies to the north of the railroad tracks was never depicted on the Sanborn maps so it can not be verified if those were additional Johnson & Johnson buildings. Notwithstanding, in the early 1900s the land itself (then named "Sunnyside Farms") was used to grow tens of thousands of Belladonna plants also known as Deadly Nightshade. This plant produces an alkaloid that Johnson & Johnson used in its plasters. Before growing its own, the company had to import the alkaloid in various grades from England or Germany. By growing it themselves, the company secured a better and more active grade at far less cost. In a timeline history of the company compiled in 1912, the column for 1903 lists the "cultivation of Belladonna" and the "erection of Belladonna Laboratories." This could possibly be the identity of the buildings depicted near the Mill Brook in the 1907 drawing.

The 1912 Sanborn Fire Insurance map indicates that the North Adelaide Avenue Johnson & Johnson factory buildings had not been relocated to the property north of the railroad track. These buildings remained and had actually received slight expansions. The largest building was the Adhesive

Plaster factory. The others were labeled grease rendering, sulfur mixing, formaldehyde torch packing, mustard percolating, storage, and steam kettle. The Cedar Avenue building had changed ownership and was labeled as the E.M. Uniak Lamp and Brass Manufacturing Company.

In 1915, the adhesive plaster factory building near North Adelaide Avenue burned to the ground. It was rebuilt and burned again on February 1, 1917, unfortunately killing the foreman Frank B. Denton. Johnson & Johnson did not rebuild its factory in this area because, by the late 1910s, the area along Raritan and Lincoln Avenues had become exceedingly residential after Watson Whittlesey's housing development spilled out of the Livingston Manor tract closer to the Albany Street Bridge.

The John Waldron Machine Company, the maker of the machines that could produce wallpaper, was another industrial company that got its start in New Brunswick and later established a presence in Highland Park. During October 1895, negotiations to buy a portion of the former Livingston property took place between Mr. Waldron and then property owner Thomas Murray. The January 11, 1896 *Daily Times* broke the news:

> Some weeks ago it was announced exclusively in the Times that the Waldron machine shop on Dennis Street was to be moved to Highland Park. At that time the deal had not been consummated but all arrangements have now been completed and the deed passed conveying to John Waldron a piece of land fronting for 500 feet along the tracks of the Pennsylvania Railroad in East New Brunswick and extending back 125 feet.

That March, a Trenton company was selected to construct the Highland Park factory, which was a one-story, 300- by 72-foot brick factory with three wings designed by George K. Parsell. (*See p. 76.*) On June 2, 1896 the factory's wood floor had just been installed and, at the invitation of the architect, a number of wheelmen were treated with the ability to ride their bicycles on the new floor unobstructed by any pillars.

The company employed over 100 men and, by the turn of the century, many were members of the International Association of Machinists. In May of 1901, forty men went out on strike protesting management's refusal to accede to the union's demands for a shorter work week. The average pay at the time was twenty-two cents per hour. Many of the strikers had been with the company for years, and some had never worked anywhere else. The strike was declared over in July, but it made no difference to the company's functioning. Most of the strikers had gotten positions in other factories and the management,

Waldron brothers William and Herbert, refused to take back any of the men in the union who had gone out on strike.

The John Waldron Company incorporated in 1903. The company's founder John Waldron and his two sons continued to run this company that would become an outstanding manufacturer of all types of machines used to make paper products with surface coatings. The company merged with Ross Engineering in 1924, expanded its physical plant along the Pennsylvania Railroad, and finally closed its doors in the 1960s.

The Highland Park Hotel, the brewery, and John Turner's collapsible tube factory are three other Highland Park companies that no longer exist, but were established in the last half of the nineteenth century and continued to operate well into the twentieth.

Throughout most of the nineteenth century, Highland Park lacked a tavern. On March 2, 1896 ground was broken for a brand new roadhouse at the fork of Raritan and Woodbridge Avenues. Philip Smith constructed the handsome structure for $11,000. Resembling a large Queen Anne style house, the hotel became the landmark for the start of horse races and bicycle jaunts, a locus for weddings, and also the site of Highland Park's first restaurant. Ownership of the hotel changed often. George H. Kemp bought it in 1901 and by 1905 it was known as Toft's Hotel with Hans Toft as proprietor. It remained the only establishment with a liquor license until the 1910s. By 1916, proprietor R.R. Osterwald offered both an American and European plan with rates beginning at $2 per day. Its prominent position on the transcontinental Lincoln Highway after 1914 helped make it a well-known stopping place for motorists between New York and Philadelphia.

After Joseph Schneider's brewery was destroyed by a fire in 1891, it remained in ruins for several years until a new brewer, Morris Weidmeyer of Camden, purchased the property and announced that he would build a new facility that would be able to produce 100 barrels of beer daily. By February of 1897, five buildings were nearing completion. Named the Waldschloss Brewing Company, a photograph of the new buildings appeared in an advertisement in the 1897 New Brunswick City Directory. However, this was a short-lived venture.

By July 1898, John W. Russert had become the new proprietor and the brewery was renamed the Rock Spring Brewery. According to a July 22, 1898 *Daily Times* article, "the new brewery takes its name from a spring on the grounds, the water from which comes from rock at the depth of 350 feet. An analysis of this spring by expert college chemists shows that its water is the purest of any in this section of the state." The brewery produced two products: a thick beer of malt and hops typical of German brewing traditions and a brand of pale American beer. Russert sponsored springtime Bock Beer festivals and locally became a popular man. He opened the Rock Spring grove, which must have had a pavilion and outdoor dining areas. Many large group picnics were held in this grove. Beginning in 1901, Rock Spring beer was not only bottled, but also delivered to customers by Peter Stamm of Milltown, who had the exclusive right to do so. In June of 1901, Russert signed the agreement of the Newark Brewers' Union thereby making his place a union brewery and his employees members of the union.

In 1898, John S. Turner, a foreman at the Consolidated Fruit Jar Company in New Brunswick, started his own factory producing collapsible tubes from white metal, a type of lead alloy. Workers at the factory, which was on the south side of Raritan Avenue between Second and Third Avenues, produced the tubes used for ointments, creams, and dentrifices. Johnson and Johnson Company was the company's most important client. The first building was one story and no larger than twenty by forty feet. The Turner family lived in a dwelling in front of the factory. After a series of ownership changes in 1901 and 1902, Turner regained the majority control of his company and continued to be its president until his death in 1922. He was an active member of the community and was president of the Highland Park Building and Loan Association. His company continued to operate in its Highland Park plant until his sons decided to move the business to Forsgate Industrial Park in South Brunswick in 1962.

The 1890s were marked locally by two great transportation improvements. The stone arch Albany Street Bridge was constructed in 1892 and the first trolley coursed its way into town from New Brunswick in 1897. For years beginning in the 1880s, discussions raged about the poor condition of the wood plank spans of the free Albany Street Bridge. The Middlesex County freeholders were confronted with citizen efforts calling for its replacement. In a particularly passionate plea, former New Brunswick mayor, state senator, and Highland Park resident Abraham Schenck called for a beautiful bridge that would prove an attraction, whereas both the city and the country would grow with more residents. Senator Robert Adrain, resident of the former Hoffman estate on River Road, also reiterated the sentiment stating that a new bridge would be noticed by those riding on the trains. Unmoved, the freeholders allocated money only for repairs.

By October of 1891, the Middlesex County freeholders were convinced, after continued citizen advocacy, to support the allocation of $100,000 for a new structure. The resolution of October 7, 1891 stated:

> Whereas the County of Middlesex is already bonded for the sum of $58,000 in payment of the Albany Street Bridge, and now that this Board has passed a resolution by a majority vote of its members to build a new one; therefore, be it Resolved, that it is the sentiment of the present Board of Freeholders that there be placed in the tax levy for the year 1892 a sum sufficient to pay for building of said bridge.

Eleven companies and individuals submitted plans for their versions of a $100,000 bridge during an open competition. Dean & Westbrook Company's design for seven arches of New England granite infilled with brick was selected. Each arch was to be seventy-five feet wide with a rise of fifteen feet above the water. The twenty-five-foot wide roadway was to be paved with Belgian block and ornamental iron railings edged the five-foot wide sidewalks made from slabs of stone reaching from curb to coping.

The wooden bridge that had served travelers well for over a century was dismantled during the summer of 1892 and the local newspapers gave the work of constructing the new bridge much ink. By October the foundation of the last pier was completed. Work progressed despite a small flood in mid-November, which caused delays and the need to provide a ferry when a temporary wood bridge used by the workers and pedestrians collapsed. The last arch was complete in mid-December and the arches were ready to be filled up to the roadway level. With only a few minor mishaps and no deaths during its construction, the stone arch bridge was finally opened in August of 1893, only eight months behind schedule. The original stonework can still be seen today on the north face of the bridge.

The *Daily Times* made the following announcement on June 20, 1895:

> If the Brunswick Traction Company is permitted to cross the Albany Street Bridge, a line will be built in Highland Park. . . . The company wants privilege to lay its line from the bridge up Raritan Avenue to First Avenue, down First Avenue to Benner Street, from Benner Street to Third Avenue, up Third Avenue to Raritan Avenue, and down Raritan Avenue to First Avenue. A line is also to be laid along the river road toward Bound Brook.

Civil Engineer Asher Atkinson began to survey the extension of the branch through Highland Park that July. Nevertheless, in December, despite strong public support for the trolley, there was still unsettled business. The private company was waiting for Middlesex County permission to cross the bridge and Raritan Township permission for an exclusive franchise. Debates lasted for several months and by April of 1896, the trolley company had received permission for both. Nevertheless, actual construction did not commence until August of 1897. One of the lines followed Raritan Avenue to the Bonhamtown road that is today's Woodbridge Avenue. The other coursed along the south side of River Road. Evidence of this line remains in the allée of trees skirting the edge of Johnson Park.

The *Daily Times* reported that on November 18, 1897, the first trolley ran along the line from New Brunswick to Philip Smith's Hotel at the fork. The trial trip was conducted in Car No. 111, which had been handsomely repainted and fitted up for the occasion. The car was filled to its fullest capacity with city officials, aldermen, freeholders, and prominent citizens. Hundreds of people lined the route. The car was met with cheers and fireworks when it reached A.J. Gebhardt's grocery store. Portentously, as the trolley reached Highland Park's crossroad hotel, another strange vehicle came down the road at a high rate of speed. This was the new motor carriage belonging to L.J. Phelps, manager of the Brunswick Tire Company. Spectators witnessed the very beginning of the twentieth century battle for vehicular supremacy on the roads.

The Baptists' history began in the early 1890s when they first started meeting in each other's homes for fellowship and to worship. In 1895, a census was taken and it was determined that there was a sufficient number of potential members to establish a Baptist Sunday School in Highland Park. Consequently, the First Baptist Church in New Brunswick established a local mission Sunday School. Meetings were held in a building on Raritan Avenue, the house behind 74 Raritan Avenue's storefront, that earlier had been built as A.J. Gebhardt's store. For several years the congregation collected funds and, by 1899, the announcement was made that Highland Park would be home to a new chapel. This would be constructed on recently purchased land on the north side of Raritan Avenue at the point where North Second Avenue would later be established.

The chapel was designed by Augustus N. Whitlock in the fashionable Shingle style. Wood shingles coated the entire exterior and the chapel's asymmetrical composition of simple geometric forms included a corner belfry and an elliptical arch entryway. The mason awarded the contract was Peter Hendricks, and Daniel Whitlock won the carpentry contract. The building was dedicated on June 3, 1900 in a joint celebration of its construction and the fifth anniversary of the Baptist Sunday School. Edward Kitchemeister furnished the potted palms. Many prominent Highland Park families were members of this congregation including the Zimmermans, Cronks, Schencks, and Atkinsons, to name a few.

Although there is little pictorial evidence of Highland Park's race tracks, as early as 1893 one had been established in an unknown location and several races took place on its trotting ring. By 1897, there was a push to build a half-mile driving and bicycle track on land owned by Dr. C.M. Slack on Woodbridge Avenue near Philip Smith's new hotel. Seventeen acres were sold to the Brunswick Driving Park Association for $3,750 and they actually commenced the project in 1898. Contractor John Van Deusen constructed the track and ancillary structures, including a grandstand, stables, and an eight-foot fence over 4,000 feet around the perimeter. In July, the first events, with admission fees of twenty-five cents, were match races by the Brunswick Bicycle Club and trotting races by the Central Trotting Association of New Jersey. Over 1,000 people attended the bicycle races on July 4. The following year, Judge Strong refused to grant permission for a liquor license after the expression of strong opposition spearheaded by local clergymen was taken into consideration.

The track was not a very financially successful venture for its investors. The admission price had doubled to fifty cents by 1900, but the track was sold in 1901 to a new group of investors, the Raritan Driving Association. After this group took over operations, many gala harness races and horse shows took place several times a year (usually at the end of May, the July 4 weekend, and in early September). A *Daily Home News* headline on May 31, 1904 proclaimed that the day before was "A Great Day at Driving Park, Fifteen Hundred People See Raritan Driving Association's Meet, W.G. Deinzer's Mare Wins the 2.35 Event—An Interesting Running Race Pleasing the Crowd." The article detailed the day's events and "despite the threatening weather and the trolley line taxed to its utmost, 1,500 people filled the grandstand to overflowing, sitting on the steps and in the aisles."

In July of the same year, Robert W. Johnson Jr., then ten years old, won an orange ribbon (third place) in the show that featured ponies that were thirteen hands or under. Local youths not only showed their prize ponies at the horse shows, but helped take care of the trotters from all over the state. A short-lived venture, the last race was held in July of 1906. Despite being considered one of the best tracks in the state, a January 24, 1907 *Daily Home News* article reported that "there will be no more races on the well-known speedway."

A bright-lights amusement park and showplace called Electric Park was heavily advertised to open on May 30, 1907 on the old Race Track land. However, newspaper accounts reported that Mr. Fullam, the manager, disappeared days before its opening, having not paid any workers or suppliers. A large amount of lumber had been purchased for the park that was never built. The supplier recovered its cost after the New Brunswick court ruled in his favor.

By September of 1907, Mr. Kennedy and Mr. Pfeiffer of Perth Amboy bought the twenty-five-acre property for building lots. They called their home sites "Annadale Crest" and advertised in the September 14, 1907 edition of the *Daily Home News* claiming that this area in Highland Park was "the most beautiful spot for home or investment in New Jersey" with its pure well water. The villa plots were sold one by one, and over the next fifty years the old Race Track would disappear under a cover of houses.

On January 14, 1897 one of the most important exchanges of Highland Park land took place when Watson Whittlesey purchased the Livingston estate of over 100 acres for subdivision and development. Whittlesey's real estate credentials included the development of "Watchung Heights" in a section of West Orange, New Jersey; "Hyde Park" in East Orange; and a small neighborhood in Plainfield near the Netherwood station. Although a local agent, Mr. Moffitt, began to sell lots with promised $1,500 homes beginning in 1897, the houses in what Whittlesey would name the "Livingston Manor" were not constructed until the summer of 1906. Interestingly, the names of these early purchasers are recorded in the Middlesex County grantee index but they do not appear in the grantor index. It remains a mystery because it is not known when or to whom the earliest purchasers sold their lots.

When historians conduct research using resources that were not available to earlier writers, the new research may reveal a discrepancy in those histories. This is the case with the Highland Park Fire Department. Newspaper articles now available on microfilm reveal that this group became an official organization in September of the year 1900, one year later than has been previously recorded and celebrated. On the evening of September 14, 1900, thirty-five residents assembled at John Metzrath's house on Raritan Avenue. The group decided to form an independent company fashioned after the Liberty Hose Company in New Brunswick instead of becoming annexed as a local branch of the New Brunswick Fire Department. Officers James Earle, William Blake, Edward Page, Theodore Welsh, Charles Dahmer, and William Holden were selected. Lorenz Volkert, John Dunham, and A.J. Gebhardt became trustees. An October announcement stated that the company's new headquarters at the corner of Cedar Avenue and Benner Street were to be repainted and strung with electricity. The "headquarters" was a converted one-story workshop. The young organization sponsored its first fund-raiser one month later—a two-week long fair with dancing to music by Professor Haywood's orchestra, performances, comedy acts, and door prizes held at Zimmerman's Hall in New Brunswick. The fair raised over $500 that was applied to the purchase of the first apparatus, a hose wagon manufactured by the firm of Valentine & Weeden Company of Trenton.

Once the trustees ordered a hose wagon, discussions turned to finding a good place to store it upon its delivery. An article from the June 11, 1901 *Daily Times* shows how situations were managed quickly at the turn of the last century:

> A committee of five members of the Highland Park fire company was appointed to wait on the Fire Commissioners of Highland Park. The committee found the commissioners at the store of Conover on Albany Street, and stated the necessity of the case to them. After hearing the situation the Fire Commissioners decided to hold an election within the next ten days when all voters will be given an opportunity to vote either for or against accepting the proposition to raise the funds to construct a fire house as required. The amount which will be required to construct the building will not exceed $1,500. The building will be a frame structure and will be made a town hall, with rooms on the second floor for general meetings. It is said that land for the building may be obtained in the central part of the Park for a nominal figure. It is believed that a majority of the voters will be in favor of the hall.

The special vote took place two weeks later on June 25, 1901 and the appropriation of $1,600 passed by an overwhelming majority of forty yesses to seven nays. The fire commissioners adjourned for the summer after appointing two members to secure a piece of land for the building. The firemen relocated their offices to a vacant barn on Cedar Avenue, abandoning the old headquarters on the corner of Benner Street and Cedar Avenue, which was fortunate, because that building burned to the ground just around midnight of August 18, 1901. In October, architect George K. Parsell presented plans for the new firehouse and construction was soon underway. The new firehouse on Raritan Avenue at North Second Avenue and the new apparatus were presented at a grand opening reception held on Saturday, March 15, 1902. On display were 500 feet of hose and the new hose cart with "Highland Park" painted on both sides and the fire company's motto "Ready to Save" inscribed on the back. The building still stands, although greatly altered due to its conversion into a dry cleaners during the 1950s.

On May 26, 1902, thousands of people from Highland Park and New Brunswick lined the banks of the Raritan River and the Delaware and Raritan Canal to see the iron truss railroad bridge pulled fourteen feet downstream onto expanded footings. This was done to allow the construction of a new higher and wider stone arch bridge. The spectators were treated to a fascinating, albeit short, show. The task was finished in less than ten minutes due to a well-designed system of steam powered pulleys and rigging. Earlier in 1902, the New Brunswick common council passed an ordinance allowing the Pennsylvania Railroad to elevate its tracks through the city. This was part of the company's overall plan to eliminate all the deadly level crossings in the urban centers along its route. Chief engineer William Brown designed the plans for the twenty-one span stone arch bridge, which replaced a steel span that had been erected only six years before, replacing the iron truss bridge erected in 1878. The stone arches were constructed in two parts—each one half their full width. This technique allowed the trains to continue to run on the truss bridge immediately adjacent to the half-width stone arches. Traffic on this busy rail line was not interrupted for more than an hour during the entire year it took to construct the magnificent bridge. Unfortunately, a dozen workers were killed during its construction.

The first train to cross the river on the new span was Engine No. 2042 drawing a caboose shortly before noon on May 17, 1903. Then Engine 807 pulled forty-two freight cars over the river. At 1:30 p.m., the first regularly scheduled passenger train from New York ran across the new bridge. With many passengers waving flags out of the windows, the spectators gathered at the New Brunswick station greeted this train with wild applause.

Despite the significant rise in the height of the railroad tracks and the lack of a convenient hopping off place, the tramps continued to occupy the tramp camp that had been established at the pond years before. To address this statewide problem, in March of 1903, the New Jersey legislature introduced a bill to allow hoboes sentenced to work on the streets to be secured by a ball and chain. The reaction from the local vagabonds was swift and sure. "The Amalgamated Alliance of Hoboes" held a convention at the East New Brunswick tramp camp and passed resolutions of its own stating; "that the said ball and chain bill is barbarous in its treatment, contrary to the rights granted us in the constitution, and in defiance of the principles of liberty so beautifully exemplified in the American flag, and we pray that said bill be promptly interred in the Senate burying ground." Their committee of lobbyists including Monk, Washington Tom, Brooklyn Red, Easton Whitey, Pittsburg Phil, Slim Jim, and Foot-and-a-half O'Neill went to Trenton to present their petition.

They had a delaying effect on the senators; however, only a short-lived one. On March 19, 1903 the measure was signed into law by Governor Murphy.

By the beginning of the twentieth century, with all the infrastructure components including the bridges and roads, the trolley line, a growing number of houses and industry, a schoolhouse, a fire company, two religious institutions, and several commercial places well established, the small Raritan Township hamlet of Highland Park was ready to take the next step in its growth—that of becoming an independent borough.

Chapter Five

1905 TO 1920

Every generation rewrites the past.

—John Dos Passos, 1941

Highland Park made headlines in February, 1905 as two groups of residents, those pro and con, again discussed the option of becoming a separate borough. On several occasions in the 1880s and 1890s, residents had convened to discuss this matter, but those discussions did not lead to action. At the time of the 1905 New Jersey Census, the little hamlet of Highland Park consisted of 147 houses built on several south side streets and primarily along Raritan Avenue, housing just over 700 people. Earlier residents had petitioned for a school in 1885 and many of the local men had formed a volunteer fire department in 1900 and constructed a firehouse in 1901. The funding for and control of these two institutions was at the heart of the debate over separation from Raritan Township. Highland Park residents thought that too few of their Raritan Township tax dollars were returned to the hamlet in the form of services as most of the Raritan Township budget was spent on maintaining the large network of rural roadways. Public meetings were held at the schoolhouse and petitions were circulated throughout the town. Sentiment was divided. A straw poll meant to gauge residents' support for independence lost by two votes. Nevertheless, on February 20, 1905, Senator Jackson introduced the Highland Park borough bill in Trenton where it passed the senate on March 8 and the assembly a few days later. The bill was signed into law by Governor Stokes on March 15, 1905.

The borough's first election took place on April 23, 1905 and a Democratic slate known as the "grocery store ticket" won handily. They were up against a full Republican slate headed by Condit S. Atkinson, then publisher of the *Daily Fredonian*. Shoe store owner James B. Archer was elected mayor. Councilmen included George Eden, Charles Tamm, John Whitehead, Charles P. Page, Otto F. Lindner, and the popular brewer John W. Russert, who was chosen as Borough Council president. With the mayor and council selected, the official business of running the borough began. At the first borough council meeting on May 2, 1905, funds were allocated for stationery, several marshals were named, and several committees were formed. Minutes were written in neat script in a large, bound book. A special committee was appointed to facilitate the adjustment of matters between Raritan Township and the new borough. That year, the borough budget was fixed at $3,990. In Mayor Archer's first formal address, he stated that the important issues at hand were to eliminate the dump along River Road, to ban baseball games on Sundays, and to negotiate with the trolley company to improve the condition of the macadam on Raritan Avenue.

Although the creation of the borough made the biggest headlines in 1905, other events took place that year. In May, $14,000 was allocated for an additional schoolroom and on Decoration Day, May 30, over 2,000 people attended the horse races at the Race Track. In June, the Highland Park Baptist Church Sunday School celebrated its 10th anniversary and on July 13, the Highland Park Reformed Church congregation took an excursion to Boynton Beach. In October, the Woodchoppers Association held a social at Donaldson's Woods and the final horse race of the season took place on October 28. Throughout the year, business continued at the brewery, at the John Waldron machinery factory near the railroad tracks, and at Turner Tubes. Johnson and Johnson's small mustard plaster factory located off North Adelaide Avenue employed a number of Highland Parkites and travelers enjoyed their stays at Toft's Hotel located at the crossroads of Raritan and Woodbridge Avenues. People shopped at A.J. Gebhardt's and Charles Ten Broeck's grocery stores and at Himmelman's confectionery on Raritan Avenue. Kitchenmeister's greenhouses in "Floral Valley" off North Fifth Avenue supplied the flowers that were sold at his New Brunswick shop.

As mayor of a new borough, James B. Archer's term in office was marked by the organization of the borough offices and construction of the first brick school. In 1905, the 219 voters registered in the new borough were presented with the fact that the old three-room school was extremely overcrowded with forty-five or fifty pupils per classroom. In a light turnout, fifty-nine voters agreed to have the borough borrow $15,000 for the construction of a new brick and stone structure designed by Alexander Merchant that consisted of four large classrooms, two cloakrooms, and a boardroom. The new building was planned to be built on the same lot as the old school. In fact, the new school incorporated the two classrooms that had been previously added onto the original school. Construction was underway and the new brick, Colonial Revival style school opened on December 12, 1907. George K. Parsell's original one-room school (without its additions) had been sold to the Reformed Church for $37. It was moved down South Second Avenue from the corner of Benner Street to the side of the church closer to Raritan Avenue and became the Church's new chapel.

According to his *Daily Home News* obituary printed on March 8, 1912, Mayor Archer was a staunch Democrat in politics and at the time of his death was president of the Highland Park Building and Loan Association. He had been in the shoe business, both manufacturing and sales, for most of his professional life and resided on South Adelaide Avenue.

On March 12, 1907, a tragic fire destroyed the five-story factory of one of New Brunswick's most prominent businesses—Janeway and Carpender Wallpaper Company. During very public discussions about rebuilding, Colonel Jacob J. Janeway was approached by representatives of several municipalities, including Deans in North Brunswick, who hoped to attract such an important business. However, several years earlier, around 1900, Janeway had purchased a substantial tract of Watson Whittlesey's land near Waldron's machine factory along the railroad tracks in the Livingston Manor. Janeway announced that he would rebuild his new factory on this tract and that "the new whistle would blow by July Fourth."

Designed by George K. Parsell, the factory was constructed with automatic sprinklers, firewalls, and three wings to allow for separate locations for different departments—lessons learned from the conflagration in New Brunswick. Work progressed very rapidly and by July 1, a significant portion of the factory had been constructed. Although the whistle blew three days later, it did not signal that wallpaper production had restarted. It took several more months before the new factory was ready for occupancy. New machines were built at the neighboring Waldron machine shop. The speed with which this factory was constructed was greatly admired and the new building was featured in a trade magazine titled *Carpets, Wall Papers, and Curtains*. The sprinklers were put to good use on a Saturday afternoon in 1916 when a small blaze broke out in the basement, which was quickly brought under control by alert employees.

In 1907, the brewery changed hands for the last time. The New Brunswick Brewing Company took over operations and ran immediately into trouble with sponsors of the growing prohibitionist movement, who were actively engaged in the battle to ban all alcohol sales. By 1909, brewers' advertising signs had to be removed from local saloons, and measures to ban Sunday sales were being passed by many communities. However, business at the local plant boomed and by 1909, the New Brunswick Brewing Company announced plans to enlarge its Highland Park facilities. New managers Max Berger and Carl Fischer took over and petitioned for fire hydrants after a small blaze in February 1912 burned the brewery's roof. They were never installed

Continued on page 97

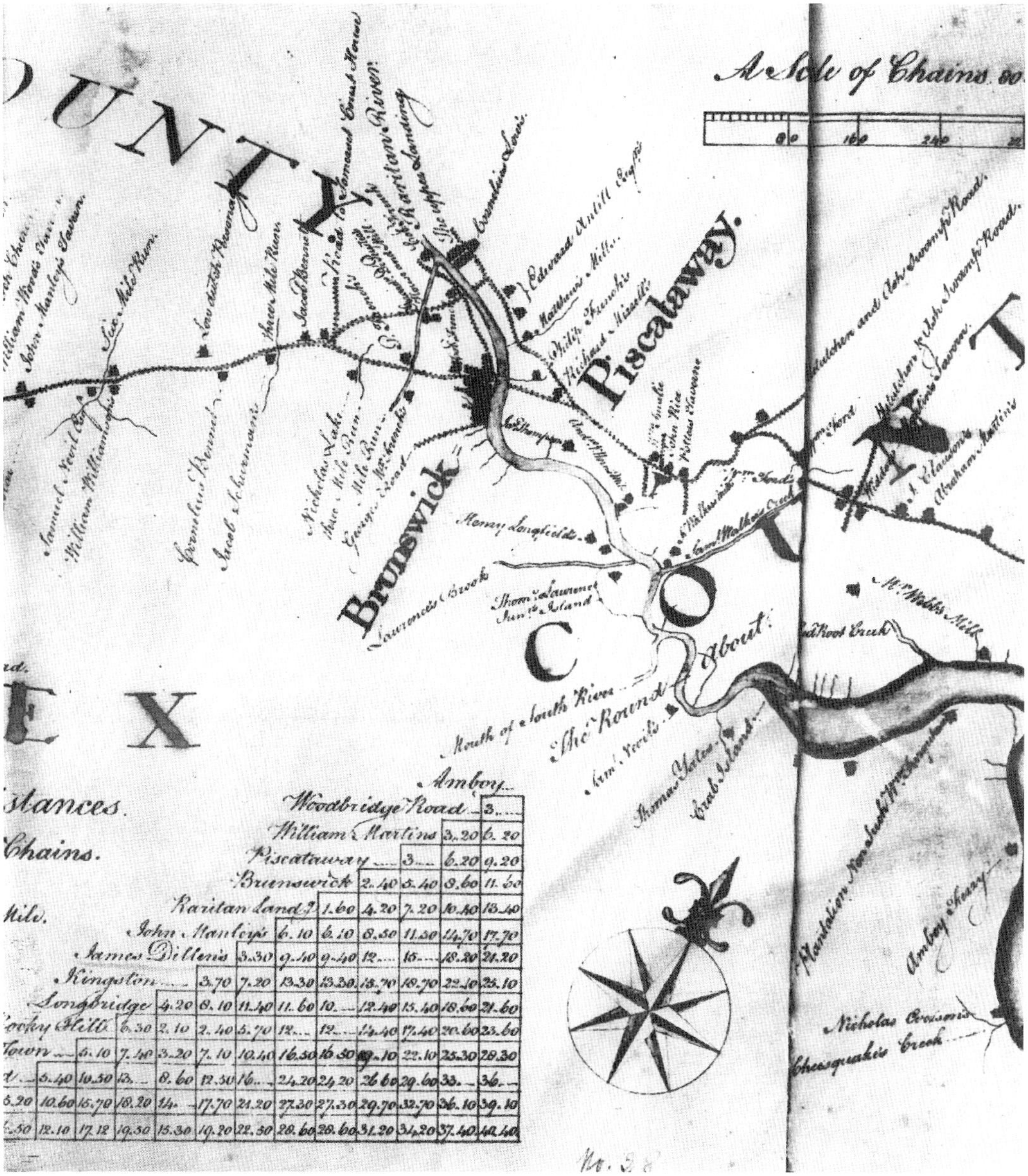

1745 Survey Map. John Dally surveyed the road from Trenton, New Jersey to Perth Amboy in 1745. The map indicates the mill and a few farmsteads that had been constructed in Piscataway on the high land across the Raritan River east of New Brunswick.

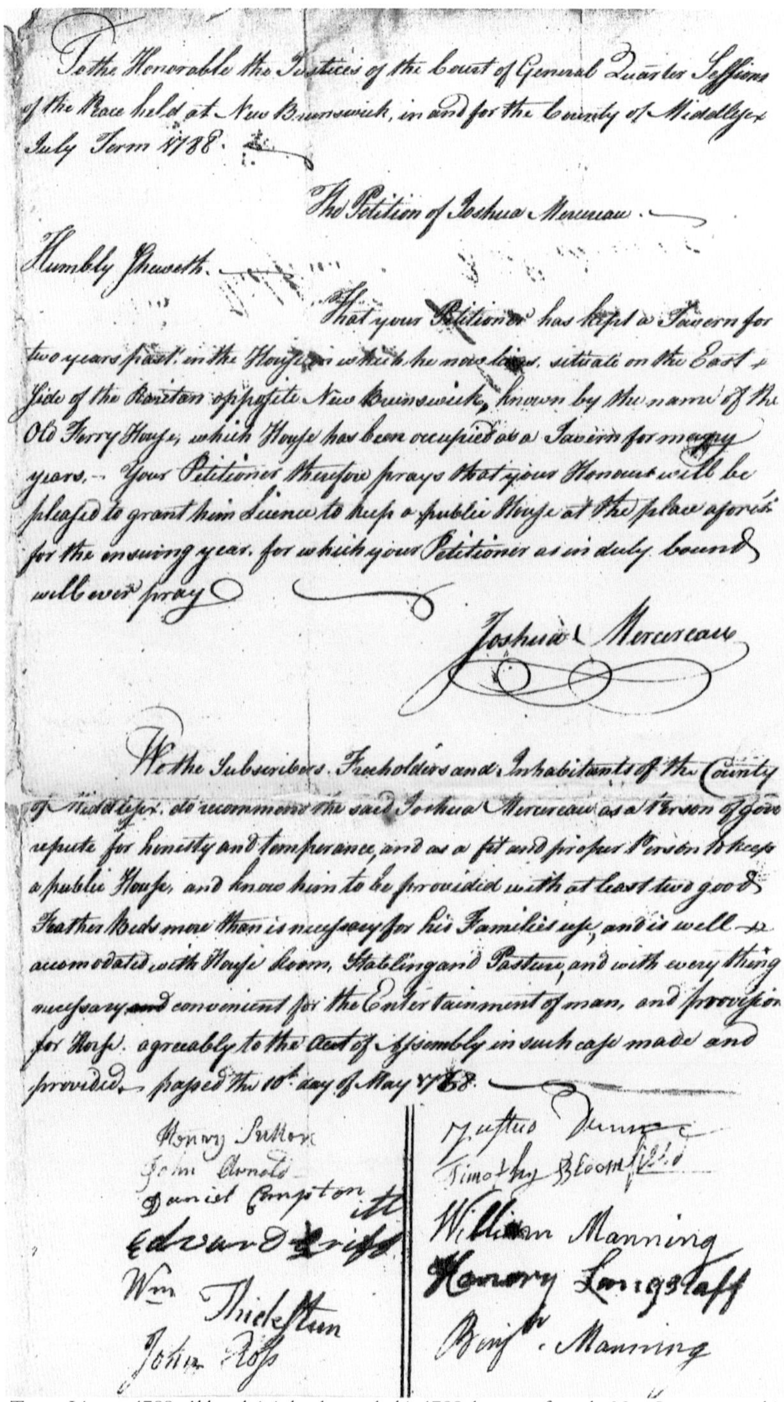

To the Honorable the Justices of the Court of General Quarter Sessions of the Peace held at New Brunswick, in and for the County of Middlesex July Term 1788.

The Petition of Joshua Mercereau

Humbly Sheweth.

That your Petitioner has kept a Tavern for two years past in the House in which he now lives, situate on the East Side of the Raritan opposite New Brunswick, known by the name of the Old Ferry House, which House has been occupied as a Tavern for many years. Your Petitioner therefore prays that your Honours will be pleased to grant him Licence to keep a public House at the place afores.d for the ensuing year. for which your Petitioner as in duty bound will ever pray

Joshua Mercereau

We the Subscribers. Freeholders and Inhabitants of the County of Middlesex. do recommend the said Joshua Mercereau as a Person of good repute for honesty and temperance, and as a fit and proper Person to keep a public House, and know him to be provided with at least two good Feather Beds more than is necessary for his Families use, and is well accomodated with House Room, Stabling and Pasture, and with every thing necessary and convenient for the Entertainment of man, and provision for Horses. agreeably to the Act of Assembly in such case made and provided, passed the 10th day of May 1788.

Henry Sutton
John Arnold
Daniel Compton
Edward [illegible]
Wm Thickstun
John Ross

Justus [illegible]
Timothy Bloomfield
William Manning
Henry Longstaff
Benj.n Manning

Tavern License, 1788. Although it is hard to read, this 1788 document from the New Jersey state archives indicates that a tavern had been established for many years on the Highland Park side of the Raritan River at Inian's ferry landing.

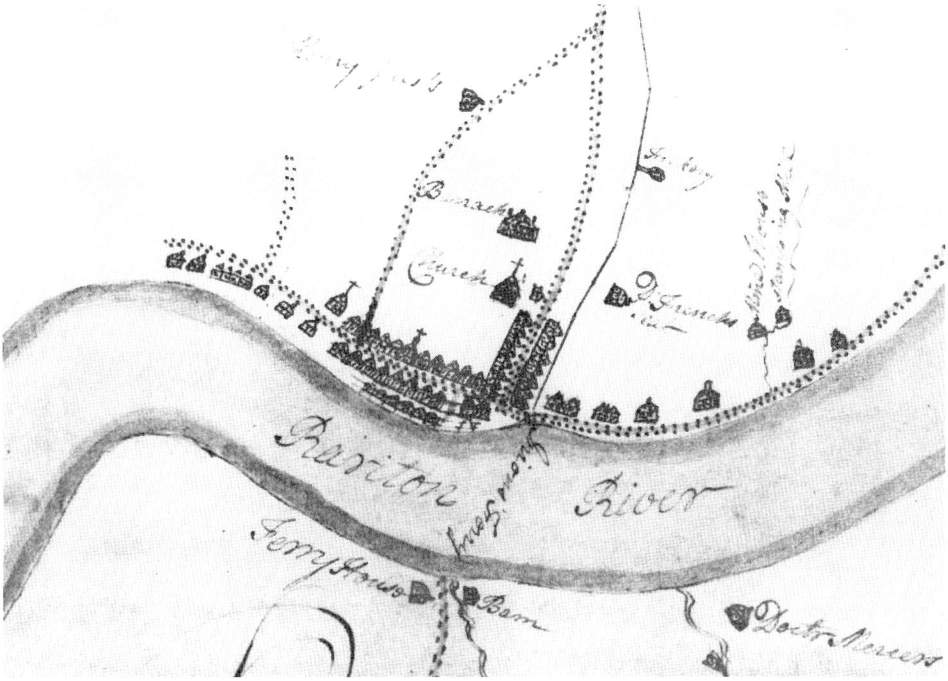

Detail of 1766 Map. A closer detail of the Raritan River and New Brunswick from 1766 shows Inian's ferry, the ferry house, its barn, and also Doctor Mercer's property at the Mill Brook on the eastern bank of the river. This is a detail from "A Map of the Division Line Between the Counties of Middlesex and Somerset."

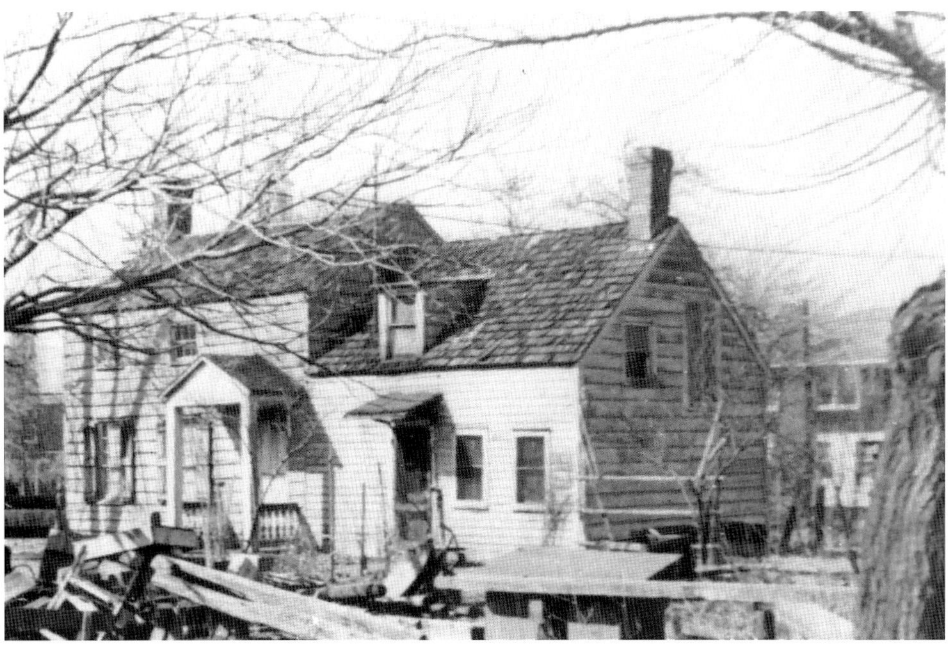

Colonial House. This photograph was taken in the mid twentieth century. It shows the small East Jersey cottage with a characteristic side gable form that had been constructed in the 1700s, perhaps by the Merrills. The house received a later, taller addition (on the left) and was known as the Lucas House until it was razed in 1959 to make way for the public library.

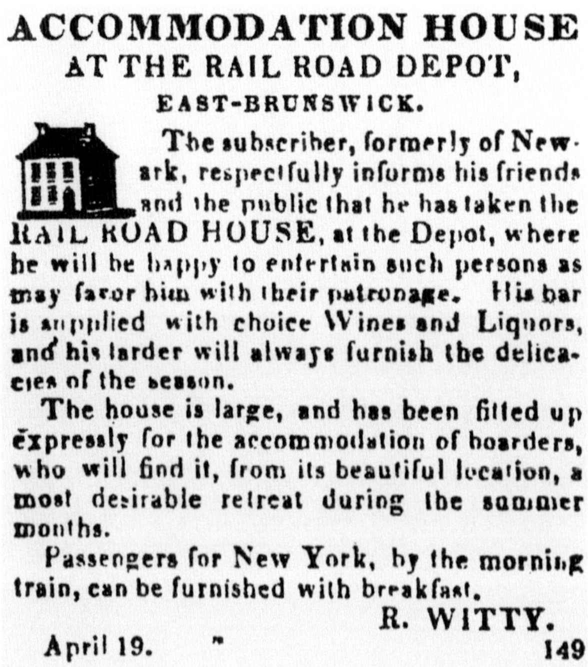

ACCOMMODATION HOUSE
AT THE RAIL ROAD DEPOT,
EAST-BRUNSWICK.

The subscriber, formerly of Newark, respectfully informs his friends and the public that he has taken the RAIL ROAD HOUSE, at the Depot, where he will be happy to entertain such persons as may favor him with their patronage. His bar is supplied with choice Wines and Liquors, and his larder will always furnish the delicacies of the season.

The house is large, and has been fitted up expressly for the accommodation of boarders, who will find it, from its beautiful location, a most desirable retreat during the summer months.

Passengers for New York, by the morning train, can be furnished with breakfast.

R. WITTY.

April 19. 149

Railroad Hotel. An advertisement from the New Brunswick Daily Times on June 7, 1837 has the only image of East New Brunswick's railroad hotel. Neither its period of operation nor its exact position on the Highland Park side of the Raritan River is known.

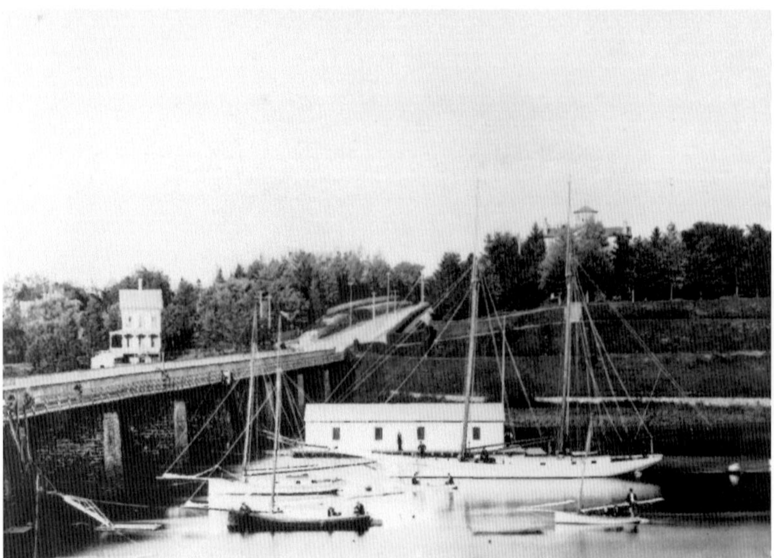

Old Albany Street Bridge, c. 1880. This photograph of the old Albany Street Bridge was taken from New Brunswick facing Highland Park. It shows the one-story boathouse, a house on River Road that has been demolished, and the old bridge, which was replaced in 1892 by the stone arch bridge still in existence today.

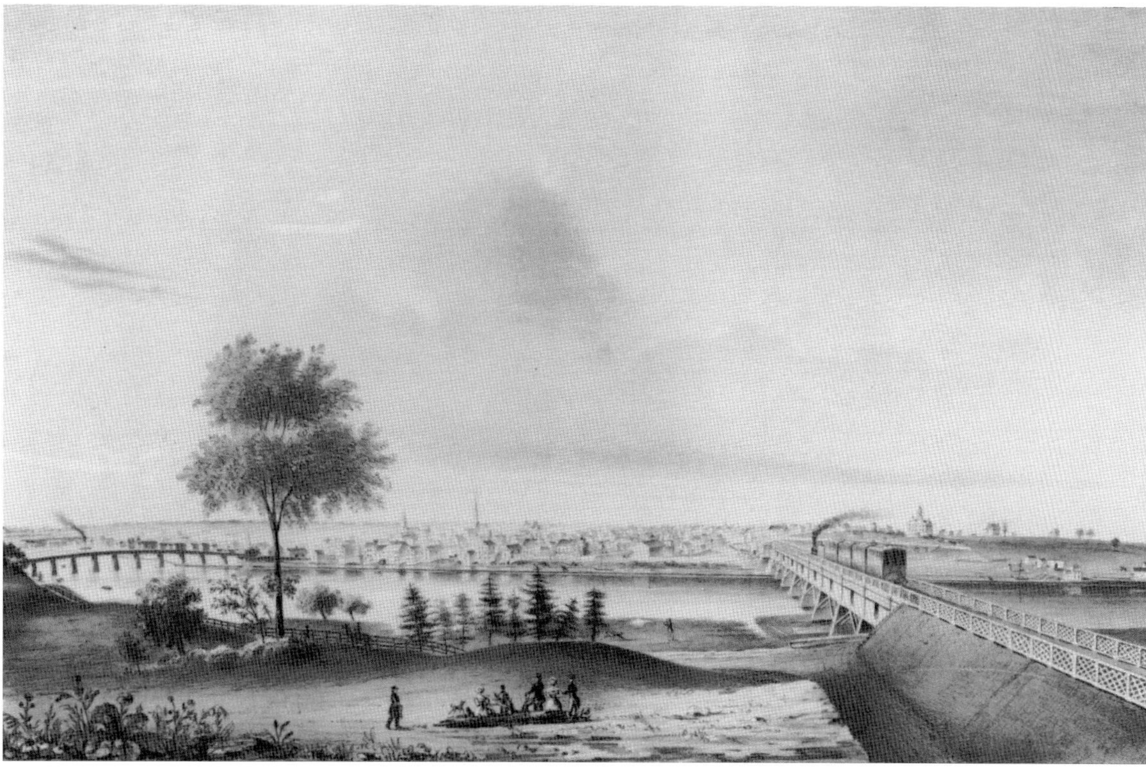

View of New Brunswick. In 1838, J.H. Bufford created a lithograph titled "View of New Brunswick, N.J. taken from the Rail Road Hotel at East Brunswick." Highland Park's rural lands are in the foreground. Two bridges, the Albany Street Bridge (to the far left) and the double deck Railroad Bridge (to the right), provided access to the city across the Raritan River.

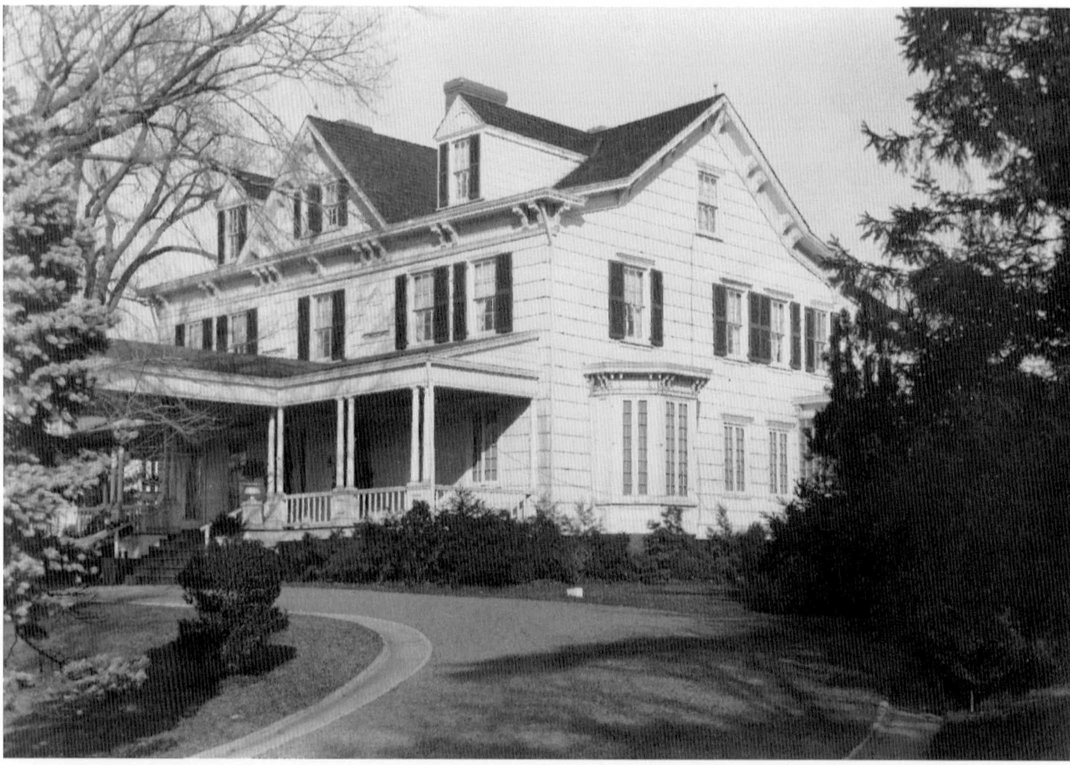

Johnson's Summer House, 411 River Road. Built around 1840 by Samuel V. Hoffman without dormers, this house has undergone several transformations. It was Robert Wood Johnson Jr.'s summer home from 1910 to 1950 and the Sisters of the Cenacle Retreat House after 1950.

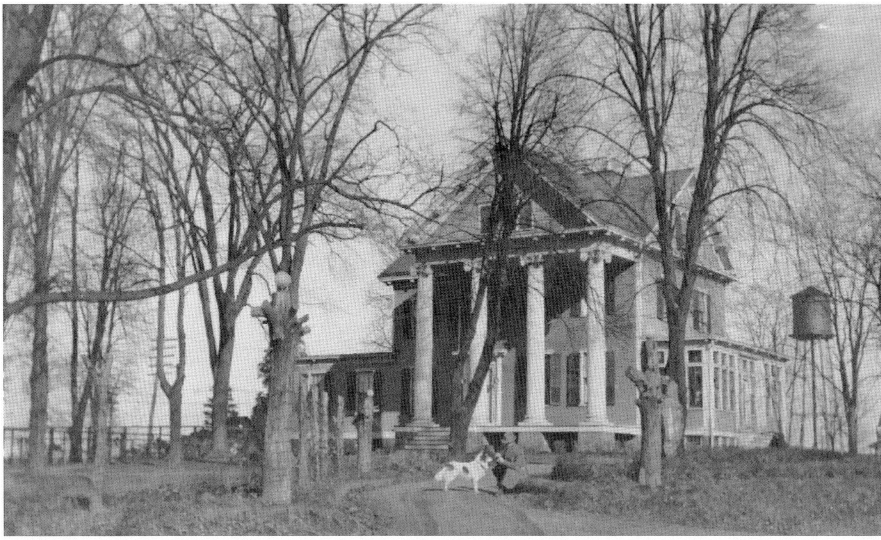

Livingston Homestead, c. 1909. Another historic house in Highland Park, the Livingston Homestead was constructed around 1843 and is located at 81 Harrison Avenue. The large portico on the front was added to the house by Watson Whittlesey shortly before this photograph was taken after 1907.

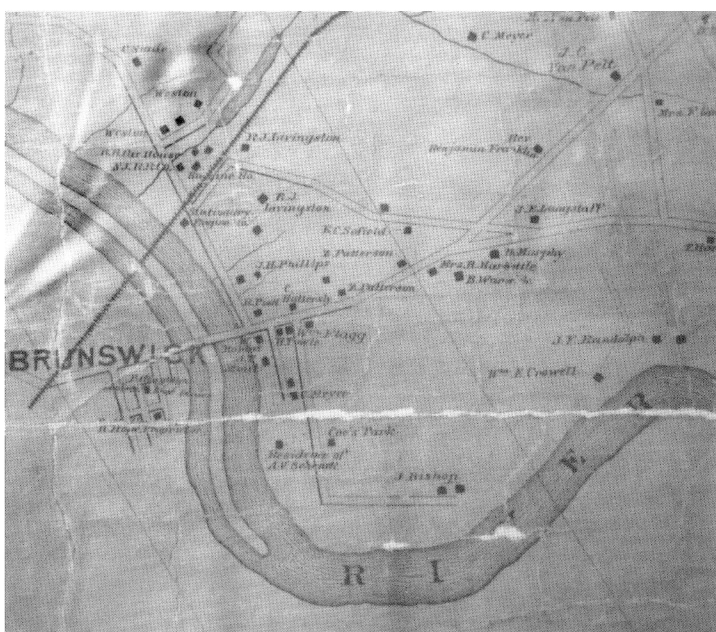

1868 Map of Highland Park. By the middle of the nineteenth century, Highland Park had become the location for a few wealthy suburbanites' dwellings. This map indicates the locations of several houses on Adelaide Avenue, Raritan Avenue, and Cedar Avenue, including Coe's Park.

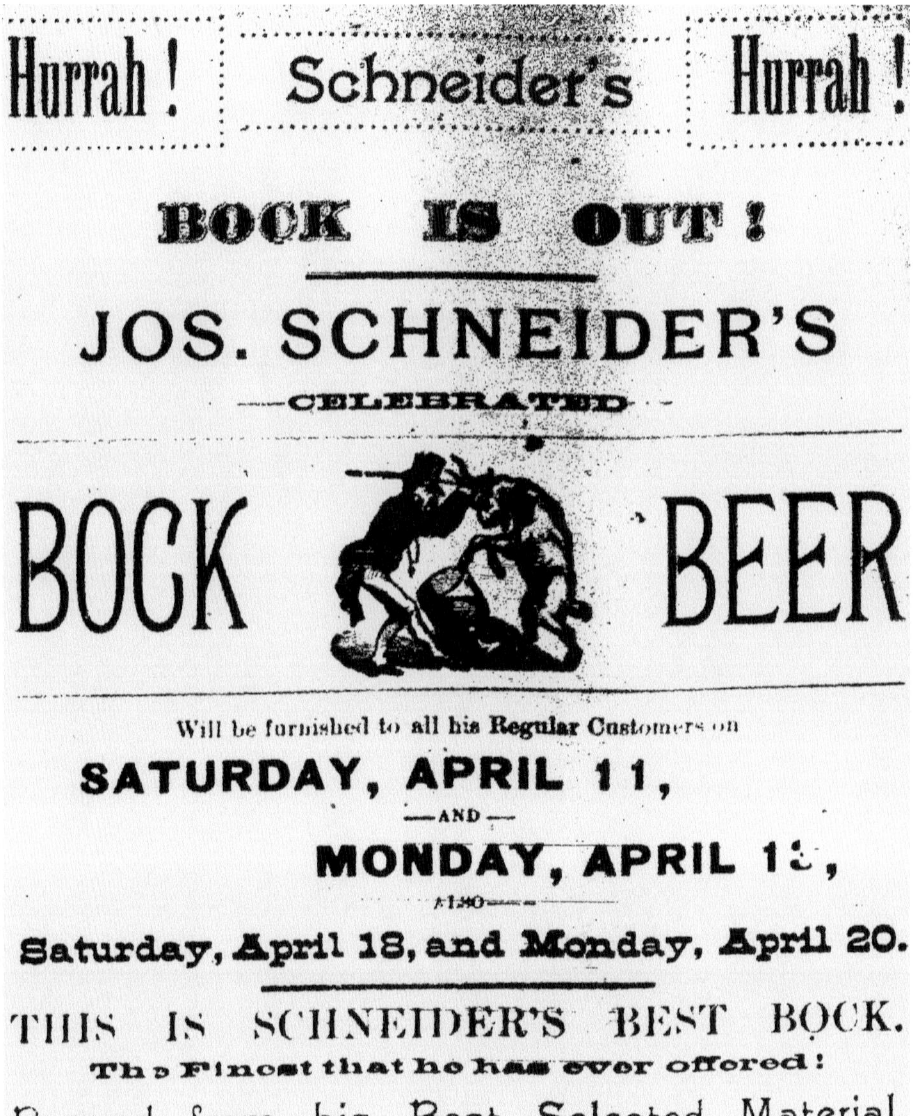

Best Bock Brewers. One of Highland Park's first businesses was a brewery, established in 1867. This is an 1891 advertisement from the New Brunswick Daily Times for Schneider's Bock Beer produced at its brewery off Raritan Avenue near today's North Second Avenue and Montgomery Street.

E. KITCHENMESTER,

Florist & Landscape Gardener

EAST NEW BRUNSWICK, N. J.

BEDDING ❊ PLANTS ❊ A ❊ SPECIALTY.

CUT FLOWERS CONSTANTLY ON HAND.

Thorough Attention given to the Scientific Arrangement of Flowers.

Early Business Establishment. This is an 1888 advertisement from the New Brunswick Daily Home News Almanac for E. Kitchenmeister, the longest on-going business in Highland Park.

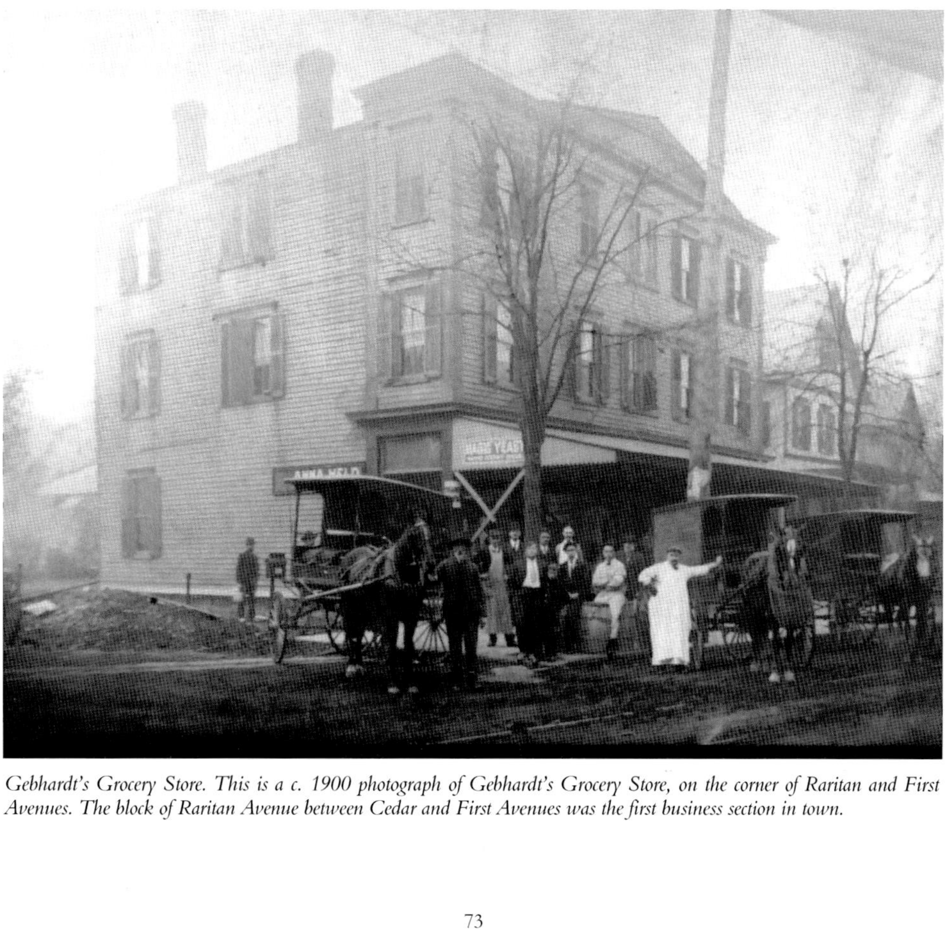

Gebhardt's Grocery Store. This is a c. 1900 photograph of Gebhardt's Grocery Store, on the corner of Raritan and First Avenues. The block of Raritan Avenue between Cedar and First Avenues was the first business section in town.

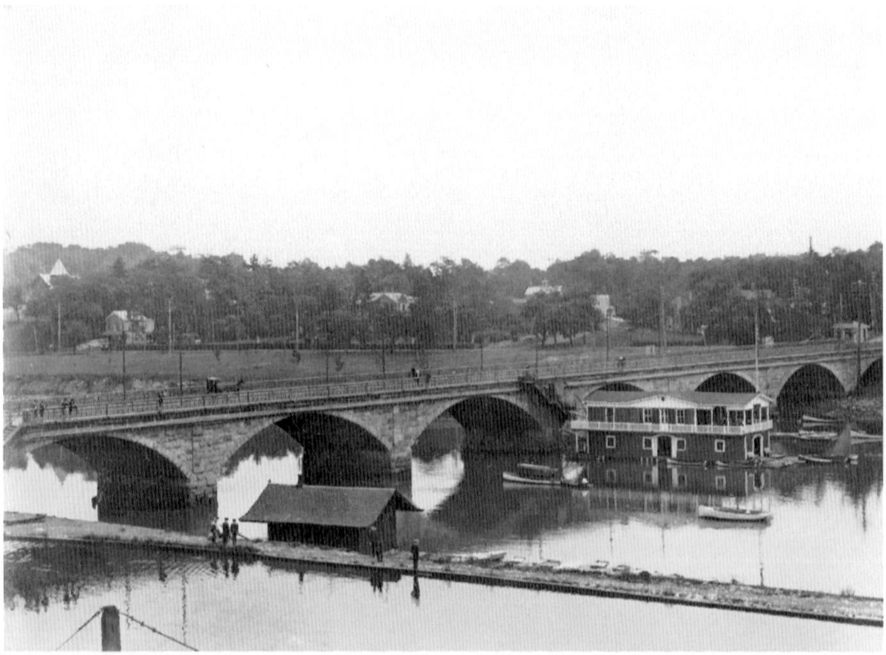

Albany Street Bridge. The graceful stone arch bridge that connects Highland Park and New Brunswick was constructed in 1892. For many years, the New Brunswick Boat Club moored its floating boat house to the bridge. In 1925 the bridge was widened and received a poured concrete extension on its south side.

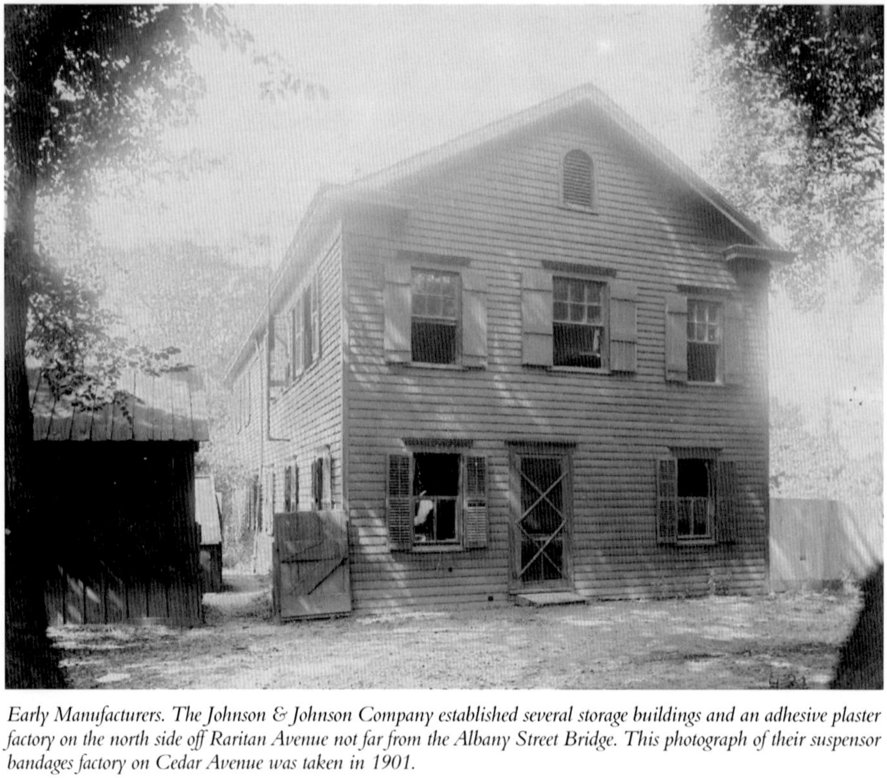

Early Manufacturers. The Johnson & Johnson Company established several storage buildings and an adhesive plaster factory on the north side off Raritan Avenue not far from the Albany Street Bridge. This photograph of their suspensor bandages factory on Cedar Avenue was taken in 1901.

GOTTFRIED KRUEGER,
PREST.

DIRECTORS:
GOTTFRIED KRUEGER,
JOHN RADEL
ANDREW RADEL
EDW H RADEL

EDW. H. RADEL
SEC'Y & TREAS.

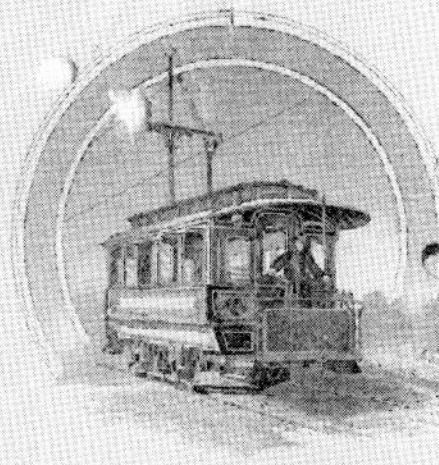

Brunswick Traction Co.

New Brunswick, N.J. March 8, 1897

J. F. Schopperkotter Esq.,

228 S. 3rd St., Phila., Pa.

Dear Sir:-

Referring to the conversation between you and Mr. M. F. Ross of this City in regard to obtaining a consent from your company for construction of an electric railway alongthe lands of The Lehigh Valley R. R. Co., at BoundBrook, I desire to say that we deem it necessary to have a consent from your company in order to enter Bound Brook. We have the consents on the River Road from New Brunswick up to this point and we also have the consents in Bound Brook, but possibly this might not cover the road in question as we understand it was recently laid out and might be considered a new road and not a continuation of either of the other two.

It is our intention to build from the City of New Brunswick to Bound Brook and from Bound Brook and Dunellen over the old stage road and also to continue our line from Bound Brook to Somerville and Raritan provided we can obtain the necessary franchises.

I understand that you made inquiry as to whether the Central R. R.. of N. J. were opposing us, up to this point there has been no indication of anyxopposition from them, but they have tied up our opponents the N. Y. & Phila. Traction Co some two years ago.

I enclose a form of consent and hope you will be kind enough to sign it and return to us., Yours truly,

BRUNSWICK TRACTION CO.
PER Edward H. Radel, Sec.

Ack. 3/12/97

The Trolley Comes to Town, 1897. A Brunswick Traction Company letter discusses the trolley line along River Road.

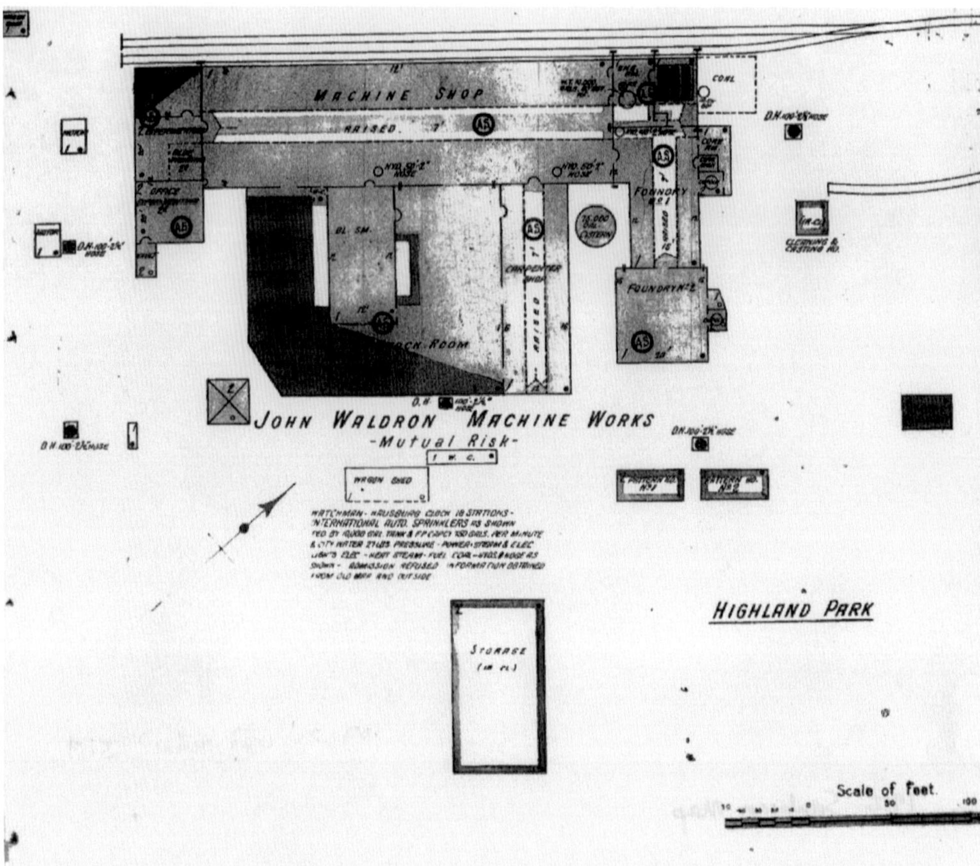

John Waldon Machine Factory. This is a detailed plan of John Waldron's machine factory from a Sanborn fire insurance map drawn in 1912. The factory was situated next to the railroad tracks just east of River Road.

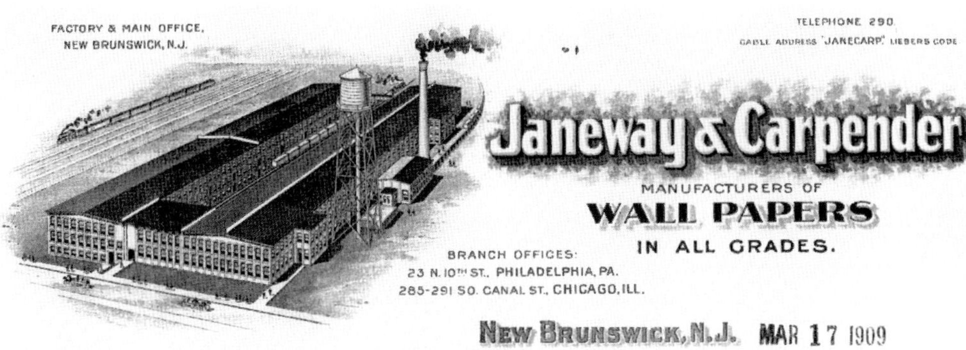

Janeway & Carpender Wallpaper Factory. Another New Brunswick company that relocated to Highland Park, this manufacturer produced wallpaper in its factory near the railroad tracks from 1907 until 1931.

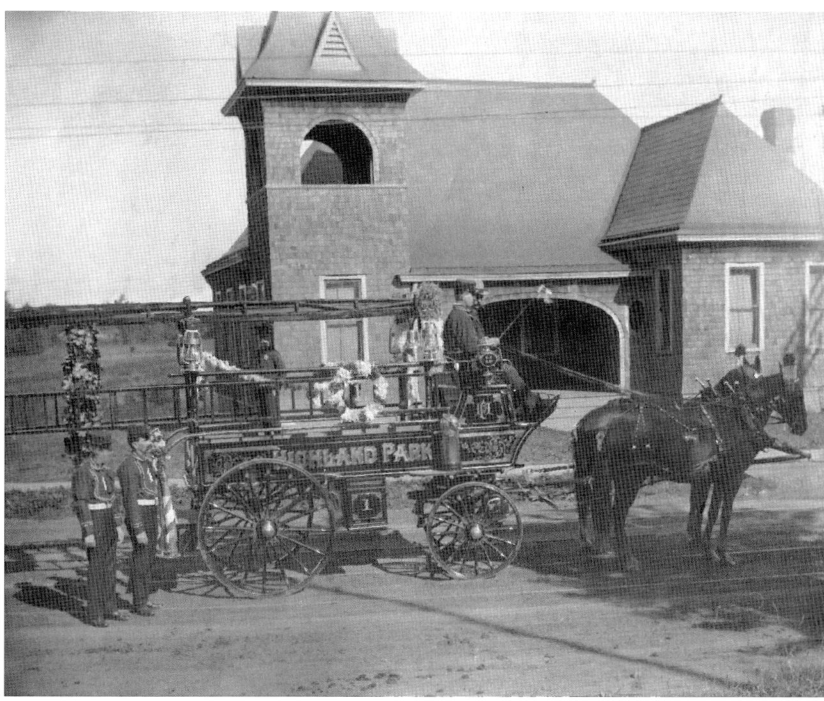

Early 1900s Firefighting. Around 1901, Highland Park's finest posed with their new apparatus in front of the newly-built Baptist Chapel on Raritan Avenue before North Second Avenue was established.

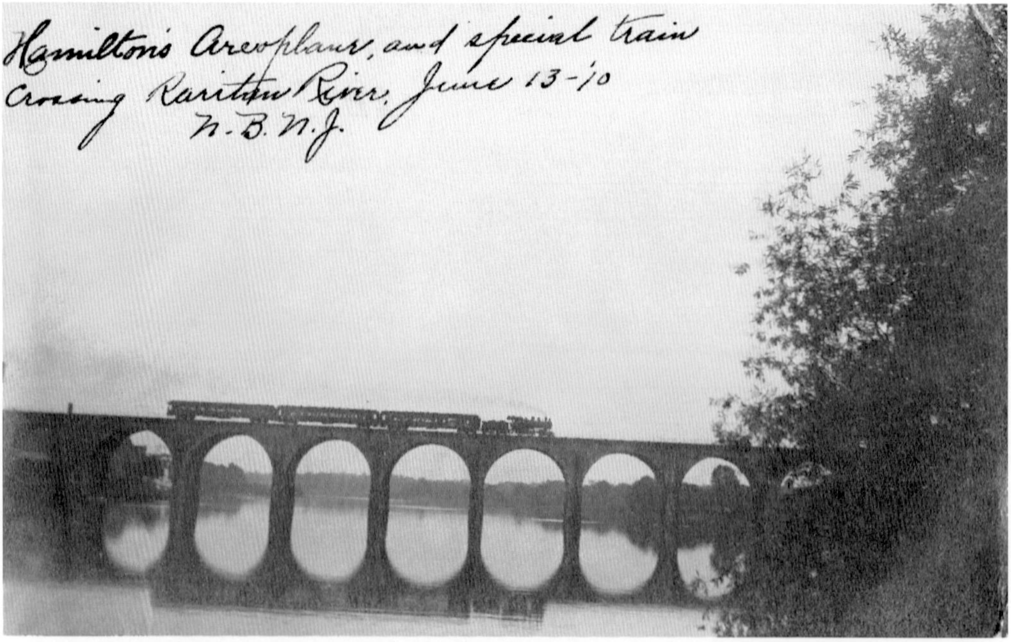

Hamilton's Historic Flight, 1910. Isaac Vandeveer produced this real-photo postcard of Charles K. Hamilton's aeroplane, the first such machine to occupy the skies over Highland Park, if only for a moment. The special train crossing the Raritan River on the stone arch railroad bridge, constructed in 1903, kept pace with the aeroplane.

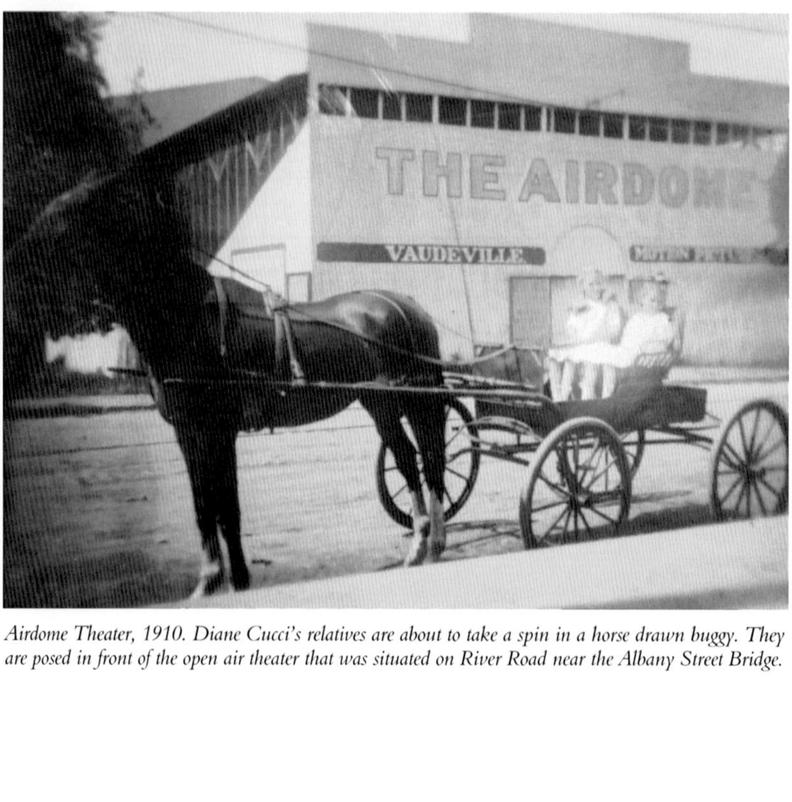

Airdome Theater, 1910. Diane Cucci's relatives are about to take a spin in a horse drawn buggy. They are posed in front of the open air theater that was situated on River Road near the Albany Street Bridge.

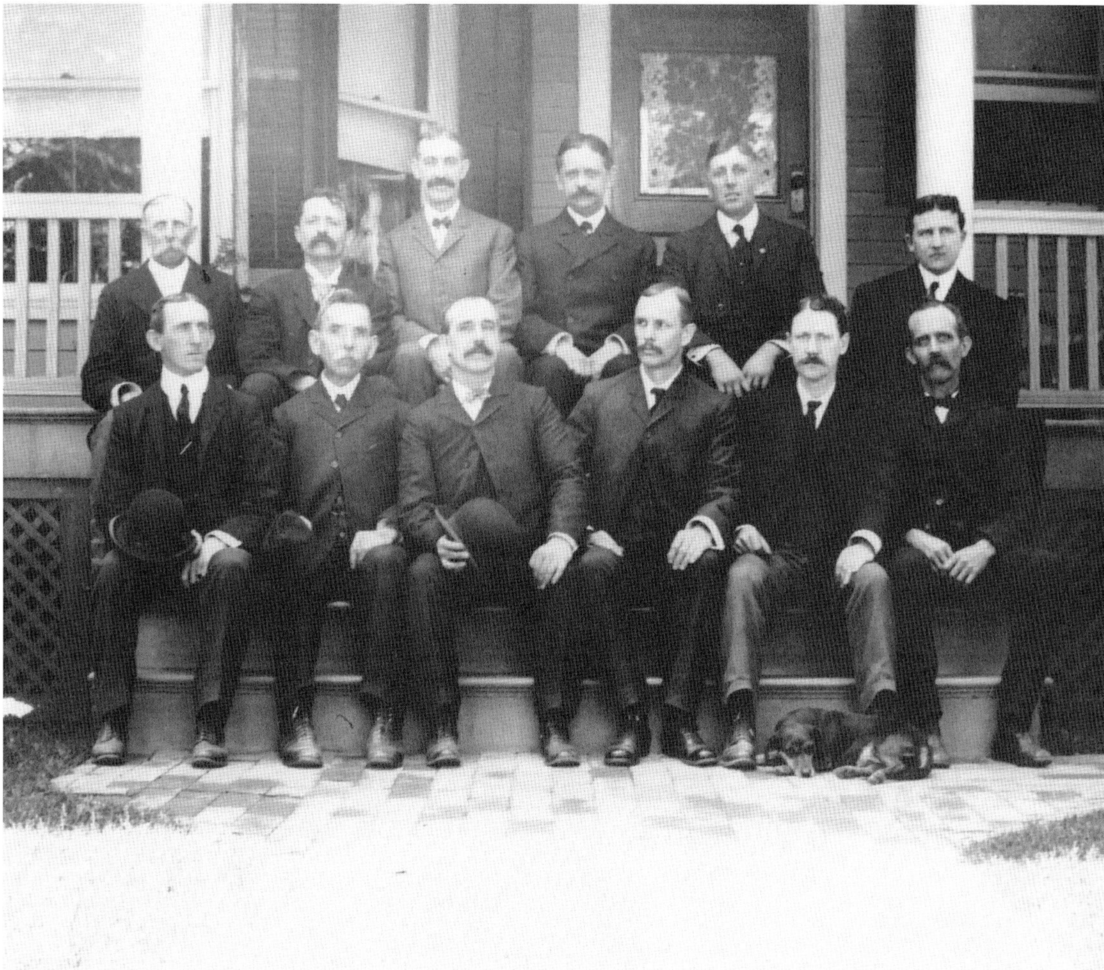

First Mayor and Council, 1905. The new borough's first mayor, James Archer (top row, fourth from left), proudly sits with his fellow elected members of council for this official portrait on May 1, 1905.

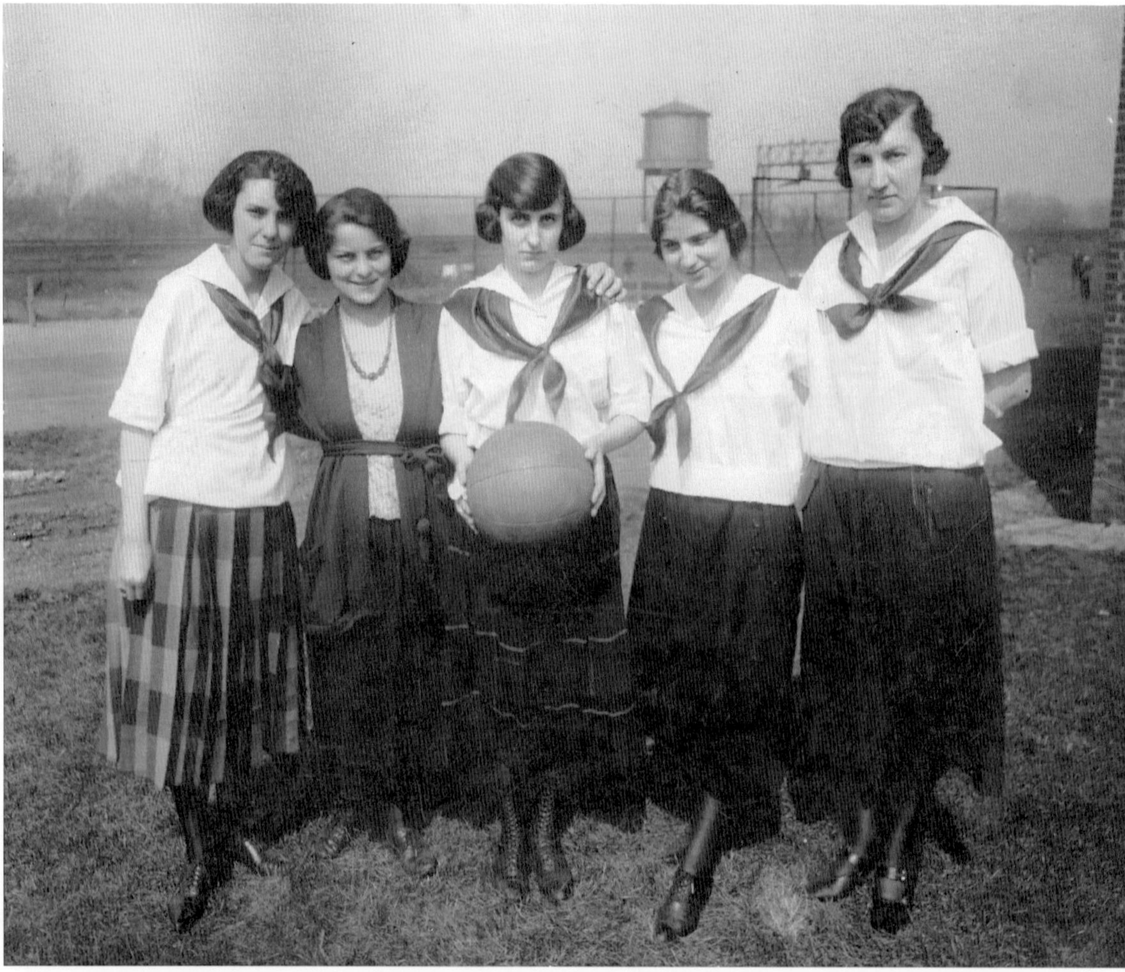

Women's Basketball Team, 1921. According to a Sunday Times article, Janeway & Carpender Company employees Eleanor Bradley, Ida Anzolut, Dorothy Drake, Dorothy Mayo, and Marie Foeriner (left to right), played "a fast and spectacular game of basketball."

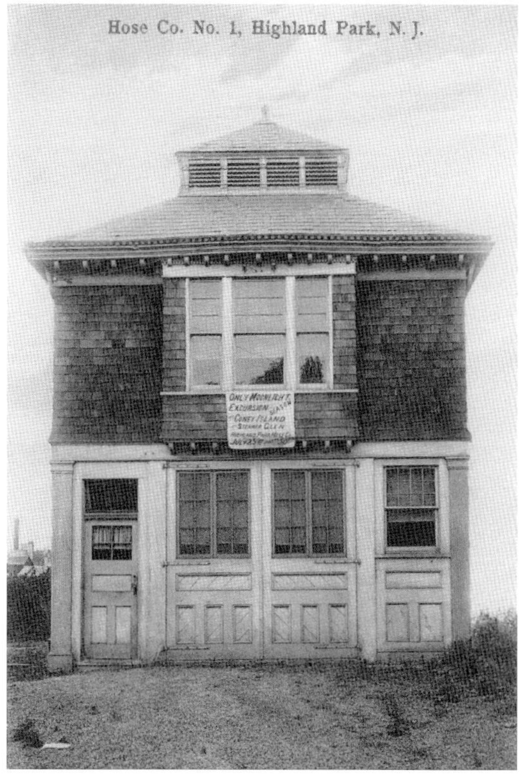

First Firehouse. This penny postcard from 1910 shows the firehouse designed by George Parsell and built in 1901 on Raritan Avenue near North Second Avenue. The banner is advertising a fund-raiser—a moonlight cruise to Coney Island.

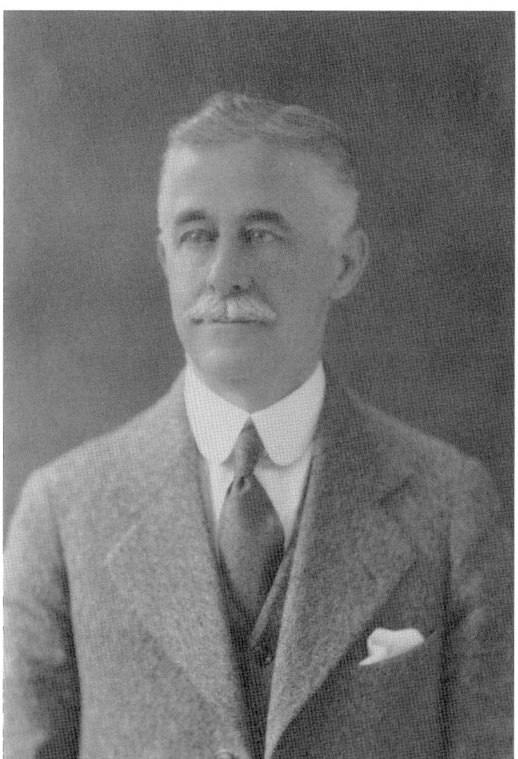

Local Architect. Alexander Merchant (1872–1952) was a prominent local architect. He designed most of Highland Park's schools, several commercial buildings, a church, and many houses throughout the borough.

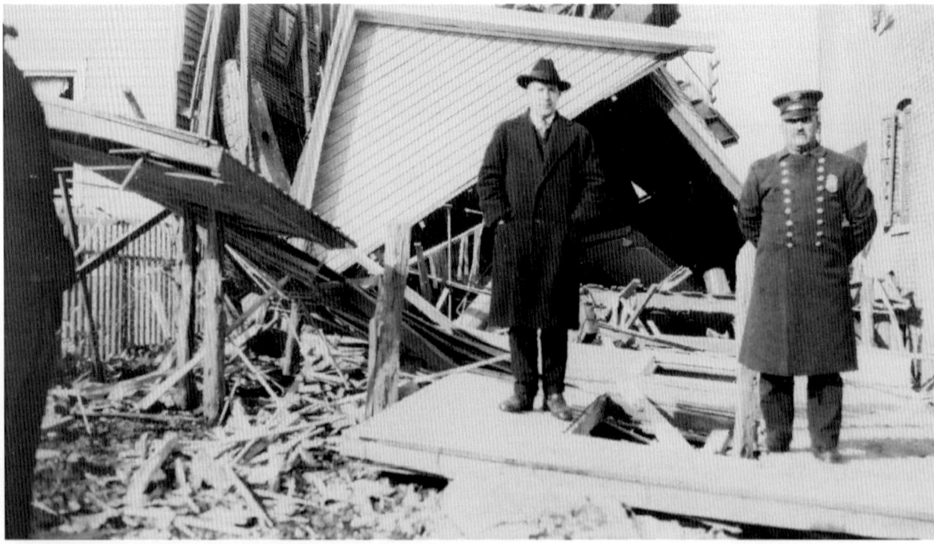

Woodbridge Avenue House Explosion. On the morning of February 20, 1922, a grand explosion destroyed three houses on Woodbridge Avenue. This photograph shows Police Chief Smith and Officer Steele as they conducted their investigation.

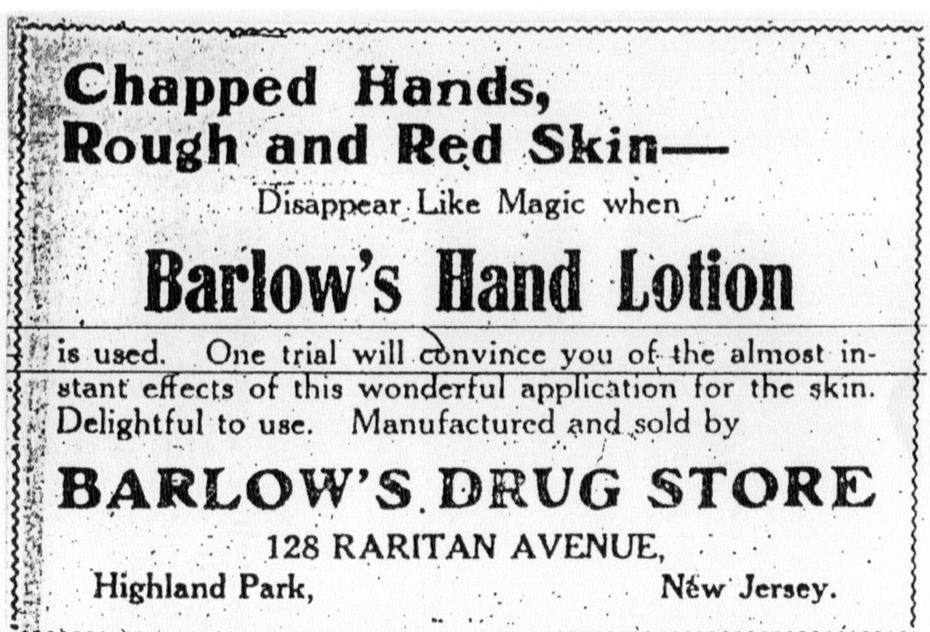

Barlow's Drugstore. From 1917 to 1923, Joseph Barlow operated a drugstore at 128 Raritan Avenue. Along with everything necessary for health and beauty, he also sold Kodak cameras and was himself an avid photographer.

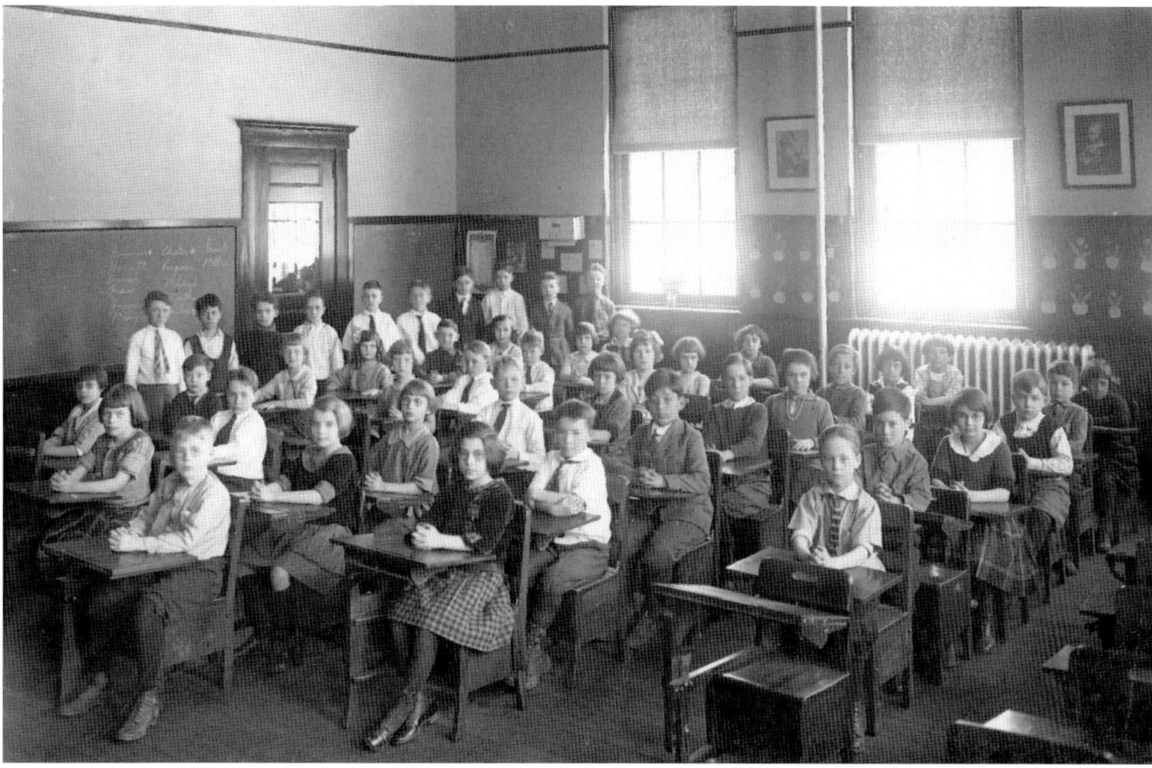

Third Grade Class, 1923. Photograph of well-groomed and well-mannered third graders in their Lafayette School classroom.

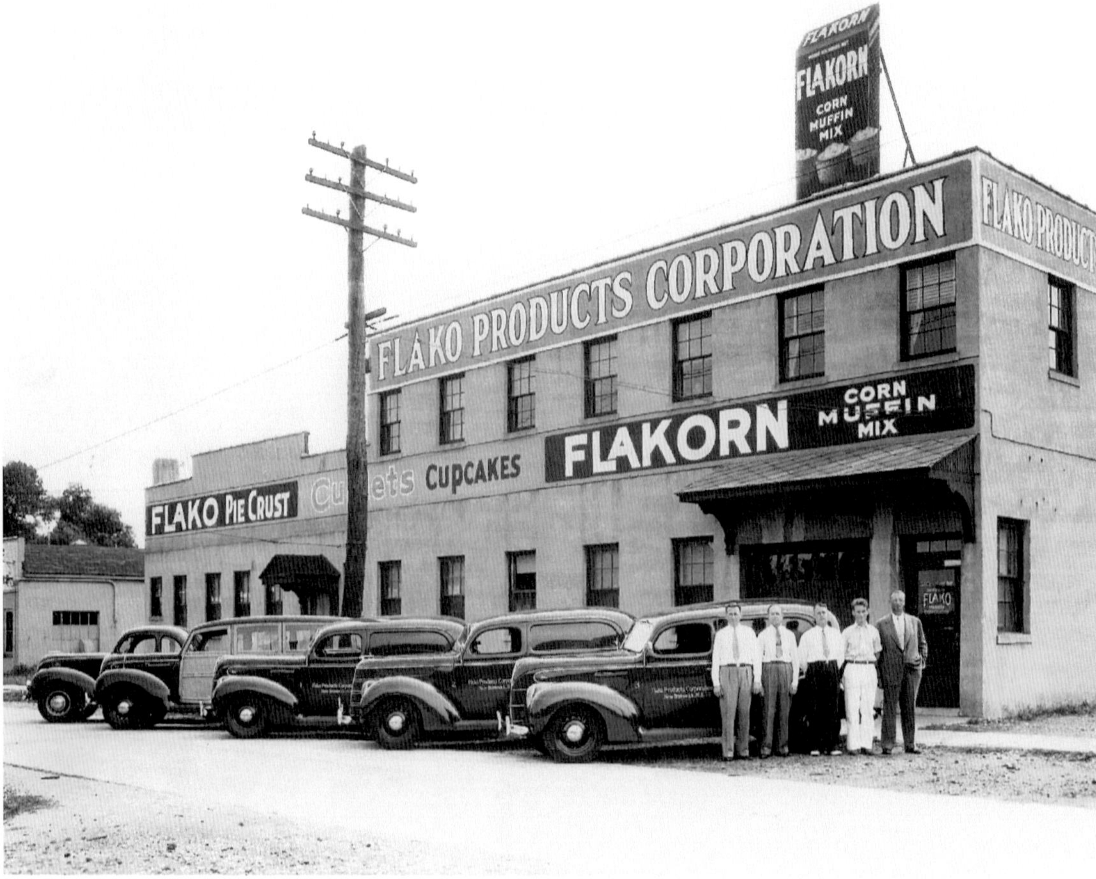

Flako Products Corporation. Highland Park can boast that it is the birthplace of two nationally known products: Johnson & Johnson's Band-Aid, and the Flako company's packaged baked good mixes. Flako president Arthur McCallum (on the far right) poses with his sales team in front of their Cleveland Avenue plant.

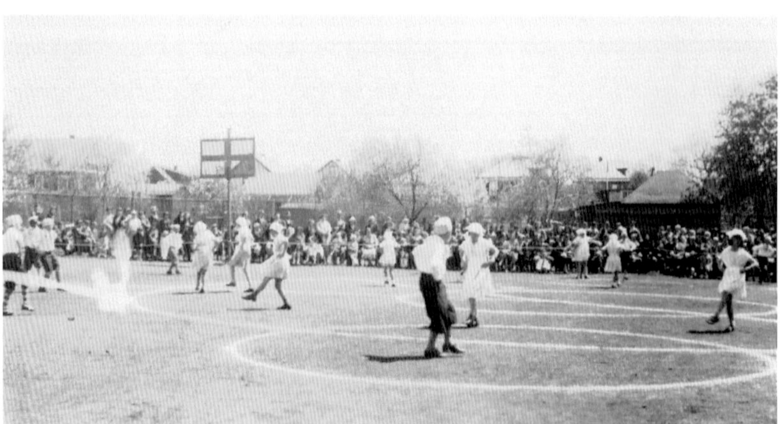

Music and Physical Education Demonstration, 1933. A colorful costumed pageant and exhibition of folk dancing took place at the Lafayette School grounds on May 4, 1933. The event was photographed by the PTA for its publicity book.

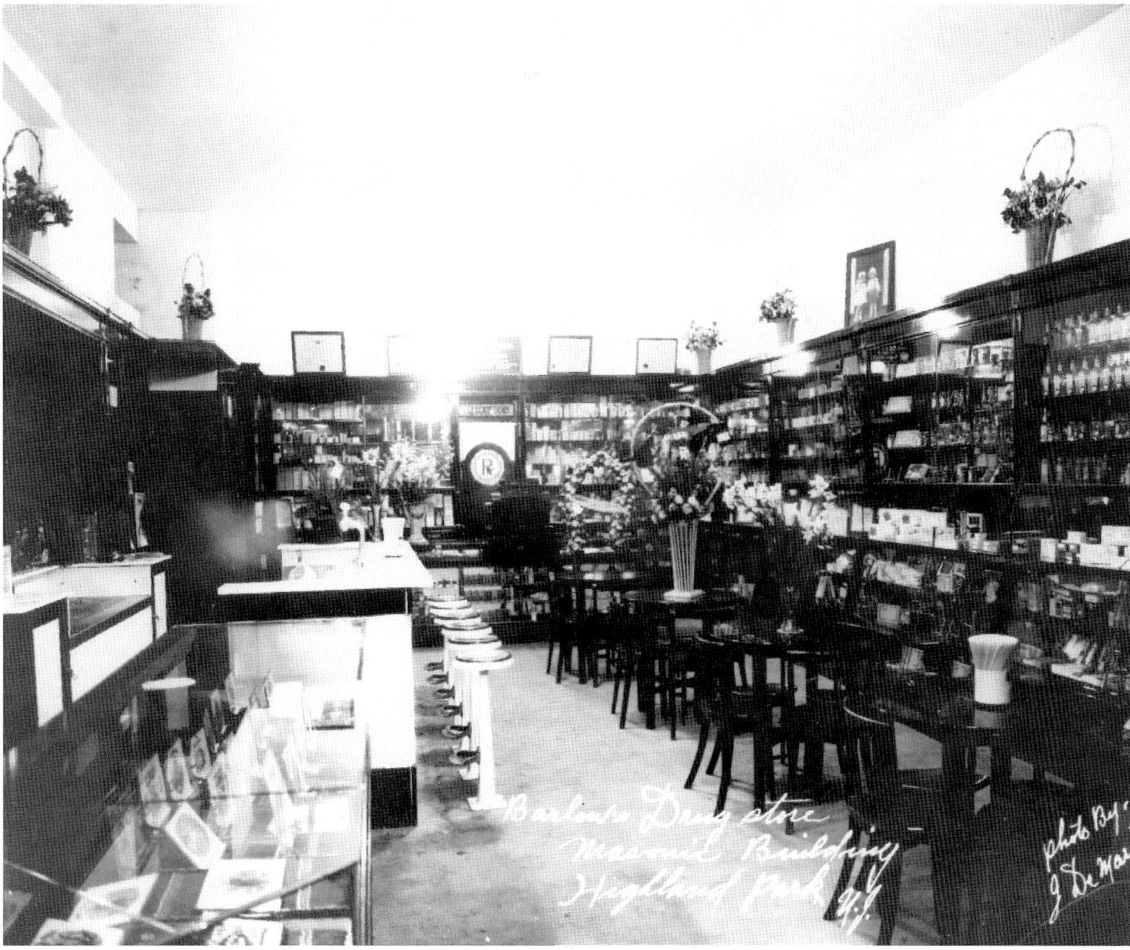

Barlow's Drugstore Relocates. After the Masonic Building opened at the corner of North Fourth and Raritan Avenues in 1923, Joseph Barlow moved his store to the coveted corner location. Local photographer Joseph DeMaria took this publicity photograph.

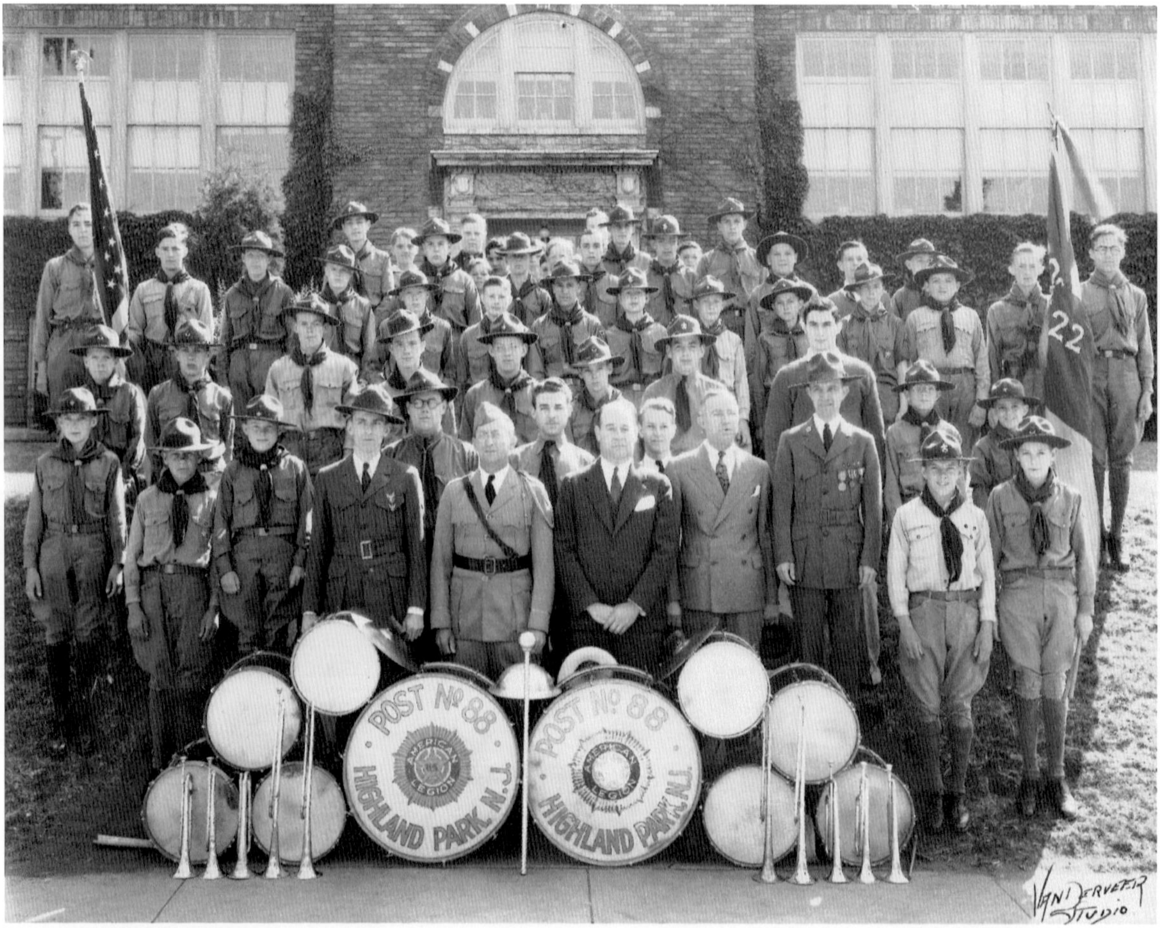

Honored Boy Scout Troop, 1937. This publicity photograph of Boy Scout Troop 22 and its sponsor, American Legion Post 88, appeared in the November 14, 1937 issue of The Sunday Times. The group was honored in Congress for its community service program.

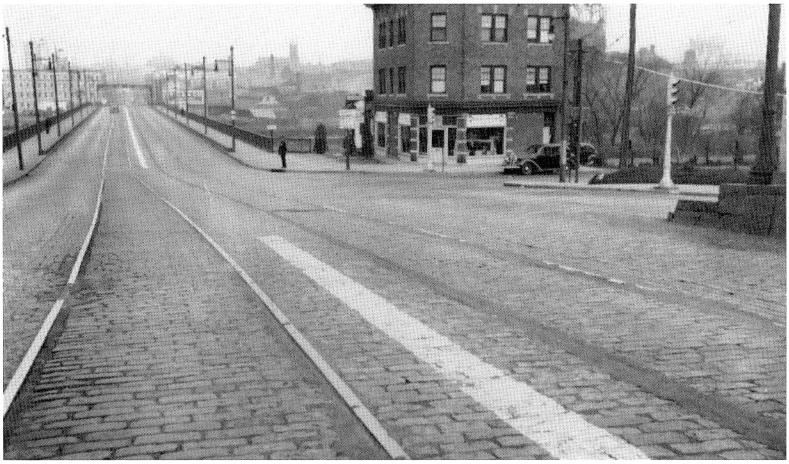

A Quiet Morning. A photograph taken in the late 1930s shows the intersection of Raritan Avenue, Lincoln Avenue, River Road, and the Albany Street Bridge. The commercial building on the busy corner was often the target for erratic automobiles. The photograph shows the new traffic signals that were installed to regulate drivers.

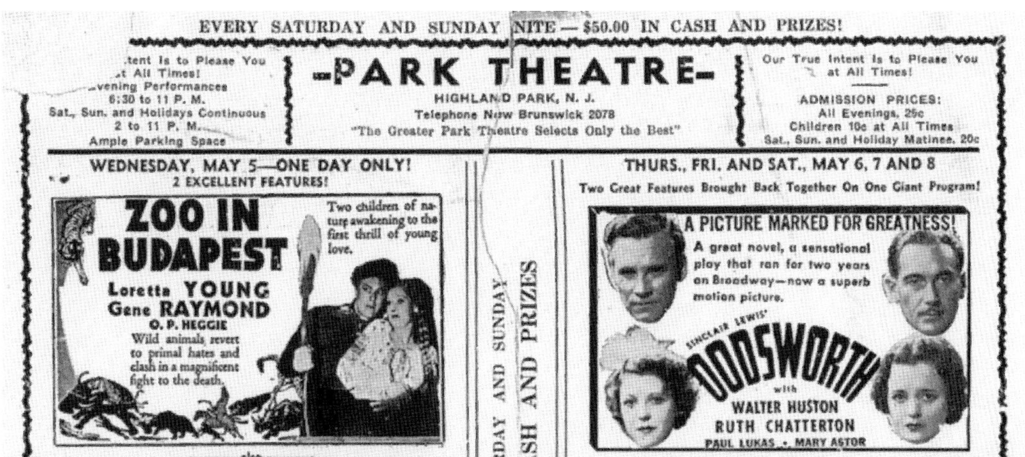

Movie Theater Program, 1937. This program for a week of movies at the Park Theatre was handed out in 1937 and kept for many years in Ray Salva's scrap book. Mementos such as these are all that remain, as the theater was demolished in 1961.

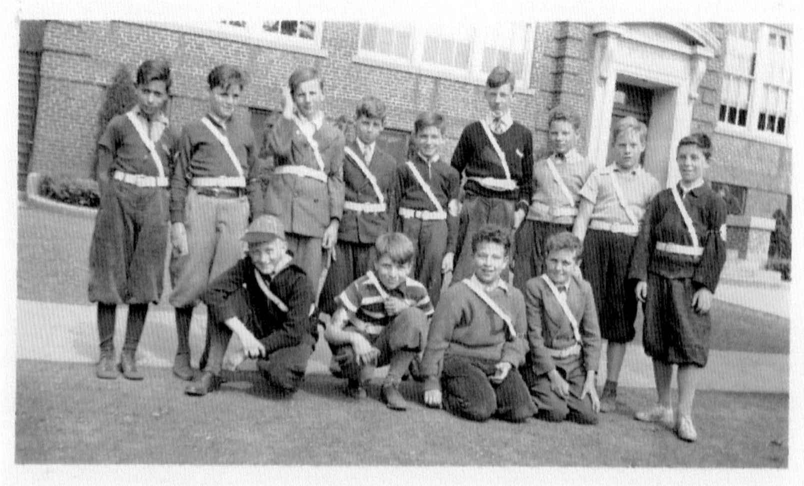

Safety Patrol, 1938. This is a photograph of Lafayette School's safety patrol, Group II wearing Sam Browne belts purchased by the school PTA.

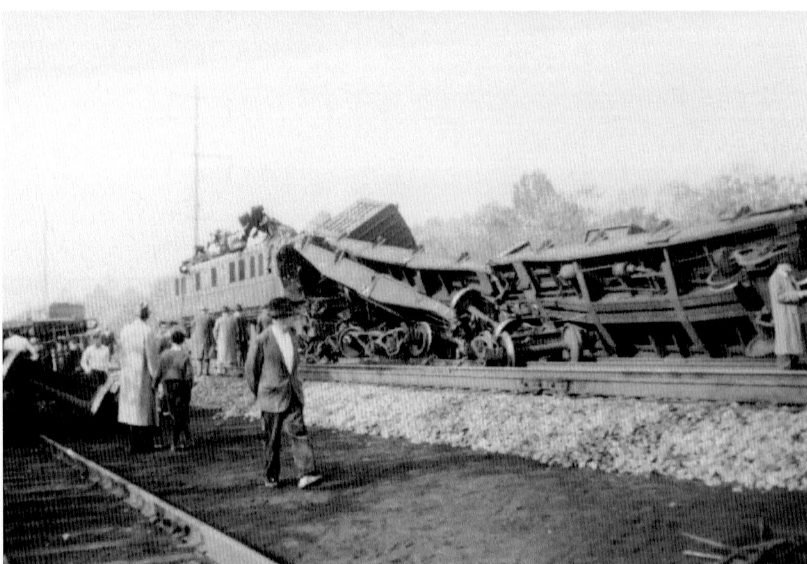

Train Wreck, 1939. One can only imagine the horrible sound this train must have made as it careened off its tracks on October 21, 1939. Lawrence Avenue resident Carl Woodward grabbed his camera and witnessed the sight first hand.

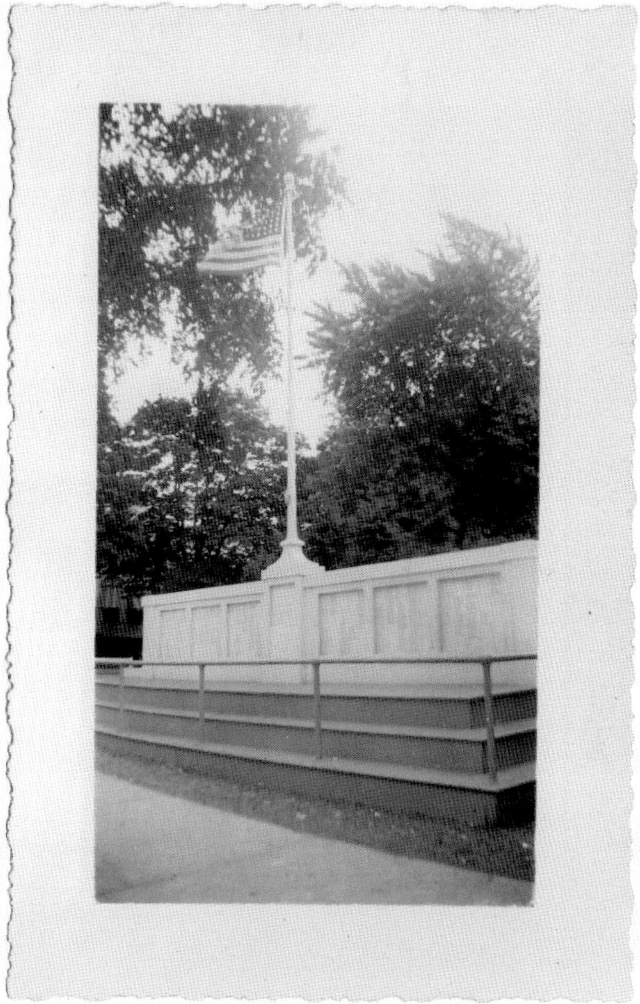

World War II Honor Roll, 1942. This is a snapshot of the honor roll that was designed by Alexander Merchant & Son and constructed by Albert Garlotti on South Fourth Avenue near Raritan Avenue. The monument listed the names of all Highland Park citizens serving in the armed forces during World War II.

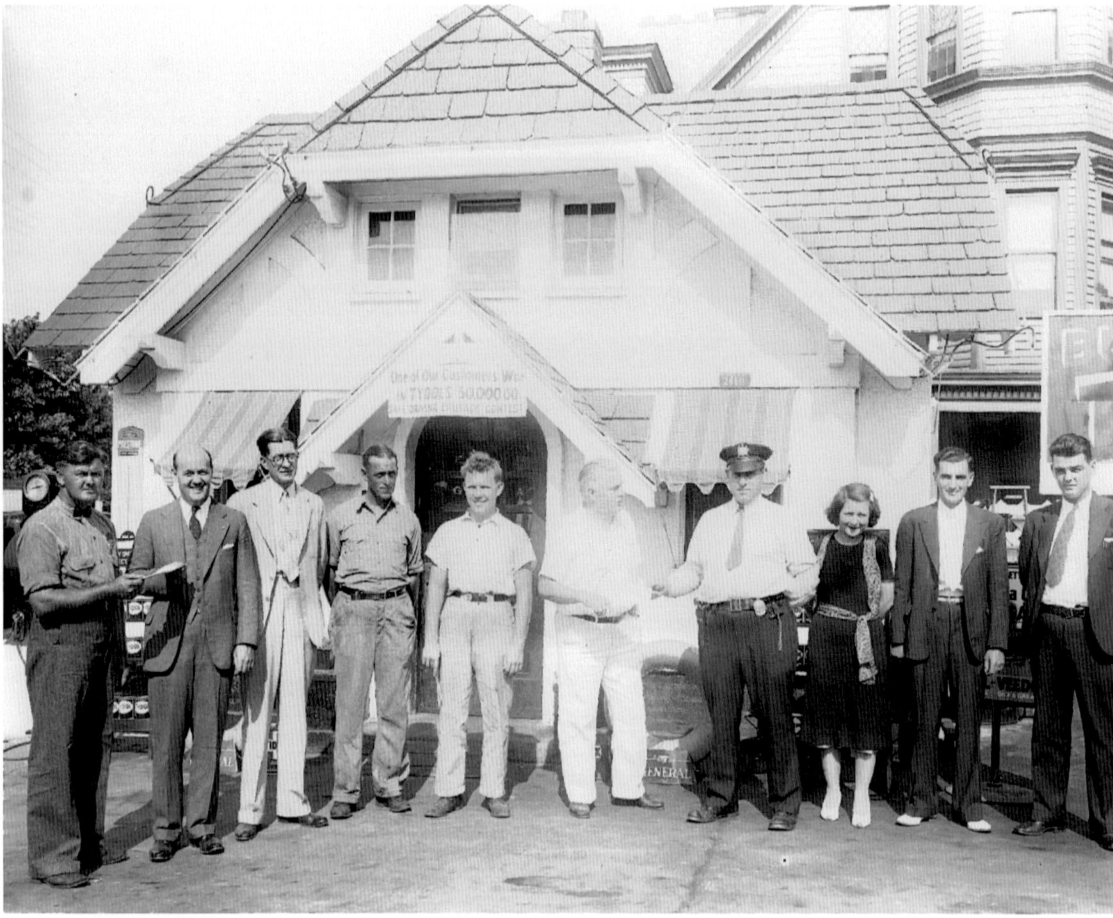

Tydol Gas Station, c. 1940. The small gas station located at the prominent point where Raritan and Woodbridge Avenues converged had one of the winners in Tydol's Safe Driving Crusade. Here, owner Jacob Young (on far left), hands over the check to the happy winner. This photograph is from the collection of Kathy Young Dalcourt.

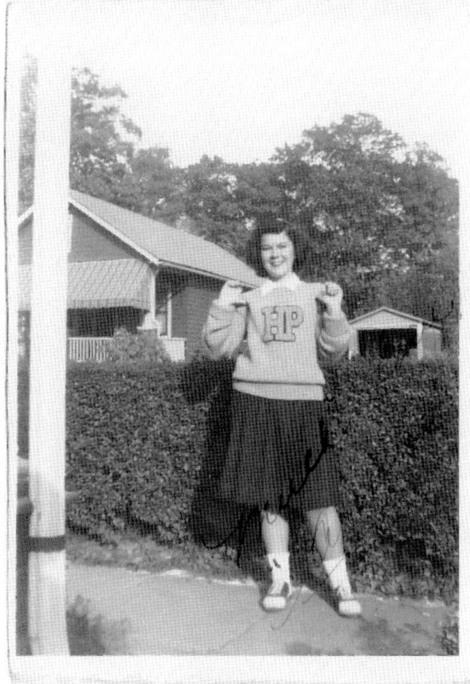

School Spirit, 1947. This is a snapshot of Annie Pfeiffer practicing her cheers near her Karsey Street home.

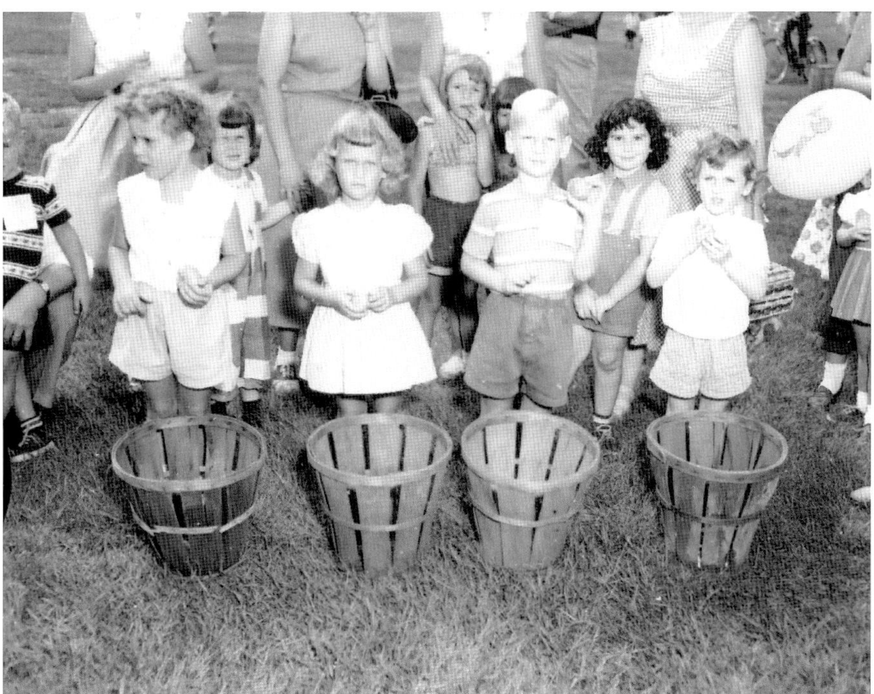

Highland Park Playground Picnic, 1948. Where can these youngsters be now? This photograph of children preparing for games at the Highland Park Playground picnic was taken in 1948 by Home News photographer Will Gainfort.

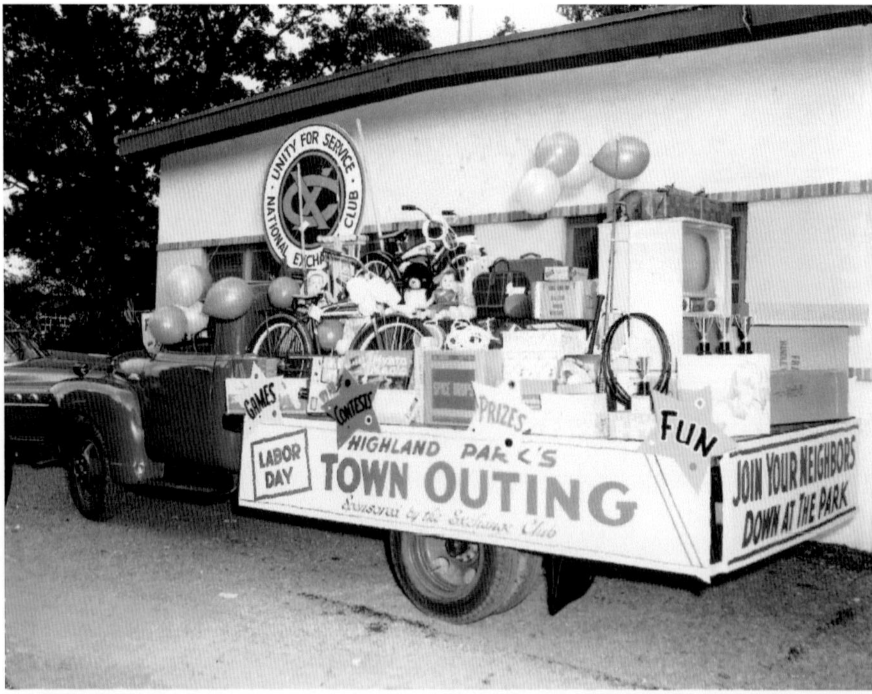

First Park Town Outing, 1953. Prizes were gathered for participants in the popular Highland Park Town Outing, an annual event held on Labor Day in Donaldson Park. Will Gainfort took the photograph.

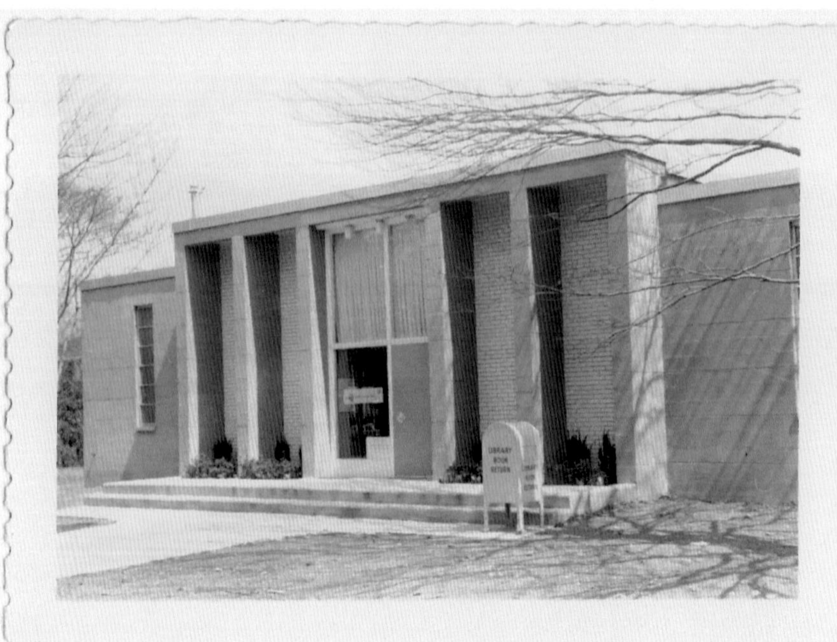

Public Library, 1959. This is a photograph of the Sixth Avenue facade of architect Ernest Levine's modern public library located where a colonial farmstead once stood between Fifth and Sixth Avenues. Renovations in 1994 incorporated this structure and gave it a Colonial Revival cladding of brick.

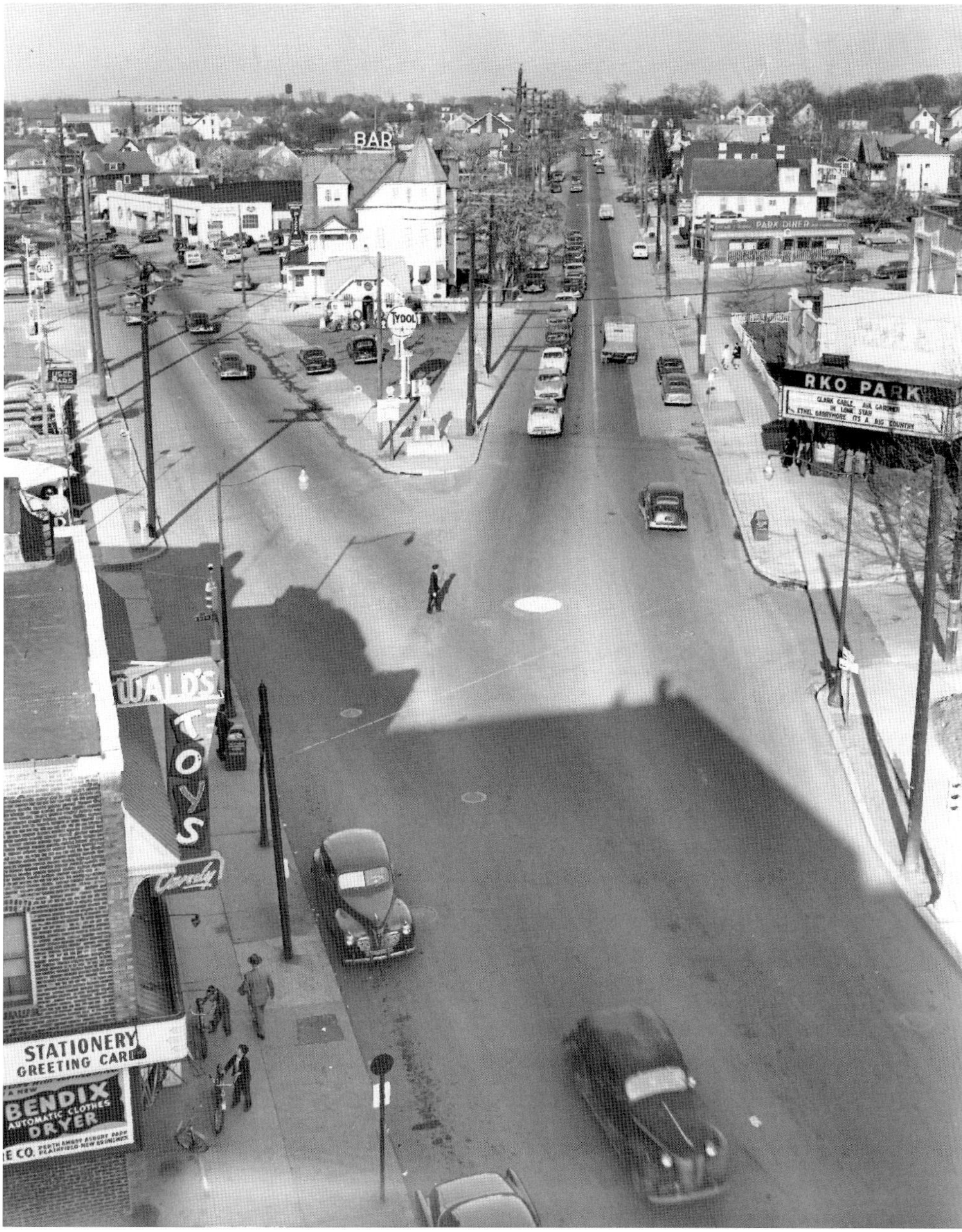

Traffic Congestion Study, 1952. Concerns with increased congestion prompted this photographic study of the traffic through Highland Park in 1952. Here we see an eleven-car backup on Woodbridge Avenue at 4:43 p.m. on April 17, 1952. Three Woodbridge Avenue institutions pictured here, the Highland Park Hotel, the Park Diner, and the RKO movie theater, are gone.

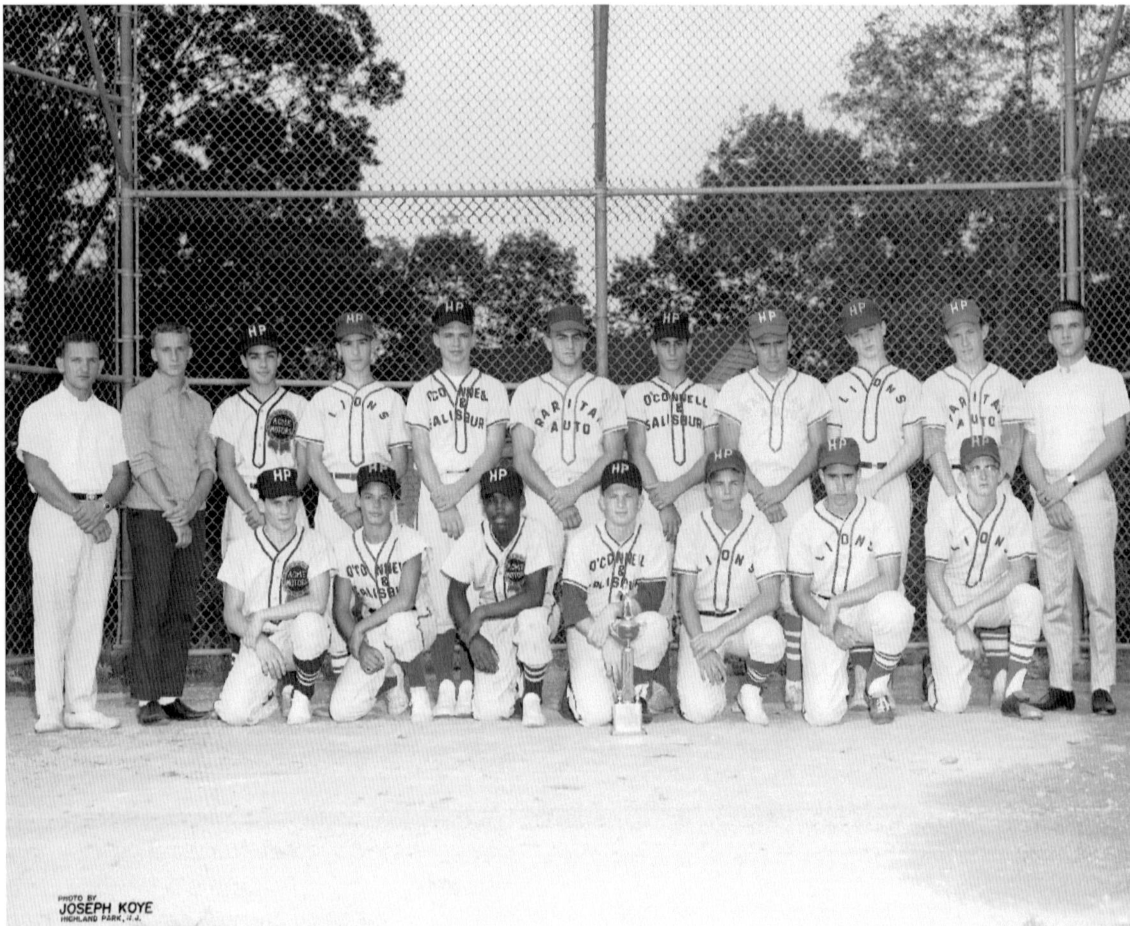

Junior League All-Star Team, 1963. Composed of players from all the little league teams, these were the all-stars for the 1963 season.

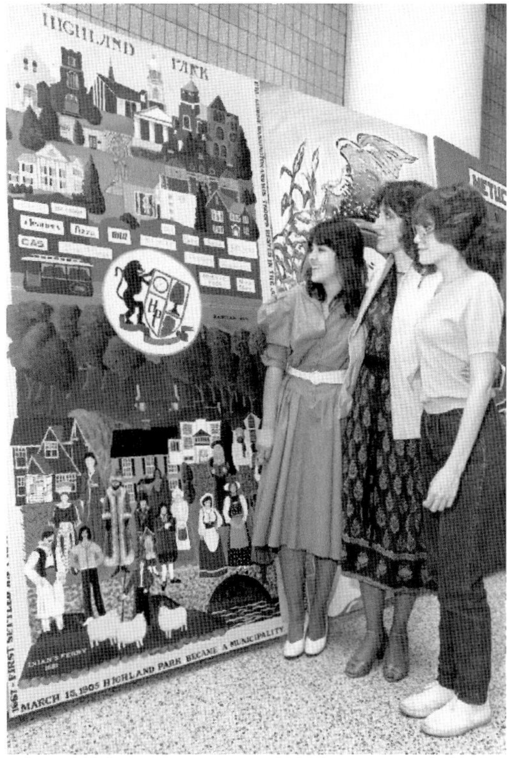

Highland Park History, 1976. The United States bicentennial celebrations of 1976 included a look at Highland Park's past. Here, Angie Daskalakis, art teacher Donna DeBaylo, and Patti Teissonniere (from left to right), admire their collage produced for a Middlesex County event.

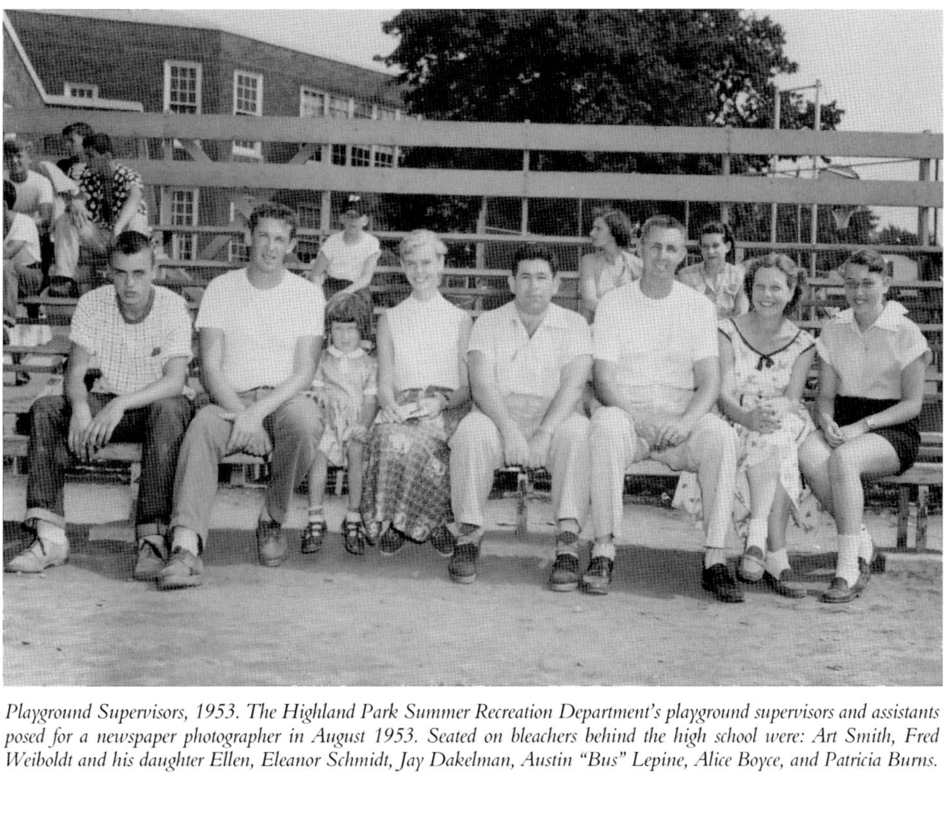

Playground Supervisors, 1953. The Highland Park Summer Recreation Department's playground supervisors and assistants posed for a newspaper photographer in August 1953. Seated on bleachers behind the high school were: Art Smith, Fred Weiboldt and his daughter Ellen, Eleanor Schmidt, Jay Dakelman, Austin "Bus" Lepine, Alice Boyce, and Patricia Burns.

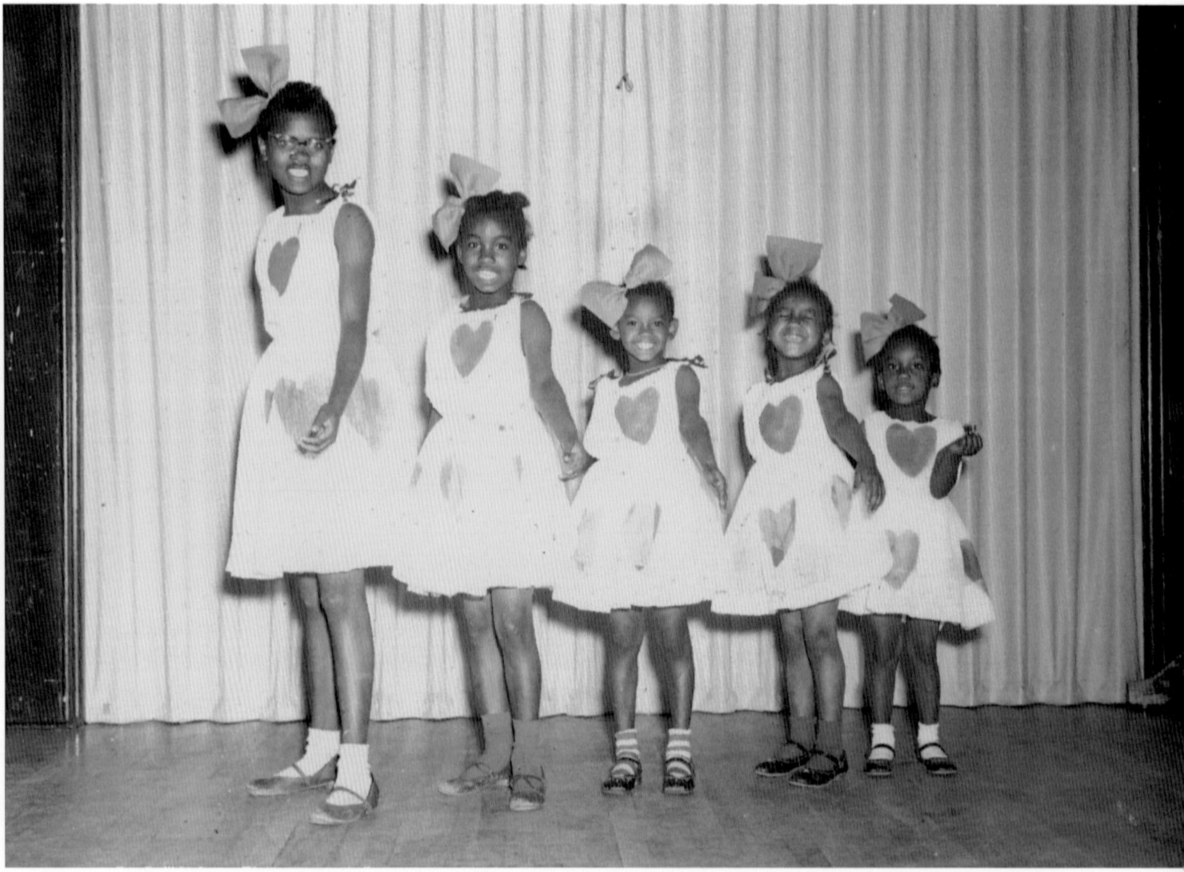

Recreation Department Performance. On May 23, 1955, the Haskins sisters performed at the annual Hi-Lite show titled "Memories Through Magic." The event was sponsored by the department of recreation and over 100 children participated. The program was written and directed by Mrs. Hector Clayton and Mrs. Alice Boyce with assistance from Patricia Burns.

Continued from page 64

and on December 15, 1912, the brewery, except for the bottling department, burned to the ground in an early morning fire. In 1929, the brewery's bottling department building was converted into the small apartment building located at 105 Montgomery Street. The remaining land and the ruins were abandoned until the 1950s, when the Montgomery Street Apartments were constructed.

The tract of land between Raritan Avenue and the railroad that made up the Livingston estate was purchased on January 14, 1897 by Watson Whittlesey for subdivision and development. Nevertheless, the development did not get underway until the summer of 1906. From then until his death on April 7, 1914, Whittlesey marketed his Livingston Manor subdivision for residential development. Whittlesey was more than a typical land speculator; he also was a community builder noted by his residency in various Livingston Manor houses from 1906 to 1914 and by his active involvement in Highland Park. Instead of auctioning lots like his nineteenth-century predecessors, Whittlesey sold lots with either a house that had been built by his company or with the promise of providing a company-constructed house. Whittlesey provided all of the neighborhood's dirt roads, poured concrete sidewalks and sewers, and paid the borough taxes for all his lots in one bulk payment. All the residential lots had a standard set of deeds with restrictions from such nuisances as chicken coops, barns, brewing establishments, and foundries. Long before the borough established zoning requirements, Whittlesey standardized setbacks and height restrictions.

Watson Whittlesey was born and raised in Rochester, New York. As a young man he learned the contracting business in Providence, Rhode Island and relocated to Newark to continue his profession as a real estate developer. By 1896, he had established business ties with nearby architects, builders, and other real estate developers. In Highland Park, Whittlesey became president of the Livingston Manor Corporation, which was incorporated on November 17, 1906. The supplier of the construction materials for the tract, the Highland Park Lumber Company, was formed earlier in June of 1906. The three investors included Whittlesey and William and Herbert Waldron. The Waldron brothers were the sons of industrialist John Waldron, who would purchase the Livingston Homestead at 81 Harrison Avenue in 1909.

During the summer of 1906, Whittlesey's crew of seventy-five workers began construction. Whittlesey made an appeal to the New Brunswick Board of Water Commissioners asking to extend the Highland Park water mains to his tract. This appeal was granted upon proof of his company's investment. By September 1, 1906 the *Daily Home News* noted that; "the old Livingston estate has undergone a wonderful change. It now bears the name of Livingston

Manor, and where once there were waving fields of corn, grain or other things of the farm, there are now fifteen concrete foundations for dwelling houses, some houses partially completed, and some under roof." The first day that deeds from the Livingston Manor Corporation transferred to two individual homeowners, December 1, 1906, meant that the first group of houses constructed on the south side of Grant Avenue west of North Second Avenue were ready for occupancy.

Whittlesey wanted to provide "villas" and "cottages" for every type of homebuyer and he succeeded by grouping small and moderate size, single-family houses with larger ones. He used plans generated by Orange, New Jersey architects George Edward Krug and Francis George Hasselman as well as plans by several local architects. Many workers in the building trades remained with the Livingston Manor Corporation and its successor, the Highland Park Building Company, for years, including Harvey E. Dodge. Dodge was noted in 1913 as "an architect of high skill, who has left gratifying traces of his work all through the Manor and has done much to establish the high standard of architectural excellence and beauty which the Livingston Manor Corporation makes it a point that all dwellings erected there shall maintain." Despite the description, Dodge was not a licensed architect, but more likely the master builder. Skilled craftsmen such as Frederick Nietscke, a carpenter; Harold Richard Segoine, a contractor; and Harvey Dodge, have been noted as both Livingston Manor Corporation employees and Livingston Manor residents. Whittlesey and his wife Anna also lived in several Livingston Manor houses including the Spanish Colonial style house at 35 Harrison Avenue.

Many prominent New Brunswick and Highland Park residents secured houses in this new neighborhood. They included Rutgers College professors, schoolteachers, bank employees, factory and store owners, and employees. Most of the women were housewives and mothers. There were many extended families. Some families took in boarders and several households included live-in servants.[1] The development became so popular that beginning in 1910, the *Daily Home News* social column changed its name from "Highland Park Notes" to "Highland Park and Livingston Manor Notes." By 1910, sixty-two houses had been constructed in Livingston Manor and the population of Highland Park had increased to 1,517.

To promote social interactions through athletic activities among the Livingston Manor residents, in 1909 Whittlesey constructed a clubhouse, athletic fields, and a playground on a triangular piece of land bounded by Lincoln, Lawrence, and North Second Avenues. Officers of the Livingston Manor Club were elected and the group sponsored "smokers," lectures,

[1]Based on data from the U.S. Census of 1910 and 1920, and the New Jersey Census of 1915.

amateur theatrical productions, baseball games, beauty pageants, and annual Fourth of July fireworks for two years. Playground equipment worth $1,300 was installed. During May of 1910, Professor Prentiss of 15 Grant Avenue gave nightly reports about Halley's Comet and set up his telescope on the playground lot. In 1911, the Livingston Manor Club disbanded and houses began to cover the former playground.

In 1910, Whittlesey convinced his neighboring landholders to allow the creation of a road extending Lincoln Avenue from Livingston Manor to Raritan Avenue near the Albany Street Bridge. It was opened with great fanfare on Labor Day, September 5, 1910. Bohn's Band played the "Star Spangled Banner" and a baby parade proceeded across the view of spectators in a grandstand.

Watson Whittlesey hired a sales agent in 1912, John F. Green, who announced the sales of bungalow lots. These smaller lots were less expensive and a set of plans for a bungalow was given to any purchaser free of charge. These lots included all the modern amenities including "macadam streets, concrete gutters, curbing, sidewalks, sewers, water, gas and electric lights, and other advantages." By 1913, 120 houses had been constructed in Livingston Manor.

Whittlesey was a well-loved man dubbed "the Lord of the Manor." Upon his early death on April 8, 1914, the local newspapers paid him many tributes. Livingston Manor residents turned out in the hundreds to attend a memorial service at his house on Harrison Avenue. Five days later, the New Brunswick Board of Trade made a proclamation as announced in the April 14, 1915 edition of the *Daily Times*:

> Whereas, Watson Whittlesey's influence upon our community has been one which will increase for good as time goes on, and whereas the spirit of progress which he evidenced has been emulated by others and has done an untold amount of good for this community, particularly in creating and disseminating a belief in the many advantages for residential and industrial location possessed by our city and its suburbs. . . . Be it resolved that this Board of Trade take this occasion to express its thanks on behalf of the community in which he lived for the work he did among us.

Whittlesey's wife Anna Wilcox Whittlesey succeeded him as president of the Livingston Manor Corporation. The Highland Park Building Company, which was incorporated after his death by long-standing members of his company including builder Robert Lufburrow and engineer Harold Richard Segoine, took over construction. Both continued to uphold Whittlesey's vision for this community of homeowners. According to the borough council minutes of June 17, 1916, Anna Whittlesey turned over Livingston Manor's privately owned streets, sidewalks, and curbs to the borough. Remarkably, there were no provisions for the borough to accept public ownership of the privately built sewers. That required a legislative act in Trenton, which was accomplished by Senator Florance and Assemblyman Edgar, and signed by Governor Edge the following year in March of 1917. Anna Wilcox Whittlesey, "The Lady of the Manor," died on August 16, 1918. She was remembered as "a woman of rare refinement and culture, and the soul of hospitality." Long-time business partner Vernon J. Miller was executor of the estate and Thomas A. Davis became president of the Livingston Manor Corporation.

Highland Park's identity as a streetcar suburb was transformed to that of an automobile suburb during the 1920s. The broad avenues once planned to allow for trolley lines provided both abundant street parking and travel lanes. In 1919, bus service was provided between Livingston Manor and New Brunswick every half hour. The route followed Grant Avenue to Lincoln Avenue to the Albany Street Bridge and New Brunswick, with the reverse order for the return trip. As indicated on the Sanborn maps, by 1922, Livingston Manor had 210 residences. The Livingston Manor Corporation continued to have deed transactions in the 1960s; nevertheless, Livingston Manor's significant development had taken place by 1925.

It has always been locally recognized that Livingston Manor is an important neighborhood in Highland Park. Its early success provided inspiration to the rest of the townsfolk and the borough's residential development became quite remarkable after Watson Whittlesey and his successors showed the way. Efforts to have this distinctive neighborhood recognized through listing on both the New Jersey and National Registers of Historic Places were successful in 2004.[2]

On June 20, 1908 the *Daily Home News* reported:

> The building boom in Highland Park continues to grow apace. There is hardly a street in any direction which has not a house on it somewhere in the course of construction. At present the following houses are under way. Alex Merchant, two on Raritan Avenue; William Blake, one, and Richard Barnwell, one on Fourth Avenue; William Hogan, ground broken on Benner Street; Charles Nourse, fine cottage at Third and Denison; George Oakley, one on Fourth

[2]Borough Historian Jeanne Kolva wrote the National Register nomination with assistance from Ruth Jansyn and with the support of a grant from the New Jersey Historical Commission. The Livingston Manor Historic District was listed in the New Jersey Register on April 1, 2004 and in the National Register on July 7, 2004.

> Avenue; ex-Mayor Archer, one on Cedar Avenue; John Deinzer, one on Cedar Avenue; L. Dunn of New Brunswick, two on Cedar Avenue; Fred Tindell, one on First Avenue; A.J. Gebhardt, one nearly finished.

In the same edition, another article announced the plans of ex–New Brunswick mayor George Viehmann, who established the Viehmann Tract housing development on the 125-acre Vandeventer Farm on the north side of Raritan Avenue between Fifth and Tenth Avenues. "Mr. Viehmann and his associates will erect forty cottages to sell for not less than $3,000 each. A lake, rustic bridge over the small stream that flows through the tract, and the nucleus of a large grove of trees are included in the plans." Construction began in 1909 after Abraham Jelin became the general contractor. Three houses on North Sixth and seven on North Seventh Avenues near Raritan Avenue were the first to be built. Others followed and by the 1910s, many fine dwellings were under construction. The Highland Park Building Company, the same company that took over the Livingston Manor Corporation, also constructed many of the houses in the Viehmann Tract.

Bungalows are compact houses with open floor plans. They constitute one of the first progressive "small house" movements—a reaction against the larger and more ostentatious houses built in the Victorian era with their myriad of enclosed rooms, each slated for a specific purpose and needing extra domestic help for care and upkeep. Many bungalows were constructed in the Viehmann Tract and throughout Highland Park during the 1910s and 1920s. Kit and plan book houses, such as Sears & Roebuck's kit house "Westly" at 223 Felton Avenue and the Loiseaux Company's plan book house at 114 Donaldson Street also became popular constructions during these decades of intensive building.

The Volkerts had come to Highland Park in the 1880s and built the stately house on Johnson Street between Cedar and South First Avenues. In November 1907, Lorenz Volkert, a well-known merchant tailor who had recently retired after forty years in the business, was elected mayor in a close vote of 121 for Volkert to 110 for Charles Nafey. Proving to be a popular Republican leader, Volkert served for three terms from January 1, 1908 until January 1, 1914 when ill health forced him to resign from his post. His terms oversaw the discussions about and the construction of additional school facilities for a growing population of school aged children that followed the housing developments. His administration established North Second and Third Avenues and tried to control free-roaming livestock, feral dogs, and the fire department. Throughout his three terms, Volkert used his veto power to defeat bond issues that would have paid for a pumper truck. Eventually, the process of calls for bids, debates over which bid to accept, and delayed action eventually resulted in the fire department's purchase of the first mechanized fire pumper, but years later in 1915, during the term of Mayor White. Volkert died on September 14, 1919. He had been a member of the Reformed Church and the Aurora Singing Society. He is buried at Elmwood Cemetery in New Brunswick.

Highland Park has always taken pride in the fact that it is a town with high rates of literacy. In March of 1909, the *Daily Home News* sponsored a readers contest with the prize of 400 books comprising the "Library of the World's Best Literature." Individuals could vote for the institution they wanted to see receive the library. Competitive voting took place at local stores in nearby towns, including Milltown, New Brunswick, South River, and Metuchen. By the end of March, Highland Park Public School was in the lead and the New Brunswick High School was second. Landsberg's Department Store in New Brunswick displayed the books, which filled its big shop windows. A Highland Park contingent canvassed the town and encouraged everyone to cast their votes for the school. In the final tally, the 400 books went to the Highland Park School, which won with over three million votes. On July 19, 1909 the books were moved to the school in a festive procession led by the New Brunswick Fife and Drum Corps and the school children. Housed at the new school on South Second Avenue, this collection became Highland Park's first lending library.

On June 13, 1910, Charles K. Hamilton accomplished quite a feat: he made the first round trip airplane flight between New York City and Philadelphia, then considered a great distance. The leading newspapers in those cities sponsored the prize-winning achievement and Hamilton conveyed messages from one newspaper to the other. Taking off from Governor's Island in New York harbor at 7:30 a.m., he flew over New Brunswick at 8:14 a.m. and was met with factory whistles, firebells, and shouts from thousands of spectators. While directly over the New Brunswick train station, Hamilton dropped leaflets that read, "The New York Times and Philadelphia Ledger Peace Bombs dropped from Hamilton's aeroplane—New York to Philadelphia round trip flight, June 1910." Moving at 45 miles per hour, he disappeared quickly over the city's horizon. Hamilton landed in Philadelphia at 9:26 a.m.

A special train followed Hamilton's progress all along the Pennsylvania Railroad's main line. On the return trip, an even larger crowd greeted Hamilton at New Brunswick when he passed over at 12:35 p.m. Hamilton flew lower to the ground than his initial passover and New Brunswick photographer Isaac Vandeveer was on the Albany Street Bridge to take a photograph of the plane and train crossing the Raritan River. (*See p. 78.*) When over Metuchen,

Hamilton ended up following a different railroad line and due to mechanical problems, he looked for a safe place to land. Seeing what appeared to be a fine, smooth field below him, Hamilton alighted in South Amboy along the Raritan River. He needed help to free his machine from the mud. After waiting some hours for replacement parts brought from his base at Governor's Island, Hamilton took off again and successfully completed his record-breaking flight and won $10,000.

The flight was so successful that the following summer of 1911, the Gimbel brothers offered a $5,000 prize to the fastest racer who would fly from their New York store to their branch store in Philadelphia. Three aviators took part in the race: Lincoln Beachey, Hugh Robinson, and Eugene Ely, who flew in Charles K. Hamilton's plane. Due to mechanical troubles, Ely did not finish the race, which Beachley won as he reached Philadelphia in 2 hours, 22 minutes, and 25 seconds.

Robinson, one of the flyers, actually landed in Highland Park just behind Robert Wood Johnson Jr.'s estate house on River Road because his fuel supply was low. Spectators raced to the site of the landed metal and canvas aircraft. James Donaldson made a ten-minute round trip to the nearest gas supplier and back. Robinson took off from the Johnson farm after many helpful spectators cleared a swatch of land creating an ad hoc runway. Robinson finished the race to Philadelphia, but in second place.

On June 21, 1910, the *Daily Home News* printed a headline declaring "Summer Theatre in Park—Work Will Be Started Tomorrow upon $5,000 Playhouse to Be Erected on the Conover Property Along the River." Located at the Highland Park end of the Albany Street Bridge, the theater featured the Charles J. Haines Stock Company, which presented dramas, comedies, and musical productions. (*See p. 78.*)

Opening day was July 7, 1910 with admission prices of 10¢, 20¢, and 30¢. Over 1,000 seats were arranged at the back of the building in tiers, "like the grand stand of a ball field," while the orchestra seats—regular camp chairs—were on the ground. The stage and orchestra areas were protected overhead by a grandstand canopy, while the tiers were open to the air. This proved detrimental to the audience as a brief rain shower dampened everybody in between acts one and two.

The modern sensation, moving pictures, were also shown during the intermissions. After operating for only one week, Fire Chief Bedford filed a formal complaint in front of borough council regarding the lack of proper equipment around the projector to protect the open-air theatre from fire. He also cited a lack of an adequate number of fire exits and asked that the movies not be shown until the owners took proper precautions.

Because of its limited operation confined to the summer months, by 1914, the Airdome operators were in financial ruin. An auction took place on August 13, 1914 with A.J. Conover buying the building for $135, John Barbour purchasing the organ for $1, and most of the scenery and fixtures going to the Star Theatre in New Brunswick for $10. In total, the building and contents sold for less than five percent of their initial cost.

With over seventy Catholic families in Highland Park, agitation for a local chapel grew after 1910. Because most of the members of this local chapel would have been their Highland Park congregants, St. Peter's Catholic Church in New Brunswick helped establish the chapel. By October of 1911, the church announced its intention to purchase several of Edwin McKeag's lots on the corner of South Sixth and Raritan Avenues. George Viehmann offered a few lots in his tract free if the church decided to build there. Citing the closer proximity of the McKeag tract to the trolley, the church chose McKeag's land. Additional lots closer to South Fifth Avenue were also secured from the Home Realty Company for the construction of a parish. In 1913, local architect William H. Boylan (1860–1927) drew up plans for the modest chapel that would be named St. Paul's Chapel and that would seat 100 parishioners. The cornerstone was dedicated on August 10, 1913. The $20,000 Gothic Revival style chapel's construction was completed by the following summer and dedicated on July 4, 1914. Attendees included over 300 Highland Parkites and visiting dignitaries from the surrounding diocese. The chapel was blessed by priests outside the walls sprinkling holy water and inside by the Right Reverend Bishop James A. McFaul of the Trenton diocese. St. Peters donated an altar and stained glass windows and the Hibernia Fire Company in New Brunswick donated a bell.

William H. Boylan also designed the church located at 9 River Road for the Greek Orthodox congregation. This was the first Greek church in the area for an ethnic group that was widespread throughout the state. The church was situated on the trolley line along River Road to facilitate attendance. The cornerstone was laid on August 10, 1919.

The Lincoln Highway is a 3,300-mile long highway that was paved specifically for automobiles coursing from New York City to San Francisco. Its creation in 1912 was the brainchild of Carl Fisher, Prest-O-Lite headlight manufacturer. Fisher was soon joined in the promotion of this road by interested parties in the automobile, tire, and Portland cement industries. The Lincoln Highway incorporated established downtown streets, country lanes, and old trails. The route was marked with rectangular signs with blocks of red, white, and blue showing an "L." By the 1920s, it had become the nation's premier cross-country thoroughfare and a testing ground for new pavements and bridge-building techniques. The roadside also became commercialized with businesses catering to the needs of motorists. Along its short two-mile route on Raritan Avenue, car dealers were quick to establish showrooms and other business owners installed gas pumps in front of their stores. Used cars were sold at 5 Raritan Avenue and new car showrooms were built at 114, 127, and 438 Raritan Avenue. The distinctive floor to ceiling plate glass windows and rear garage at the building on the corner of South Fifth and Raritan Avenues indicate that this was built as an automobile dealership. A recent Special Resource Study conducted by the National Park Service has determined that this historic roadway is a significant national corridor that is eligible for listing in the National Register of Historic Places.

George White, a Democrat, was Highland Park's third mayor with his term of office from January 1, 1914 to January 1, 1916. Some of his administration's noted acts include the opening of Fourth Avenue from Raritan to Lincoln Avenue, the purchase of the Fire Department's first pumper truck, and the construction of two neighborhood schools. By 1915, the population of Highland Park had grown to 2,901. Mayor White was defeated in his reelection attempt by former Assistant Prosecutor Russell E. Watson, who would serve in office for four years.

Despite receiving a six-room addition in 1910, the Highland Park School was becoming overcrowded again in the early 1910s. The need to build new schools finally reached crisis status in 1913 and the argument literally divided the town in half as those on the south side and the east side were presented with a difficult proposition. Apparently, Watson Whittlesey offered to sell some of his land at a reduced price and donate $1,300 worth of playground equipment for a new school in the Livingston Manor tract. This was a tempting proposition because taxpayers always enjoy bargains. However, the location was not ideal, for the town center had shifted to the east and many residents wanted the new school to be built closer to the Viehmann, McKeag, and Home Realty Company tracts on both the north and south sides east of Fourth Avenue. East New Brunswick Heights, the old Race Track lots, were also being purchased by potential homebuilders and the population there was expected to rise significantly. The main point of discussion centered on children crossing the dangerous streets. Two new school sites were proposed—one near Livingston Manor and the second in the old Race Track area on Central Avenue. However, several prominent members of the community were shocked when the second location was announced. They could not stand the idea of funding a new school out in the middle of the country, for at the time, the Race Track district only had a few houses as indicated in a map published in the *Daily Home News*. Despite the purchase of the two tracts of land, that following July a new proposal was offered. This plan called for the construction of one new school on Abbott Street between Fifth and Sixth Avenues. On September 30 and then again on December 1, 1914, voters expressed their wishes in one of the liveliest school contests ever waged in Highland Park. Voters defeated the one-school plan by supporting the construction of two four-room, neighborhood schools.

Alexander Merchant drew up one set of plans and the schools, Irving and Hamilton, became identical twins. Hamilton was completed first and dedicated on November 30, 1915. Irving was completed six weeks later and opened on January 13, 1916.

The history of the early mayoral and council elections shows that the town's political affiliations alternated from Democrat to Republican and back again. Highland Park's fourth mayor, Russell Watson, was a Republican who headed a council that was divided between Democrats and Republicans. Council members included Democrats Frank Deinzer and Edward Waldron, and Republicans Page, Baier, and Wendt. A.H. Wykoff, newly elected in November 1915, was an independent and would balance the council if he voted with the Democrats. The issues this group had to face included an infant paralysis epidemic of 1916, the debate over a ban on rabbit hunting (which passed into law on April 10, 1916), the first World War, and the rising ire of taxpayers who wanted lower taxes and higher levels of municipal services. In Mayor Watson's state of the borough speech on January 1, 1919, he stated that increases in appropriations were due to the provision of additional services, such as an additional police officer and a borough engineer to oversee the Streets and Roads Committee developments:

> These appropriations supply only the barest needs of municipal life, and none of the needed things can be supplied without adding to our revenue. If there is a demand upon the part of the taxpayers, direct or indirect, for a progress of public improvements, the tax levy will be larger, and the rate or the valuations, or both will increase.
>
> It is not a problem peculiar to Highland Park. It is the experience of all municipalities. The cost of everything else has increased. Highland Park not only has to meet these higher costs, but also labors under peculiar difficulties. It has no means of indirect taxation, such as a municipally owned water system or light system, it receives relatively no revenue from excise licenses, and it has relatively small manufacturing and business sections subject to assessment and paying taxes.

In 1918, Livingston Manor and the Viehmann Tract had pavements of stone lightly dressed with oil laid upon graded streets, the borough clerk announced that there were 524 telephones in town, Lafayette Place and Cliff Court were new side streets off Adelaide Avenue, and on February 5 Robert Wood Johnson Jr. was appointed to borough council. The municipal budget was estimated to be between $18,000 and $20,000. Several streets in the Race Track area received new names. During World War I, house building came to a halt the year the country was at war. Public Service, the electric company at the time, reduced street lighting due to the coal shortage. Mayor Watson served as the Middlesex County fuel administrator and donations poured into the Home Defense League. The flu epidemic took its toll on the borough, and schools were closed for a week in October. Advocacy for social improvements also kept residents active.

The power of democracy's most valuable tool—the secret ballot—was given a passing grade during the spring of 1918 when petition drives were carried out throughout town calling for a special referendum to institute a borough-wide ban on all liquor sales. The petitions garnered 335 names, more than forty percent of the voters. However, when the actual vote using secret ballots was held on May 21, 1918, by far the majority of the 508 voters actually wanted the town to remain "wet" and only 200 voters truly wanted to outlaw alcohol. Unfortunately, the town had to raise taxes to pay for the vote, which cost $208.26. A good lesson in democracy; nevertheless, by the next year, Prohibition would become the law of the country and Highland Park would ostensibly go dry for the next thirteen years.

Chapter Six

1920 TO 1945

History takes time. . . . History makes memory.

—Gertrude Stein, 1932

In 1920, the population of Highland Park was 4,866. The decade of the 1920s was one of tremendous growth and possibilities. There was women's suffrage and the creation of the League of Women Voters, "Lucky Lindy," Prohibition and the social problems it brought, and closer to home, the Halls-Mills murder, which dominated daily headlines for two months in 1922. Highland Park had its own distinction. On November 4, 1919, Councilman Robert Wood Johnson Jr., son and nephew of the founders of Johnson & Johnson Company, was elected to become Highland Park's youngest and most famous mayor. The twenty-six-year old Republican received 412 votes, placing first on the ticket. Henry F. Miller and Amos Wheatly won positions as councilmen.

In his inauguration speech, January 1, 1920, at the firehouse on Raritan Avenue, Johnson called paving "our first consideration." At the time, the firehouse also housed the borough offices. Because new fire equipment would be stored in the building, Johnson suggested that the town arrange for other office space. Beginning on Monday, March 8, 1920, council meetings were held in the rooms over Charles Meseroll's garage at 10 North Second Avenue, now B. Beamesderfer's Art Gallery.

Most of Johnson's first year in office was devoted to the paving of streets and the adoption of a building code. In addition, all firemen, soldiers, and sailors received a property tax abatement of $500. During his second year, a campaign was started to raise funds for a memorial to the local soldiers who served in World War I. Jitney bus licensing was issued, Benjamin F. Gebhardt became borough office manager, and J. Ford Flagg was appointed borough clerk. Johnson declined to run for re-election in 1922, citing business concerns. It was during the 1920s when the Johnson & Johnson Company gained its international stature. During World War II, Johnson became a brigadier general and led the corporate business section of the War Department.

A philanthropist, the general was involved in local fund-raising events and celebrations throughout his lifetime. In 1950, Johnson donated his Belleview estate to the Congregation of Our Lady of the Retreat in the Cenacle. In 1955 he was the featured speaker at Highland Park's Golden Jubilee. Johnson died January 30, 1968 at the age of seventy-four. He is buried in the family mausoleum at Elmwood Cemetery in New Brunswick.

In November 1920, Earle E. Dickson (1893–1961), a cotton buyer for the Johnson & Johnson Company, created what would become Johnson & Johnson's best known product world-wide: the Band-Aid. Dickson resided at 326 Montgomery Street with his young wife Josephine. The Band-Aid reportedly arose out of a need to have bandages readily available for her because she often cut her fingers when preparing food. The first Band-Aid consisted of a piece of gauze preattached to a strip of adhesive tape. It was created in Dickson's kitchen. He told a co-worker, who told Johnson & Johnson management, and the production of this product commenced soon thereafter. At first they were handmade and quite large. In 1924, the first Band-Aid Adhesive Bandage machine was perfected, and the company introduced smaller bandages with medicated pads. Dickson's career at Johnson & Johnson was long and successful. He became head of the Hospital Division in 1924 and remained in charge until his retirement in 1957. By that time, annual sales of his and Highland Park's most famous creation reached the $30 million mark.

On May 17, 1920, a license was granted to Forest Park, Inc. allowing this company to run a three-acre amusement park. Around the turn of the century the Aurora Singing Society, a New Brunswick based German-American club, purchased a tract of land between Crowells Road, Karsey Street, and Aurora Street for its social functions.

Aurora Grove was renovated at great expense to its owners and opened as Forest Park on Decoration Day, May 31, 1920. There was a dance pavilion for 600, a motion picture theatre for 300, a mammoth carousal, a shooting gallery, and a miniature bowling alley. An ad in the New Brunswick Directory from 1921 stated, "Forest Amusement Park; Dancing—A place to have a good time under refined and pleasant surroundings—Vaudeville Entrance at the foot of Hilton Street, Highland Park." Visitors could either bring their lunches or purchase food on site. There were tables for family picnics and enough benches to seat several thousand people. Shore dinners or clambakes could be provided and various organizations booked events. There was no liquor due to Prohibition.

It was not long before the ministry of the Highland Park Reformed Church protested the opening of Forest Park on Sundays, the "American Sabbath." Petitions both in support of and against the park were signed by a large number of residents. Other churches, namely the Presbyterian, Baptist, and Methodist denominations, voiced their opposition to Sunday openings. New Jersey had "blue laws" that had been passed by the legislature in 1874 and amended in 1893. Financial problems due to the blue laws closed the park for good after only two summers of operation. However, parts of the amusement park remain. Several houses at the end of Karsey Street are believed to be original park structures and, in 1926, a team of horses moved the wooden dance hall to a corner of Hilton Street where it stands today at 168 Woodbridge Avenue, renamed the Forrest Park Professional Building.

One of the organizations that held events in Forest Park was the Rice Memorial School, which held its twenty-fourth annual closing exercises on the amusement grounds in June 1921. Students made speeches and recitations and the Jenkins Band from South Carolina performed.

The Rice Industrial School for Colored Children was organized in New Brunswick in the summer of 1897 by Reverend W.H. Rice. Ella H. Rice is credited with continuing her husband's work after his death in 1899. She relocated the school to Highland Park in November 1920, where it was located on Drier Avenue near the Lincoln Highway just above the Veihmann Tract. The Drier Estate, which is no longer extant, was formerly a sanitarium.

Reverend Rice had organized the State School for Colored Children at Bordentown, before moving to New Brunswick. His primary motive was to uplift and educate African Americans. The school's purpose was to prepare children for a useful life and give them elementary instruction with Christian influence. There were thirty boys and thirty girls from New Jersey residing in the boarding school. Many of the children were orphans. The tuition was approximately $120 per year and students performed household chores. Private donations and entertainment fund-raisers secured necessary school funds.

Mrs. Rice, the principal for twenty-three years, died on November 25, 1920. In addition to holding positions in numerous organizations, Mrs. Rice was treasurer of the New Jersey State Federation of Colored Women's Clubs and vice-president of the State Association of Teachers of Colored Children. She was interred at New Brunswick's Elmwood Cemetery. In February of 1922, a lively debate about whether mixed race schools offered better education than "colored only" schools took place between students of the Rice School and a team from New York City. The team from the Rice School took the position that colored only schools provided political and psychological advantages to African Americans that were not available in mixed schools, which primarily catered to the most favored white youths. The judges rendered a unanimous decision in favor of the Rice School debate team. The school continued to operate until 1924 when a fire devastated the facility.

Patriotic fervor earmarked the decade of the 1920s. In May 1921, a committee of former soldiers and sailors voted to form a local social organization to be known as the Veterans Association of Highland Park. The members petitioned the American Legion's county executive committee for a charter. On July 25, 1921, Highland Park Post 88 received its charter, the thirteenth such post in Middlesex County. John Hunter was the first post commander and meetings were held in rooms over Hodge's Garage on North Second Avenue. A woman's auxiliary soon followed. In addition to protecting the rights of veterans, the Legion held many community activities including bazaars, poppy sales, Christmas Eve celebrations, and Community Nights. In 1925 the group donated "a large caliber captured German field gun" to the borough, which eventually was placed on the front lawn of the High School.

The post received title to a house at 127 Benner Street in 1931 that served as its headquarters until 1949. In June 1950, Post 88 moved into a new building at 808 Raritan Avenue. The group consisted of 150 members at the time.

That building was sold in 2002. After paying off debts, the post had $160,000. Frank Conover Jr. and Frank Ferguson formed a committee to disperse the money. Among the donations was a gift of $70,000 to the New Jersey Veterans' Memorial Home in Menlo Park for a glass enclosed solarium and a $60,000 scholarship fund for Highland Park High School students. The group continues to meet in member's homes and at other posts.

Patriotism extended to the younger members of society and scouting was an important function in the 1920s. Many churches and organizations sponsored Boy Scout troops. Serving as a social opportunity where boys learned to tie knots, went on hikes, and marched in parades, scouting also engaged them in community service, assisting during fires and natural disasters. During World War I, scouts aided the Red Cross, liberty loan, and food conservation workers. Scouts helped direct traffic on November 18, 1922 when the construction of State Highway 1 required detours through Highland Park. The Reformed Church organized Troop No. 2 in April 1912. Troop 22 was founded by the American Legion in 1923 by Denton E. Brome and Duke S. Leonard. (*See p. 86.*) In the 1940s, the troop had the drums and bugles that had been used in the past by Post 88.

Another organization promoting Americanism was the Daughters of the American Revolution (DAR). On Columbus Day, October 12, 1922, the Jersey Blue Chapter of the DAR aided in organizing the Colonel John Neilson Society, a branch of the Children of the American Revolution, at the home of Mrs. George H. Brown, 59 Adelaide Avenue. Over 100 children were enrolled as charter members. Mrs. James Neilson of New Brunswick presented a picture of Colonel John Neilson to the society.

On March 11, 1921 G. Frances Eden, president of the Third District Republican Club of Highland Park, declared it was time to honor the town's war heroes. Sentiment favored a monument to be erected at the intersection of Woodbridge and Raritan Avenues on state and county owned land. The monument would be on the Lincoln Highway and it was hoped that it would become a tourist landmark noted in the Automobile Blue Book. Mayor Robert Wood Johnson became chairman of the World War Memorial Association Committee. Volunteers canvassed door to door and donors' names were printed in the *Highland Park Press*, then the local weekly newspaper. A carved granite statue of an artilleryman, called a doughboy, standing at parade rest was purchased from L.L. Manning & Sons of Plainfield. The monument's unveiling was held on Armistice Day, November 11, 1921 before a crowd of nearly 2,000 people. It followed a parade—one of the biggest ever held in Highland Park. Local dignitaries spoke, including Professor E. Livingston Barbour, who read a poem written specifically for the occasion by William J. Fitzgerald. Marguerite and Kathleen Wheatley, daughters of Councilman Amos Wheatley, laid a wreath at the foot of the statue. The American Legion held an invitational dance that evening.

On January 1, 1922 Republican Cornelius B. McCrelis Jr. became mayor. Council consisted of six men, all but one of whom were Republicans. Among McCrelis's goals was improved law and order. He wanted to build a small "lock-up," create a zoning ordinance, and construct a garbage disposal plant. He also felt consideration should be given to projects in the Viehmann Tract and the Race Track section. Highland Park's Zoning Ordinance was unanimously adopted in February 1923. The Technical Advisory Corporation of New York City assisted in its drafting. McCrelis ruled out a disposal plant and decided to purchase a one-ton truck to be used for collecting garbage and ashes. In July, William Ten Eyck offered 378 acres of unimproved lowland in Raritan Township as a dumpsite for $11,000. John McCarthy, superintendent of streets, was in charge of refuse collection. Mayor McCrelis did not get a jail, but he did get a new office. During his administration borough council chambers and offices were moved to the new Masonic Building at North Fourth and Raritan Avenues. The first year lease came with the privilege of renewal at a yearly rate of $780 beginning August 1, 1923. On Monday, August 6, 1923 at 8:00 p.m., council held its first meeting in its new quarters, rooms 8, 9, and part of 7 on the second floor of the Masonic Temple. Mayor McCrelis ended his two-year term on January 1, 1924, but continued to serve in local government.

The borough's previous growth spurts pale by comparison to the one that took place in the 1920s. The growing development of the Viehmann Tract and Magnolia Heights and Riverview Terrace on the south side followed that of the Livingston Manor and composed a major step in residential growth. As early as 1921, the need to regulate the explosive and uncontrolled growth was acknowledged and a building code ordinance was introduced. The increased development raised other issues and created pollution that plagued the area for years. Complaints were made to the Health Department that the vacant lots on Denison Street between Second and Third Avenues were used for the dumping of garbage and that the stench was unbearable. Developers such as Dr. Walter Atwood, who built twenty-two houses on Becker and Graham Streets between South Third and South Fourth Avenues, wanted sanitary sewers extended to his tract. The problem with the lack of sewerage in the north side Viehmann Tract remained unresolved. An installation of a sewer from the area adjacent to the Mill Brook to the Raritan River was suggested, but never implemented.

Great changes in both the residential and business area had been made. The demand for local services and stores resulted in the emergence of small factories and many types of stores. Raritan Avenue was the logical choice and in the month of March 1921, six new stores were scheduled to open. Some residents disapproved of the haphazard manner in the development of business properties, fearing it would reduce property values. By the end of 1923 Highland Park had a variety of stores. There were three meat markets, six grocery stores, three delicatessens, four confectionery stores, two fruit stands, three bakeries, and two lunchrooms. There were three drug stores, four barbershops, four tailor shops, one shoe shop, one toy store, and two dry goods and notion stores. There were also many garages, several of which were also motor sales agencies. Almost all were located on Raritan Avenue. There were also a number of industries other than the large manufacturers of Janeway & Carpender and the John Waldron Company. The Francke Company, the Kompak Company, Highland Park Building Company, and Cronk Manufactories were situated along the railroad. J.S. Turner White Metal Company and New Brunswick Knitting Mills were on Raritan Avenue. J.S. Bergen and Sons, makers of paper bags and allied products, were located on North Third Avenue and the Unshrinkable Metal Company was on Cedar Avenue.

Along with Turner Tubes, the New Brunswick Knitting Company, 431 Raritan Avenue, was one of the factories along the borough's main street. It was organized in 1919 by DeWitt B. Strauss and Daniel Rheinaner and was the only business of its kind in the area. Highland Park was chosen as its site because of its central location, wonderful transportation facilities, availability of labor, and room for expansion. Everything for the manufacturing of bathing suits, jersey cloth, street clothing, and knitted outerwear was found in the two-story brick building, which still exists. Three thousand garments were made weekly and 2,000 yards of cloth were woven. The plant employed about fifty people, mostly girls and women. By 1923, the company was successful enough to warrant a night shift.

In 1924, the old plant received an addition. A gala celebration was held, including dance music supplied by Galipo's Orchestra and an impersonation of Rudolph Valentino's "Spanish Fandango" by Ben Baron, the chief traveling salesman of the firm. The new building contained 6,000 square feet of floor space. Three stores were built and rented and new machines were installed on the upper floor. The company continued to produce knitwear into the 1950s.

One other nationally known brand name product other than the Band-Aid was created in Highland Park. This was Flako boxed mixes produced by the Flako Products Corporation, a company that started small in the early 1920s. Arthur McCallum took an old family recipe and developed it over a three-year period. The pre-mixed, packaged ingredients required only the addition of water. First labeled "Flaky" Pie Crust, the boxed mixes had immediate retail success. Flako was born in a small factory at 213 Cedar Avenue in September 1921, and the company was incorporated in January 1922. Arthur McCallum was the company's president and his wife Helen, reporter for the *Daily Home News*, became secretary-treasurer. In December 1925, the company moved to 314 Cleveland Avenue. Three years later the company expanded and the factory received a second addition, constructed in July 1931. The pie crust and corn muffin mix company survived the Depression and eventually was purchased by Quaker Oats in the 1950s.

Arthur McCallum, a Republican, served on the Borough Council from 1934 through 1939. Both he and Helen McCallum were instrumental in establishing Highland Park's First Aid Squad. In 1949, through their Flako Products Corporation, they donated a fully equipped 1949 Meteor Cadillac to be Highland Park's first ambulance.

In the early twentieth century, the Raritan River was used for boating, regattas, and water carnivals. Some national and international athletes participated. In 1922 Gertrude Ederle, internationally famed swimmer, set a record in the 440-yard freestyle, beating Hilda James, England's champion.

Another entertainment spot was Ayres Beach on the Highland Park side on the first bend of the river downstream from the Albany Street Bridge. In June 1922, Highland Park farmer and former milkman Frank Ayres imported several truckloads of white sand to create a beach. He also constructed a beach house. The area, a popular swimming place for many years, had been known as "The Elms." His improvements drew even larger crowds. The building had a screened-in front porch, a thirty-foot square dance hall, and a small kitchen on the first floor. Soft drinks, sandwiches, and dinners were served on the porch. Fish dinners were the specialty of the house. On the second floor were twenty bathhouses with large windows that offered good ventilation. The house was wired with electric lights and lights also cascaded down the road off Cedar Avenue and down to the riverbank. In 1939, a small allotment of WPA money paid for a new road leading to Ayres Beach and a boat basin. Additional funds were sought to continue improvements and to create a park named Ayres Beach Park for Middlesex County residents. The federal money would have employed 100 men for ten months, but apparently it never arrived. Nearby Donaldson Park did not open to the public until after World War II.

Boaters took advantage of the dock. In the later years of its operation, Ayres's business transformed from bathing beach to marina. Frank Ayres ran a dry docking facility for motor boats and sea planes until his death in 1945. Pollution put an end to the aquatic events and, eventually, Ayres Beach. In the last half of the twentieth century the area was known as Red's Marina. Oral histories suggest that Red had quite an eccentric personality. Middlesex County bought the property in 2003 and demolished the beachhouse, which had become derelict through neglect.

On September 17, 1923, the Masonic Temple opened at the corner of North Fourth and Raritan Avenues, becoming Highland Park's new grand community center. Its prominent position also shifted the town's hub from Second to Fourth Avenue. Discussions regarding the construction of a Lodge began in January 1922, when approximately 150 Masons met in the Hamilton School and made preliminary organizational arrangements. Ex-mayor Russell Watson was the principal speaker. There were over 400 Highland Park resident Masons, including Mayor McCrelis. Highland Park Lodge No. 240 of the Free and Accepted Masons was granted its charter on April 20, 1922. The group met in New Brunswick until a suitable meeting place in town was created. Alexander Merchant designed the building and the Highland Park Masonic Building Association was in charge. Groundbreaking ceremonies were held before a large crowd. Ex-mayor Robert Wood Johnson Jr., Mason and member of the finance committee, turned over the first spade of dirt. The cornerstone dedication was held Saturday, December 16, 1922. Mason and Governor-elect George Silzer gave a speech and numerous Highland Park organizations took part in the ceremonies. The $300,000 lodge officially opened on September 17, 1923, changing community life in Highland Park. It became home to borough offices, the post office, and the library. The seventy- by ninety-foot auditorium hosted, among other events, boxing, indoor circuses, and dance marathons. There was retail space for the First National Bank and several other stores. Joseph Barlow relocated his drugstore from 218 Raritan Avenue to the corner store. A Cadillac showroom and parking garage were located on the North Fourth Avenue side. The Masonic Temple was the borough's entertainment center until March 10, 1965 when the building was nearly destroyed in a double-alarm fire. The first floor still stands as a one-story commercial building.

By the 1920s, Highland Park had a population of sufficient size to seek its own library and post office. In January 1922, Elmar Boyd, publisher of the *Daily Home News*, assigned reporter G. Wallace Conover to establish a library in Highland Park. Within forty-eight hours the task was completed. The library was in a twelve- by twenty-eight-foot room located at 9 North Second Avenue. Books were contributed by the *Daily Home News*. There were tables, six chairs, and a librarian's desk. Reverend Quinn of St. Paul's donated a complete set of the *Book of Knowledge*. The New Brunswick Sign Company donated a swinging sign with the words Highland Park Free Public Library on both sides. Miss Viola Weiss of the Christian Endeavor Society of the Reformed Church was the first volunteer. Mrs. John Green volunteered to be librarian.

In March 1922, Mayor McCrelis reported that council had no provision in the budget to maintain the library and had no authority to do so without a referendum vote. He felt the citizens would support the library until the borough was in a position to take over. Fundraisers were held. There were Highland Park Library Days at the Reade State Theatre in New Brunswick. In addition to the regular feature *Moran of the Lady Letty* starring Rudolph Valentino, twenty-five local girls of the Highland Park Amateur Artists presented a local vaudeville act. Councilman Harry Drake held a sale in his store and donated five percent of the proceeds to the library. The *Highland Park Press* offered two newspaper files to hold copies of the *Daily Home News* and the *Press*. By the time of the referendum, at least 3,000 books had been donated. At the general election on November 7, 1922 voters passed the referendum. In 1923, the Highland Park Free Public Library moved, along with the borough offices, to the new Masonic Temple. From 1923 to 1946, the library occupied four different locations within the Masonic Building. From 1946 to 1959, it occupied larger quarters next to the Masonic Temple.

It is not known when postal services were no longer offered at local stores, but, in 1922, the first steps toward the establishment of a branch post office in Highland Park were taken at a community dinner held in the Reformed

Church. Pastor Anthony Luidens stated that all government projects engaged in by Park citizens were carried out as if Highland Park was "merely an organic part of New Brunswick" and that residents had to go across the river to register letters, insure packages, send parcel post, and buy stamps. A committee made up of A.J. Gebhardt, Klemer Kaltelssen, Councilman Harry Drake, and Frederick Gowen was formed.

Postmaster James Morrison of New Brunswick encouraged the creation of a station in Highland Park, which would have been a branch of the New Brunswick post office under his supervision. The Men's Bible Class of the Reformed Church and the *Highland Park Press* circulated a petition. Signed by 1,300 residents, the petition requesting the United States Post Office Department to establish a "classified" post station in Highland Park was forwarded to Washington.

Facilities for the Highland Park Branch Post Office were established in the Masonic Building. It was officially opened September 1, 1923 with John Sutton the clerk-in-charge. On December 1, 1926, superintendent James Quakenboss took over. The borough had three carriers and a fully equipped office. Mr. Quakenboss was superintendent; Charles Thompson, clerk; and Lester Giles, Joseph Schalosser, Walter Dicke, Eugene Pries, and Percy Tunison served as carriers. In 1940, the post office moved to 300 Raritan Avenue. In 1949, it was relocated to 17 North Fourth Avenue, and in 1960 to its current facility on Raritan Avenue at South Fourth Avenue.

George F. Leonard became Highland Park's seventh mayor on January 1, 1924. The only elected Democrat in a Republican controlled administration, Leonard's difficulties were evident from the start. He appointed Leon A. Campbell, fellow Democrat, to fill the vacancy necessitated by the ex-councilman's rise to the position of mayor. That was the bright spot of Leonard's day. Almost every one of his other appointments failed to be confirmed by the Republican controlled council. In his mayoral message, Leonard presented his plans for his administration. He hoped to repair streets, install trunk sewers along the easterly boarder, establish an organized police department with a police chief, and establish a water commission to study the extension of water mains. He also wanted a permanent non-partisan borough improvement commission made up of six volunteers to assist in creating more civic pride and consider the possibility of public parks and playgrounds.

Town safety was an issue. Councilman Joiner called for substitutes when the patrolling marshal and paid fireman had their regular days off. The Police Committee acquired a $505 Indian motorcycle with a side car and tandem seat. Fire Chief Page asked for a new alarm system and the replacement of worn equipment.

The age of the automobile worsened traffic problems. In 1925 the Albany Street Bridge was widened, adding to the problems of unregulated traffic. Parking regulations were suggested for the main thoroughfare. Gasoline stations were springing up throughout the town and automobiles were speeding along Woodbridge Avenue. Public transportation was unsatisfactory. Trolley and bus service was scheduled for every four minutes during the rush hours; however, surveys showed haphazard and irregular service was the norm. The 5¢ fare limit extended only to Seventh Avenue, the terminus of the Highland Park trolley and bus lines.

Health issues were also addressed. A milk ordinance was proposed to regulate the delivery and sale of milk, which was required to measure up to a certain standard. Mrs. Whitney, president of the PTA, urged support of Dr. Haight's recommendation for a full-time Health Officer.

The Democratic mayor lost his only ally, Leon Campbell, in the second year of his term when Councilmen McDonald and Schermerhorn, both Republicans, were elected. Leonard did not even attempt to make his own appointments, stating, "the appointments I am about to make are the appointments of Council."

Reviewing his first year in office, Leonard expressed satisfaction with the improvement of the police system with a lieutenant in complete charge and the addition of a motorcycle. He was disappointed that the trunk sewer was still in the process of review. Leonard felt the lack of extension of water mains retarded Highland Park's proper development.

It was during Leonard's second year that plans were made to erect a "brick and hollow block" police headquarters next to the firehouse on Raritan Avenue and an addition to the fire house. Alexander Merchant was selected to design the building and the construction contract was awarded to Nora and Nora Construction Company. This building at 137 Raritan Avenue is now an international delicatessen. Also in 1925 the New York Telephone Company installed a telephone on its pole at the northeast corner of Raritan and Fourth Avenues for the use of the Yellow Taxicab Company.

In 1926 there were 350 residential houses under construction. This residential population explosion was reflected in the increase in religious organization activity. Two new churches were constructed.

The All Saints Episcopal Church began as a mission in 1924. Services were held in the Masonic Building until a house was purchased for use as a church and rectory. In the autumn of 1926 ground was broken and by November 1927, the Gothic Revival style church at Magnolia Street and South Third Avenue was completed. The Trinity Methodist Church also had begun as a smaller organization forming a Sunday school on July 6, 1924. Meetings were held at the Masonic Temple and later at the American Legion rooms over Hodges Garage. Dedication of the new church on Montgomery Street was June 3, 1928. In the 1920s, the Baptist Chapel on Raritan and North Second Avenues had become too small for its increasing membership and, in 1925, the members started collecting money for a building fund. This church was relocated to the first lot on North Second Avenue, raised up onto a higher foundation, and covered with brick. This move left the corner lot available for the construction of an extraordinary limestone Gothic Revival style church, which never materialized.

By 1920, Highland Park had three neighborhood elementary schools—Lafayette on the south side, Hamilton on the north side, and Irving in the Race Track area. Older students continued to attend high school outside the borough. The growing population resulted in increasing school enrollment and a need for greater facilities at both Hamilton and Irving. On November 12, 1920, contracts were awarded for the construction of four-room additions to both schools. On June 3, 1921, the school board granted permission to Julius Kahn to open a dental clinic in the Hamilton School. It was the first school dental clinic in Middlesex County and one of the first in the state.

As larger numbers of Highland Park's high school age students traveled out of town to Metuchen or New Brunswick to continue their education as tuition students, demand for a local junior high school began. But it was not realized until 1924, when the Solomon-Maher tract, seven acres of land at the intersection of Montgomery Street and North Fifth Avenue, was purchased for a local high school. Noted Highland Park architect Alexander Merchant submitted plans for the Georgian Revival style school with its stunning central tower. Construction began after a $280,912 contract was awarded to Nora & Nora Construction Company. The total expenditure was closer to $362,000.

Opened in September 1926 for Highland Park's seventh through ninth graders with Alger Maynard as principal, a formal dedication ceremony took place later on October 14 that included placing a cannon donated by American Legion Post 88 on the new school's front yard. The name Franklin Junior High School was chosen one month after dedication day. From 1927 to 1935, the school served children only up to the tenth grade. In 1935, over 1,000 residents signed a petition calling for a complete high school curriculum. The 1936–1937 school year found eleventh graders in the hallways, and the twelfth grade was added the following year. On May 11, 1937, Franklin Junior High was officially renamed "Highland Park High School." The first yearbook published in 1938 took its name "Albadome" or "white dome" acknowledging the school's distinctive architectural detail. The first graduation at the new high school was held in June of 1938.

Additions of the "Science wing" in 1958, the "English wing" in 1968, and the 1990s expansions that included a gazebo-like cafeteria, reflect not only Highland Park's growing student populations, but also the enduring commitment to providing adequate facilities for them. Highland Park High School remains one of the most beloved of the town's landmarks.

In the 1920s, Highland Park acquired its first and only castle. Merriewold was built in 1926 by J. Seward Johnson, brother of ex-mayor Robert Wood Johnson Jr. and heir to the Johnson & Johnson fortune, for his wife Ruth Dill Johnson. Located at 433 River Road, near the Piscataway border, the castle and its outbuildings stand on a hill across from Johnson Park, obscured by dense woods. The turreted twenty-five-room structure has two hidden stairways, eleven fireplaces, and six bedrooms. There are 150 lead glass windows and a walnut paneled ballroom. In 1928, architect Thomas Harlan Ellett (1880–1951) won the New York Architectural League's silver medal for Merriewold's design.

The castle has had a varied past. There was a robbery and an attempted kidnapping of the Johnsons' baby daughter. In the early 1940s, actor Michael Douglas, son of Kirk Douglas, lived there until he was six weeks old. The castle was used as a nursing home beginning in 1945. Later it became home to Charles and Barbara Farmer and their three children and was the site of the notorious Farmer murder when Charles shot and killed Barbara. The Kaplan Organization currently owns the main house and most of the grounds next to a small section of the original estate owned by the Francis Parker nursing home. This northernmost acreage contains architect Thomas Ellett's Chauffeur's Cottage (also known as the Crockett House) and, until 2003, a nineteenth century barn. As the boyhood barn of sculptor J. Seward Johnson Jr., it was recently dismantled and relocated to his farm in Hopewell.

In 1926, Benjamin Erickson became mayor. Robert Hayden and Edwin Eden were the new councilmen and the borough had a completely Republican administration. In a brief speech, Erickson outlined his recommendations for the coming year. He wanted paving and sewer programs started in early spring, better streetlights on Raritan Avenue, and a tax sale every year. He also stated consideration should be given to the creation of a police department and a water department. The formation of a police department granted the patrolmen a legal standing that they did not have before. Provisions were made for three additional patrolmen; two had already been appointed. Council acquired a site for a sewage disposal plant and it was hoped financing for its construction would be forthcoming.

The traffic situation along Raritan Avenue was dangerous and, in 1926, the Highland Park PTA urged Council to install a system of centrally controlled overhead lights to supplement the work of the traffic officers. It was not until Patrolman Sorenson was seriously injured on May 10, 1927 that steps were taken. On September 5, 1927, the DeLaplaine Brothers Company was awarded the contract to install traffic signals at Raritan Avenue and River Road.

The most thrilling event during Erickson's tenure became David Bobker's application for a license to operate a motion picture theater on behalf of developer Mark Block.

Despite several previous announcements of movie theaters coming to Highland Park, it was not until November 21, 1927 that Highland Park gained one when Block's Park Theatre held its grand opening. Situated at the corner of South Sixth and Woodbridge Avenues, it stood across Woodbridge Avenue from the doughboy monument. Senator Morgan Larson dedicated the building. Other dignitaries included Mayor Benjamin Erickson, ex-Mayor McCrelis, and Mayor-elect Edwin W. Eden. The feature presentation was *Clancy's Kosher Wedding* starring George Sidney.

The interior was lavish. Golden brown with decorations of gold and silver leaf and a fountain and fish aquarium in the center foyer, it was considered one of the most beautiful in the state. The theater could seat 1,400 people. Depending on the day and time, admission was either 20¢ or 35¢ for adults and 10¢ or 20¢ for children. The building also contained two stores.

It was not long before problems with blue laws emerged and the theater owner was fined for operating on Sundays. As with Forest Park, petitions were presented for and against Sunday openings. Borough Attorney Horace Barwis found employees of the theater in violation of the State Vice and Immorality Act. In March 1928, the situation escalated into a war between the theater manager and the borough fathers. The theater was never very profitable and closed and re-opened several times under different management. Talkies were introduced in 1929. The theater continued to operate into the 1950s and was demolished after becoming a derelict building in 1961.

Edwin Eden ushered in another all Republican administration and inherited the controversy of Sunday openings at the Park Theater when he became mayor on January 1, 1928. Patriotism and godliness were present that inaugural day of January 1, 1928. Mayor Eden suggested an American flag for the meeting room and invited Reverend Luidens to offer an opening prayer.

In a lengthy report, Eden presented his mayoral message to the council. Much of this address was a review of Highland Park's achievements over the years. By his inauguration Highland Park had five churches; four public schools; St. Paul's parochial school; business houses including the Masonic Building, the Stein Building, the Singer Building, and the Park Theater; one nineteen-family apartment building and several others contemplated; and numerous four- and two-family apartments. The school system, according to Eden, was "one of the best in the state." The program of street paving, which started in 1919, resulted in fourteen miles of permanent pavement. Traffic lights had been installed on Raritan Avenue at the town's entrance from New Brunswick. The water system had been in operation by Highland Park for one year. There was an additional sixteen-inch main laid across the Raritan River that increased the water pressure from twelve to twenty pounds. Two major problems that continued into the late 1920s were pollution and traffic.

One of Eden's first actions was the creation of a committee to study the polluted Raritan River. In 1929, Robert Wood Johnson Jr., Ben Erickson, Robert Hayden, J.L. Matthew, and Mayor Eden served as members of the sewerage committee. Eden hoped to create a sewage treatment plant. Borough Council received a number of complaints against the soft coal smoke from Janeway & Carpender and an eighty-six-name petition requesting an ordinance to control the emission of smoke and other obnoxious gases from local plants. Fire Chief Malmros recommended an ordinance to prohibit automobile service stations from dumping oil and gasoline into sewer catch basins and onto unoccupied lands. Protests were made against the automobile junkyard on Woodbridge Avenue, which was so cluttered that made it difficult for residents to pass.

Traffic problems worsened. Mayor Eden hoped the State Highway Commission would provide uniform traffic lights and signs for Raritan Avenue, "one of the heaviest traveled thoroughfares along the Lincoln Highway." Traffic regulation was provided by police at the borough's expense putting a significant burden on the police department. Eden believed the planned bridge over the Raritan (the U.S. 1 bridge) rerouting traffic to the outskirts of the town would benefit the town enormously. The extremely high volume of truck traffic along Raritan Avenue prevented patronization of local merchants.

Eden sought to refine the borough and to create an ideal residential community. The Shade Tree Commission was established. He wanted to provide a police pension fund, a small yearly payment for firemen, and accident insurance for both. Eden wanted wires along Raritan Avenue to go underground and backyard lines in the residential sections.

In 1929, the borough of homes was in very good standing. In January 1929 Eden stated, "the whole finances of the Borough are in a very healthy condition and our standing is very high in the bond market." Unfortunately, this prosperity and positive attitude of the 1920s, just like the decade itself, would soon end with the crash of the stock market.

The bleakness of the 1930s actually began on October 29, 1929 with the New York Stock Exchange crash. The Great Depression changed lives, shattered dreams, and brought poverty and desolation. It was also in the 1930s that the government's role expanded to exert greater control over individuals. This was true on the local, county, state, and federal levels.

On January 1, 1930 when Richard T. Parker became mayor, the shadow of impending doom had not yet reached Borough Hall. The Republican mayor stated, "There is at this time very little which especially requires your attention." The town's infrastructure was in place. Needs were to clean streets, erect street signs, and install higher power street lights. The water supply contract with New Brunswick was to expire in 1932 and the town needed to begin investigating its next source of water. Sewer disposal was still a question, but that decision was bound up with the greater problem of the Raritan River ecosystem. Mayor Parker concluded, "if no unforeseen emergency arises, it is my opinion that the present tax rate can be lowered substantially during the next few years." As an omen of the difficult times ahead, in February 1930, a resident approached council for assistance in obtaining work. He was referred to the police committee.

A new nuisance that may have also been a reflection of the economic environment was emerging. Boys insisted on "minding" parked automobiles for a fee while the owners attended social affairs. The job situation had worsened by November 1930 and Chairman Smalley of the Streets and Roads Committee suggested the possibility of giving temporary employment to needy men to relieve the unemployment condition.

Mayor Parker began his second year on January 1, 1931. In his annual message, the mayor stated that the "key note of my message is again economy without the loss of efficiency." He considered his first year's accomplishment to be the installation of traffic lights on Raritan Avenue that eliminated accidents. Street signs were also being installed around town as were new arc lights. Parker continued, "The present is a period of financial depression. I urge our taxpayers to make prompt payment of taxes as they fall due."

In the 1930s, the Jewish population became more prevalent. Many were from New Brunswick and many were newcomers. The Jewish Civic League was active in community events, requesting council to send speakers to its meetings to discuss local government, presenting recommendations for the establishment of a rabies clinic, and recommending methods to rectify the economic situation. Highland Park acquired its first temple in 1930.

The construction of the synagogue culminated a five-year project. Planning for a temple began in 1926 with a meeting in the Masonic Hall where officers were elected and early pledges totaled $5,000. In 1927, Rabbi Horowitz was engaged to teach Hebrew School and conduct services. For three years the Hebrew School was located in a rented store at 10 North Fourth Avenue. Land was purchased on North Third Avenue near Montgomery Street and the Hebrew School moved to the Masonic building where classes were conducted until the synagogue was complete. The new Highland Park Conservative Temple held dedication services on September 12–14, 1930. Rabbi Ravetch delivered a sermon entitled "The Voice of God" and Mayor Parker extended greetings. Dr. Latham, pastor of the Trinity Methodist Episcopal Church; Louis Beck, president of the Congregation; and Mrs. A.H. Freeman, president of the Ladies Auxiliary were among the speakers.

It was not long until the increasing Jewish population grew too large for the small temple and in 1944 fund raising began for a new structure. In September 1949, the Highland Park Conservative Temple moved to a larger building designed by Ernest Levine on the corner of South Third Avenue and Benner Street. In 1964 an addition, housing a school, gymnasium, auxiliary worship room, kitchen, library, and offices, was constructed.

During Parker's administration, neither the PTA Civics Committee nor the Highland Park Civic Club noted the seriousness of the Depression when presenting their recommendations for borough improvements to the council. They wanted covers on loaded garbage trucks, the Raritan Avenue traffic lights re-timed to improve pedestrian safety, and to curb the problem of heavier traffic on the side streets after the installation of Raritan Avenue traffic lights. The groups were also concerned with the proposed installation of a water spray for the children at Lafayette School Playground and the problem of ice cream wagons on the streets on Sundays.

But in 1931, the failing economic condition was quite evident. Chairman Buttler of the Police Committee reported that due to the business conditions, the police department had withdrawn its request for an increase in salaries.

The fire department requested permission to conduct a motion picture fundraiser on a Sunday to re-finance the department. The Republican Club also requested permission to hold benefit motion picture performances and Herman Kahn, the new operator of the Park Theater, proposed a series of Sunday benefit motion pictures to raise money for unemployment relief. The situation worsened. Councilman Buttler stated the need for additional funds for aiding the poor and unemployed and the necessity of providing adequate funds for relief work during the winter. An Emergency Relief Committee was established. Highland Park created many local projects such as sidewalk grading, tree trimming, and landscaping around the schools to take advantage of the Employment Relief state aid funding.

Parked cars of theater patrons caused traffic problems on South Sixth Avenue and the police committee proposed making South Sixth a one-way street between Raritan Avenue and Magnolia Street. Public Service Coordinated Transport was granted permission to run the Highland Park Line buses from Raritan to Woodbridge Avenues to Seventh Avenue to Magnolia Street to Eighth Avenue and back to Woodbridge Avenue at Raritan Avenue. This eliminated the dangerous practice of backing the buses from Woodbridge Avenue into Seventh Avenue, which was used as a turn-around.

Citizens needed an escape from their dispirited reality and in the 1930s, novel and sometimes unusual entertainment venues arose. Miniature golf courses were found up and down the Avenue. In September 1930, the borough clerk was directed to write to the managers stating that the courses should be closed earlier and that gambling should not be permitted or Council would take necessary steps to stop them. Russell Chevrolet Inc., operator of a miniature golf course on Raritan Avenue near First Avenue, offered to close its course no later than midnight on Saturday nights.

Ham radio also became popular as an inexpensive source of entertainment. In February 1932, Walter Ambler of North Fifth Avenue conducted a meeting of over 300 amateur radio operators. It was the first "hamfest" or gathering of ham radio operators from New Jersey, New York, and Pennsylvania. Representatives from various manufacturing companies of radio equipment demonstrated new developments in short-wave radio communication.

The one craze most representative of the 1930s was the dance marathon. Joblessness drove singles and couples to compete in walkathons and dance marathons. Monetary prizes lured dancers to travel from coast to coast to shuffle over wooden floors day and night, sometimes for months at a time. One such Walkathon-Marathon, "Red Head Night," was held at the Masonic hall in the early 1930s. An undated newspaper photograph shows the energetic, well dressed men and women posed on the stage and floor of the auditorium and a large banner advertising Station WAAM 1250 "for the latest events direct from the marathon floor." Signs posted on the walls gave the vital statistics. Classification was by "boys" and "girls." The last contestant out was no. 31, with 1,584 hours.

Not all Parkites embraced the practice of holding public dances for financial gains. The Board of Education condemned the dances as "demoralizing" to the youth of the community. Religious leaders asked that the entertainment ordinance be amended to forbid public dances on Sundays. One such leader called the dances "degrading" and stated that people who took part in them were of low mentality and would probably become charges of the state in later years.

In January 1932, when Republican Irving D. Buttler took office, Highland Park was experiencing financial problems and the new mayor was forced to assume a role not unlike that of future president Franklin Delano Roosevelt. In his mayoral message Buttler remarked that his administration began during "the most critical period of economic stress that has existed since the incorporation of Highland Park as a Borough."

Buttler, who had been chairman of the Poor Committee, recognized government's need to help the poor and unemployed. He stated, "we cannot let any of our inhabitants freeze or starve and, while private contributions to funds for this purpose have been generous, our local government must do its part." He recommended an increased appropriation going to the streets and roads department for unemployment relief and also an increase in the appropriation for the poor to be used for dependency relief. The number of delinquent tax payers had increased and Mayor Buttler urged taxpayers to make immediate payments of past due taxes.

Public transportation in Highland Park was also affected by the economy. In 1931, Public Service Coordinated Transport asked for and was granted approval to substitute buses for trolleys on the Highland Park Line. In 1932, the transport service claimed that the economic conditions would not permit the company to furnish frequent services and the half-hour schedule was reduced to an hourly one. Plans to remove the unused trolley rails on River Road was not accomplished because the borough could not afford the project. In 1933, the borough's service was cut in half and the only recourse was to seek legal restoration of the former bus service.

The condition of the Raritan River was a critical issue, and in July 1931 the State Department of Health ordered Highland Park, as well as other local municipalities, to furnish a statement by December 1, 1931 of what had been done to cease polluting the River. Engineer Wilson stated the borough's plans were ninety percent completed and requested an extension until January 1, 1932. Highland Park had approved detailed plans for a sewerage disposal plant and Mayor Buttler was behind the movement to clean the Raritan River. However, financial conditions would not permit its construction until the late 1930s.

Mayor Buttler delivered a somber annual message in January 1933. The economy was the primary concern. Employees had already contributed five percent of their salaries and wages could not be further reduced. The major problem was still the relief of the poor. The mayor stated that foreclosure was the only method to force payment and must be continued. By 1933, general unrest increased and the citizens began demanding results. In January, a delegation of Highland Park's unemployed appeared before council with complaints about the administration of emergency relief, which was tied to New Brunswick. One outcome was an arrangement that, through the overseer of the poor, medicines could be obtained from Barlow's Drug Store.

In February a large delegation of taxpayers attended the budget meeting. John Parsons, representing the Highland Park Taxpayers Association, presented a list of recommendations for the reduction of taxes. It was suggested that the borough offices be moved back to the firehouse, but the fire department protested, stating that would deprive the volunteers of their recreation room, the men would lose interest, quit, and a paid department would then become necessary. The meeting apparently was a spirited one. Former Mayor Erickson criticized the faultfinders, claiming they were to blame through past insistence for local improvements.

Economic conditions were so poor and competition so great that, in 1934, local restaurant owners complained to Mayor Buttler that the increasing number of church suppers open to the public were injuring their business and that they were unable to compete with the low rates charged by the churches. Foreclosures continued in greater numbers. Buttler stated the town could not be "too sympathetic" to individual delinquents. Fortunately, Highland Park had only taken titles to two properties with dwellings, neither occupied by the owners.

Throughout the Depression, citizens and organizations recommended methods to raise money. A fifty-signature petition was presented to council to adopt an ordinance imposing strict regulations and a license fee of $150 for each marathon or walkathon, $10 for each dance permit, $10 for each basketball game, and $20 for boxing bouts in the borough. Daniel Feller, president of the Jewish Civic League, recommended the publication of a list of delinquent taxpayers. The Lafayette, Hamilton, and Franklin School PTAs advised the appointment of a citizen committee to aid in the collection of taxes.

Moe Englehardt of the Highland Park Bakery started a mini-war when he proposed a $200 increase in peddler's fees. A petition signed by thirty-seven local merchants supported it and a petition signed by nine local peddlers was against it. The merchants claimed they paid taxes and needed protection from the peddlers. The peddlers said they provided door to door service and that larger companies would use tax-exempt war veterans to peddle for free, thereby depriving the town coffers. Council decided not to change the fees.

In 1934, a Citizens Committee, headed by W.C. Kerringan, was formed to contact every delinquent taxpayer in Highland Park in an attempt to collect back taxes. More than ninety citizens volunteered their services. Many volunteers were surprised to find the names of prominent and wealthy residents on the list of those in arrears.

One of the most influential changes to the economy came at the end of 1933 as Congress allowed the sale of beer. Although opposed by several citizens, on April 7, 1933 it became legal to sell and distribute 3.2 percent liquor provided a license had been obtained from the borough. Licenses were first granted to grocery stores, delicatessens, and drug stores, but were later expanded.

Prohibition officially ended when Utah became the thirty-sixth state to ratify the 21st Amendment on December 6, 1933. Local builder Abraham Jelin celebrated the event with figurine bottles specifically created for his 1933 New Year's Eve party, two of which are in the collection of the Highland Park Historical Society.

As Highland Park was no longer a dry community, the Protestant ministers of the town, concerned with its moral condition, expressed their disapproval of the fire department holding its annual New Year's dance on Sunday evening, December 31. A letter to the mayor read, "we expect that you and our Council shall take all necessary steps to prevent any further events of this nature occurring on our Sunday."

In 1933, Mr. Harry Simon, on behalf of Herman Kahn, new manager of the Park Theater, presented a petition signed by 1,200 Highland Park residents requesting Sunday showings of motion pictures. The petitioners met resistance from the Irving School PTA. The question of the blue laws was placed on the November ballot and borough voters repealed them.

In the 1930s, Highland Park was strongly Republican and Buttler's re-election in 1933 was almost assured despite an aggressive Democratic campaign. Among those challenging Democrats was school teacher Christie M. Bartle who appeared on the ticket for a council seat along with John Sokoloff. The Democrats lost to Republicans Lyman Schermerhorn and Arthur McCallum, president of Flako Products Corporation. Bartle School is named after the life long educator and first woman to run for borough council.

In 1934, there was a serious fire at the Stein Building. The Boy Scouts, Legionnaires, and off-duty policemen aided the Highland Park, New Brunswick, and Raritan Fire Departments. The cause was attributed to unwarranted fire hazards and it was decided other buildings should be inspected. Chairman Long of the Fire Committee stated the fire showed the lack of fire equipment and that many of the vehicles were obsolete.

The most important event in 1935 was the offer by the U.S. government to finance the construction of a sewage treatment plant. Highland Park received a grant from the Federal Emergency Administration of Public Work for forty-five percent of the cost of the project upon completion. The money was not to exceed $119,045. The plant was slated for a Valentine Street property.

Buttler's final year as mayor began on January 1, 1935. In his annual message he referred to the town's financial situation and inability to provide financing for several capital improvements. Surprisingly, the financial condition of Highland Park had actually improved during 1934. The bonded debt was reduced and tax collection improved. Mayor Buttler took advantage of Chapter 60 of the Laws of 1934 and put Highland Park on a cash basis. He thought the town should consider restoring either part or all of the salaries that had been reduced. In a gesture of public spiritedness, Frank R. Jones donated his River Road property and Highland Park had its first land for park purposes.

On January 1, 1936, Republican Russell C. Smalley became mayor. Councilmen Russell Long and Harold Drake also took the oath of office. Highland Park, for the eleventh straight year, had an all-Republican administration. In his mayoral message, Smalley expressed concern over the budget and promised to explore ways to reduce expenditures. County and local school taxes were increasing and the federal government was withdrawing its contribution to the state for the poor. Highland Park was operating on a cash basis, which required an increase in the budget. Council needed to use every means possible to collect taxes and assessments.

A court order was forcing the town to construct a sewage disposal plant and the contracts had already been awarded. Only part of the cost was going to come from the federal government's grant. Taxpayers were to pay for the balance. The plant would only prevent the dumping of raw sewage into the Raritan River. Despite this and other plants, the Raritan would remain unfit for boating, bathing, or fishing as manufacturers were still permitted to discharge industrial waste into the river. Mayor Smalley thought that this was an unfair practice and wanted the various municipalities involved to meet to discuss the problem and to suggest new legislation.

In 1936, Highland Park had an ambitious summer recreation program. Paul Hancock was the salaried director of playgrounds and used his own money to pay for assistant high schoolers. The remaining costs were financed through federal WPA funds. Activities were held at Irving School, the former lands of Forest Park, the junior high school field, a field at Eighth Avenue, and at Lafayette School. On their own, the boys cleared the Irving School lot for a baseball diamond. The determined and energetic youngsters developed into one of the best baseball teams in the borough. Frank Pfeiffer was team captain and James Vasnelli helped organize the team. The younger boys and girls of the Irving School District held their activities under the oak trees of Forest Park with Miss Donna Shannon in charge. There they wove crepe paper baskets and shaped brightly colored flowers. On the Eighth Avenue field, a group of boys practiced golf, using loaned clubs. Games were held on the Rutgers golf course. Roger Thatch directed activities at the high school, which included a hardball league. The high school program also provided handicrafts and dramatics for girls under the direction of Helen Rosen and Ruth Klaus. Lafayette School playgrounds reopened and sported the younger boy's league games, but handicrafts were the main activity under the tutelage of Mildred Mansier and Louise Pino. In the afternoons sprinklers were turned on and the children cooled off in the cascading waters. Weekly high points were free swims at the New Brunswick YMCA pool for the boys and at the New Brunswick Natatorium for the girls.

In 1937, Hancock, chairman of the WPA Recreation Committee of Highland Park, announced that 982 residents had benefited from the winter program. The men's and boy's activities were the most popular. After-school events included basketball, boxing, wrestling, and tumbling.

There was a smaller recreational program for women, elementary age, and older girls. There were also art and craft classes along with dressmaking and knitting. For the first time, a social program was offered and the WPA Orchestra played dance music for 125 young men and women.

In addition to the recreational program, the WPA formed an artist project, the "Index of American Design," headed by R. Rodman Van Voorhees of River Road. This project's purpose was to document in watercolors, crayon, and ink, domestic and household articles found in New Jersey during the seventeenth and eighteenth centuries. Although it furnished jobs to many citizens, the WPA regulations presented obstacles to some borough residents seeking work. Highland Park men who were not on relief prior to November 1, 1935 were disallowed and the jobs were given to other county residents. The borough had entered into a restrictive agreement with the federal government and was unable to change the terms. Nevertheless, there were different agencies and organizations working to support many needy residents and, in 1936, F.M. Ritchie of the American Legion suggested that a committee for social welfare be created to coordinate welfare activities in an effort to prevent overlapping services.

In 1937, the Middlesex County Board of Freeholders met with council to discuss its request for a plot of ground in the county for parkland. Johnson Park, located in both Highland Park and Piscataway, was made possible through the WPA's grant of $317,043 for labor. The county provided materials and equipment. J. Seward Johnson and Robert Wood Johnson Jr. donated 120 acres of land to the county through the Johnson Foundation. County Engineer George R. Merrill, with the cooperation of the WPA executives and engineers, drew up plans. One hundred men began clearing the land in May 1937. The work force grew to 400 men, who landscaped a mile-long strip from the Pennsylvania Railroad Bridge to Metlar's Lane between River Road and the Raritan River. They deepened streams, made a pond, built rustic bridges, and constructed macadam driveways and cinder walks. Today this park remains as a tribute to Franklin Delano Roosevelt's New Deal public works program and the Johnson family's generosity.

Despite the Depression, there were building plans in the 1930s on individual, county, and state levels. In the middle 1930s, David and Sarah Tishler opened a tavern on the corner of North Third and Raritan Avenues. It was later enlarged and became the popular Sally's Steakhouse. Victor Fais opened a sweet shop on the opposite corner and started one of the longest continuously operating confectioneries in town, now today's Corner Confectionery. In 1936, Angelo Lenetti opened his gasoline station on Woodbridge Avenue. Commissioner Magee of the Motor Vehicle Department requested that any contemplated street improvements in the area of the proposed Motor Vehicle Testing Station on Raritan Avenue and Washington Street be completed before the station's opening in 1938.

By 1937, Highland Park's Police Department, which in the past had mostly traffic control responsibilities, had developed into a sophisticated organization. Police Chief Alfred Smalley instituted corrective methods in an attempt to control a general increase in traffic violations and crime. That year the department investigated 1,147 cases, including eighty-nine motor vehicle accidents that resulted in thirty-five injuries. Among the measures adopted were the fingerprinting of all peddlers and canvassers, and a commendable public relations campaign.

Highland Park's first uncontested mayoral race took place in November, 1937. On January 1, 1938, Republican Russell B. Howell became mayor. The mayor's most important recommendation was the undoing of the borough employee pay cuts. Promises had been made the previous year, but the employees agreed to forgo raises for one more year. Howell thanked the Committee for Coordinated Charitable Agencies appointed by Mayor Smalley. As others before him, he requested that taxpayers pay fully and promptly because the town was still under the "cash basis" plan. During Howell's second year in office, in 1939, three high school civic classes under the direction of Alfred Buschhorn made a motion picture depicting the activities of the Police, Fire, and Street Departments. The students compiled footage of the Police Training School, pistol-range practice, a simulated fire at Irving School, and street cleaning.

The 1930s saw governments gain more power over the lives of individuals. One example was the institution of mandatory motor vehicle inspections. New Jersey established a Motor Vehicle Testing Station on the corner of Raritan and Washington Avenues. As one of twenty-eight such stations, it opened on Monday, January 10, 1938 at 8:30 a.m. and initiated the compulsory inspection of all motor vehicles. Mayor Russell Howell and Councilmen Lyman Schmerhorn, Arthur McCallum, Walter K. Wood, Russell Long, Harold Drake, and John Ochs celebrated the grand opening by forming a parade of borough cars and trucks for the first official inspections. These seven passed. Cars eight and nine, driven by Police Chief Alfred Smalley and William Gonch, also passed. The tenth vehicle, the Highland Park water department truck, was rejected because of defective headlights. Only six of the next ten vehicles were not rejected. One of the automobiles that passed was operated by Jack Pisciotta. Each inspection cost 50¢ and a green certificate signified a pass.

During the two decades of the 1920s and 1930s, the weekly newspaper, *Highland Park Press*, "covered the borough of homes like the sky above." Little is known about this newspaper and its operators because only a few issues were located during Rutgers University's small New Jersey newspapers recovery project in the 1990s. One of the *Press's* editions reported that in 1938, F.M. Ritchie, attorney for the Highland Park Publishing Company, the *Press's* publisher, took legal action against the borough. The *Press* alleged that the town failed to make a public notice of intended liquor licenses. This culminated in a failed attempt to print the borough's legal notices, which went to Middlesex County's newspaper of record, the *Daily Home News*.

Governor A. Harry Moore urged a civil holiday on June 28, 1939. He called for "New Jersey Day" at the New York World's Fair and the municipal offices of Highland Park were closed to allow residents to participate. Mayor Howell and most of the municipal employees joined Mayor Mulligan of New Brunswick to journey to the fair. There were even special Public Service buses with round trip fares of $1.50 for adults and $1 for children.

The 1930s ended but the Depression did not in 1940 when architect and planning board chairman Walter K. Wood became mayor on January 1. There was no traditional mayoral message that year due to an accident that Wood had just experienced. He sent a short note to Council stating he was with them "in spirit" and extended a happy new year to one and all. During the year, the finance committee recommended to council that the old factories of the Janeway & Carpender and Kompak Company be demolished. Also, the borough's fire school held its graduation on September 3, 1940. Certificates were awarded to the twenty-nine members of the department who had completed the course of instruction. On January 1, 1941, Wood delivered a mayoral message. Stressing strict economy, he stated again there would be no major capital improvements. He discussed drivers' carelessness and that the police would become more stringent in enforcing laws. Because of the increased activity in the real estate market, in 1940 Highland Park was able to dispose of a substantial number of parcels acquired due to unpaid taxes. The borough hoped to sell more properties by putting "For Sale" signs on the lands. Mayor Wood wanted the foreclosures to continue.

In the early 1940s, there were a few signs that at least the local economy was improving. The First National Bank of Highland Park enlarged its quarters and held an open house on January 7, 1941. Alexander Merchant & Son, Architects, prepared plans for alterations and an addition to the police headquarters and a referendum addressed the question of increasing police and firemen's salaries.

Local economies are affected by larger forces and the economic situation may have been improving in Highland Park, but there was foreshadowing of another major catastrophe about to befall the country. Even before the Pearl Harbor attacks on December 7, 1941, there were signs of the nation's pending wartime involvement. Public Service Coordinated Transport, which had reduced services during the 1930s, requested permission to extend the route of buses on the Newark–New Brunswick route to Fort Dix. Emergency defense arrangements were made with New Brunswick so the police and fire departments and the American Legion would be prepared for any calls for defense maneuvers. The New Jersey Defense Council requested that Mayor Wood, as chairman of the defense council, survey all houses and rooms potentially available to rent to defense workers. After a discussion with council, it was determined that there were few houses in the borough within the specified rent limits. The American Legion Auxiliary submitted a list of services that twenty-two of its members would offer in case of emergencies. The State Department of Health stated that supplies of chlorine for sanitation work at the sewage treatment plant would be available on the same priority as for defense work.

The Japanese attack on Pearl Harbor plunged the United States into another World War and Highland Park entered an unknown and difficult era. The 1940 census counted 9,004 residents. By 1944, there were more than 1,000 Highland Park men and women in the nation's armed forces.

When Republican Harold W. Drake became mayor on January 1, 1942, the United States's involvement in the war was only a few weeks old. Drake stated it was difficult to offer a message of cheer as the future was an unknown. He advised to view the days ahead "not with alarm, but with courage and a prayer." Economy and efficiency were still the basis of the borough's business affairs. Mayor Drake spoke about the need for recreational facilities "to check juvenile delinquency" and to uplift the morale of the town's younger residents. He hoped to construct a community building where the "young folks" could meet. In order to begin the process, Drake created a Park and Recreation Committee. In 1942, there were two new items in the budget: local defense, $2,500; and parks and recreation, $2,000.

Highland Park welcomed a new neighbor, Camp Kilmer. Ground was broken for the camp in January 1942. In March, Colonel L.S. Dillon, New York district engineer, requested that Highland Park extend a water main to the Stelton Staging Area to provide a standby connection to protect the water supply at the new camp. As Highland Park had no funds, the town suggested that the federal government pay for the lines. The War Department also requested the use of the railroad siding on the site of the former Janeway & Carpender plant for unloading materials needed for the construction of Camp Kilmer. By June the $25 million construction project was complete. The camp's first ceremony was held June 14, 1942, dedicating a plaque in memory of the poet and Sergeant Joyce Kilmer, member of the "Fighting 69th" in World War I who was killed in France on July 30, 1918. Born and raised in New Brunswick, he was the author of the well-known poem "Trees."

Uplifted morale was important during these difficult times and those citizens remaining home contributed to the war effort by engaging in activities to support those in uniform. Service flags were hung throughout the town, several men constructed an Honor Roll, women tended Victory Gardens, and the Boy Scouts held scrap drives. There was a shortage of materials during the war and scrap drives collected metals and paper. Borough trucks were used and house-to-house campaigns gathered piles of metal hair curlers, dented aluminum pots, and camera equipment. These items were sold to authorized smelters in accordance with State Defense Council regulations and the proceeds went to national defense. The Victory Garden Committee, headed by Dr. Charles Connors, was part of the New Brunswick–Highland Park Defense Council. Interested in promoting victory gardening as a war measure and to conserve the food supplies, in 1943 the committee held a Victory Garden Contest in the two towns. Sponsored by the RKO theaters, the Kiwanis Club, and the *Daily*

Home News and the *Sunday Times*, the entries were divided into different classes with a grand prize of $150 in war bonds and stamps.

In August 1942, Theodore Klaus of 224 Wayne Street was granted permission to hang a service flag across Wayne Street at North Third Avenue. It was the first of its kind in town and it bore eleven stars to honor the boys of Wayne Street in the armed forces. The wife or mother sewed on a star representing her loved one. There was also a small plaque bearing the names of the servicemen. These men were Donald W. Jackson, Harold D. Salkin, William Altman, Floyd Mehrof, David McCorvey, George A. Pancza, Arthur E. Mets, Norman V. Hawley, James G. Walker, Milton Cohen, and Robert G. Heinold. On September 21, 1942, Borough Council voted to obtain a service flag for public display and a roster of names of those in service. In October, permission was granted to the air raid warden of the 4th Election District to display a U.S. flag and a service flag over the street at the clubhouse of the 4th District Republican Club on Benner Street near Sixth Avenue.

Mayor Drake stated that 1943 would be a year of "hope and determination." He praised the community for its efforts and cooperation with the Defense Council activities and the salvage drives. He was proud of our sons and daughters in service, some of whom had already made "the supreme sacrifice." In May, the borough contracted Albert Garlotti to erect an honor roll in accordance with drawings and specifications prepared by Alexander Merchant & Son, Architects. (*See p. 89.*) The PTAs instituted a "Block Mother" program to take care of children during air raids or other emergencies. Red, white, and blue "V" stickers were displayed on those homes where children could go to seek shelter while their parents were away at work.

Due to its proximity to New York City and Newark, the town, under the Civilian Defense Council, expanded fire units in preparation for potential bomb attacks. Men were trained in first aid and to fight fires. They conducted regular drills and a government issued truck and pump were stored in John Cost's garage on North Fourth Avenue. Air raids were a particularly onerous aspect of civilian life during wartime. On September 22, 1942, there was to be a practice air raid outside Hamilton School with a mock bombing. In an ironic twist of fate, there was an actual air raid alert at the same time when a blue alert, the final step before an actual air raid, was broadcast by the First Interceptor Command.

With so many men overseas, there was a labor shortage and women were compelled to take on work that once had been reserved for men. The Women Ordnance Workers, or WOWs, was a group of women who helped guard the nearby Raritan Arsenal. It was one of the first army posts to employ women in this capacity. These "pistol-packing mamas," and grandmothers, guarded ammunition plants, shipped out material, drove trucks and buses, and filed reports. Because "loose lips sink ships," all correspondence was subject to censorship. Mail addressed to enemy countries was discontinued and all letters to foreign countries were read and censored.

By 1944, Highland Park had become a "war-minded community." Mayor Drake, starting his second two-year term, cited the development of our Defense Council and our proximity to Camp Kilmer. He stated "nothing we have ever done has brought our people closer together than the shared activities and the smooth-working organization of the Defense Council." He thanked the commanding officer of Camp Kilmer for a pleasant relationship. Also by 1944, the country was looking toward the end of conflict and Highland Park was making plans for peace time. Mayor Drake appointed a Post-war Planning Committee and the American Legion Post 88 wanted a central meeting place in town for the "upwards of a thousand Highland Park boys" in the armed forces when they returned home from war.

The final year of Drake's second term began on January 1, 1945. The Republican stronghold in Highland Park was chipped away by the election of Councilman Alfred H. Buschhorn, the first Democrat in office since 1925. Mayor Drake's 1945 message echoed that of the previous year. Reviewing 1944, he noted that a Post-war Planning Board had been appointed and three years before, the Parks and Recreation Committee had been created. In the summer of 1944, approximately 275 people took part in the program. Drake still hoped for a community building and a year-round recreational program. Drake hoped the war in Europe would be over in 1945 and the country could "see the light of day" in the Pacific. Highland Park had 1,122 people in the armed forces. The mayor extended his appreciation and gave his deepest sympathy to those families with gold stars. Those in attendance then rose and paid tribute to the thirteen servicemen who had been killed. By April of 1945, it was evident that the war would soon be over. Mayor Drake made recommendations for V-E Day to the merchants, giving specific times of closing. On May 8, 1945 the war ended in Europe. September 2, 1945 was V-J Day, the day Japan signed a formal surrender.

The recreation program was a major topic in 1945. Councilman Buschhorn wanted the Board of Education to give permission for the use of one or more school buildings. Chairman MacKinney of the Parks and Recreation Committee reported the proposal to invite several teams from New Brunswick to join the Senior Basketball League being organized in Highland Park to make the league workable. Due to the war, there was a shortage of players. Reverend James Mulder of the Highland Park Reformed Church pledged his congregation's support to establish a youth center. By the end of the year, an extensive program was planned. There were basketball teams, Community Nights, which included dancing, games, and refreshments, and a possible bowling league for both men and women. Councilman Denhard suggested that flood lights be installed at Johnson Park for night basketball games and skating.

One of the most important actions taken in 1945 was the Postwar Planning Commission's selection of Russell Van Nest Black as a planning consultant. He was hired to prepare and provide maps, surveys, and studies including a revision of the zoning ordinance. He was to compose a master plan by 1946. Black stressed the need for Highland Park to plan for essential municipal improvements such as a borough hall, a firehouse, a library, and an incinerator. Highland Park was only one of a few municipalities in the state that did not have its own borough hall. There was also a need for housing for the returning servicemen and Highland Park was viewed as a desirable residential area. A substantial amount of borough-owned property was being sold for development. The postwar tract developments would leave a different impression on this borough of homes.

Chapter Seven

1946 TO TODAY

History is the memory of things said and done in the past.

—Carl L. Becker, 1931

On January 1, 1946, Republican George W. Miller became mayor of Highland Park. In his mayoral message, Miller stated that it was the first time since 1941 that the world was at peace. Members of the armed forces from Highland Park were returning home in increasing numbers.

Highland Park real estate was in demand. Over $50,000 worth of land was sold in 1945. This, plus the building of new houses, put over $100,000 of new assessments on the books for 1946. The ratable would be used to reduce land assessments that, although still high, were more uniform in Highland Park than elsewhere in the county. Except for the sewage plant and a few paved streets, no major improvements had been made in the borough for almost twenty years. This was partially the result of the Depression and then, later, the war, the lack of manpower, and materials. Miller stated, "this condition should change very shortly."

Early in 1946 a committee consisting of representatives from the PTA, the school board, local churches, and businesses was appointed to study the feasibility of a year-round recreation program. There had been a full program at all four schools, including an eleven-team night softball league and a seven-team night baseball league. Picnics took place at Johnson Park and trips to major league baseball games were organized. Later that year, the Reade RKO Theater offered Saturday morning movies for young people.

Returning veterans needed housing and employment. In January, the state asked Highland Park to participate in the New Jersey Veterans Employment Plan. Arrangements with the Emergency Housing Administration were made to construct two eight-family and one three-family unit. Because of the housing shortage, council went on record stating that the Army should provide housing at Camp Kilmer for personnel living outside the camp. Concern for the veterans "found expression" in a contract with the federal government for the nineteen housing units in the easterly section, near the Raritan Township border. In 1946, a contract was awarded to Reiss and Weinsier Contracting

Corporation for the construction of veterans' temporary emergency housing to be built on borough owned land between Raritan and Central Avenues. The borough supplied required utilities to the building line for connection to the structures. There were to be three buildings containing nineteen apartments. Two buildings contained eight units and a third, three apartments. It was estimated that it would take approximately ninety days to complete.

On Saturday, February 8, 1947, in a severe snowstorm, a formal dedication ceremony was held for the opening ceremonies of the Veterans Housing Project. Councilman Maurice A. Chaffee, supervisor of the project, presented the keys to the first apartment to Mr. and Mrs. Richard J. Pisciotta. A citizen's committee selected the couple from among a list of more than eighty-five veterans. Mayor Miller and Irving B. Baker, area supervisor for the Federal Public Housing Administration, greeted Pisciotta and Laurence E. Rosshirt, another of the veterans selected for one of the three apartments. The four-room apartments were located in a one-story building and were constructed from a former barrack brought to Highland Park from Swinburne Island in New York harbor. Each contained a refrigerator, a unit heater, and a hot water heater. Two other two-story buildings, containing eight apartments each, were expected; however, a lack of funds resulted in a downscaled development. In June of 1947, council asked Public Service Transport to establish a bus stop on Raritan Avenue at the entrance to the development.

The *New Brunswick Daily Home News* and the *New Brunswick Sunday Times*, which were major influences chronicling the development of Highland Park, were getting competition from the airways. A permit was granted to Chanticleer Broadcasting Company, WCTC radio on the third floor of the People's National Bank in New Brunswick, to erect a radio transmitter and antenna on the north bank of the Raritan River near Donaldson Park. The radio station broadcast its first hour of recorded music at 6:00 a.m. on December 12, 1946. Two years later, WDHN, run by the *Daily Home News*, began broadcasting on 93.5 on the FM dial.

Even at the middle of the twentieth century, Highland Park still had rural characteristics. In March of 1947, dairyman William W. Ten Eyck presented a bill for $18 to borough council for nine hens that had been killed by a feral dog. In December, Elwood N. Richardson presented a claim for $30 for eight New Hampshire Red Roosters killed by a dog and valued at $3.75 each. The Highland Park Field and Stream Club was popular and a Junior Sportsmen's Club was organized in February 1947 to foster interest in hunting and fishing among young sportsmen. The initial meeting was attended by more than twenty-five young men and was held in the rooms above the firehouse on Raritan Avenue.

On January 1, 1948, Alvah H. Cole, Republican, became mayor. The planning consultant, Russell Van Nest Black, had prepared a map indicating all one-family, two-family, and multi-family houses; also, the location of public parks and public buildings and schools, a map showing borough-owned and tax-lien properties, and auxiliary maps showing possible locations for new public buildings and parks. Cole hoped that some of the post-war planning board's thoughtful recommendations would be carried out and he advised an improvement in water, sewer, and paving. There would be more building by individuals this year that would ease the housing shortage. Many private residents bought lots for future development, including Theodore and Mary Pisciotta, who purchased lots 6 through 9 in block 54 on Hilton Street for $600. There was an expanded building program in 1948. New homes required the extension of public utilities into formerly undeveloped areas. In 1949, the town would continue to make more sites available, complete with water, sewage facilities, and paved streets. The high cost of materials, equipment, and labor made a major building program problematic given consistent taxpayer complaints about municipal expenditures. Cole wanted to construct a new firehouse; however, this would not become a reality until 1955.

One building that was constructed started out as plans submitted by Alexander Merchant & Son, Architects. A spacious concrete block municipal garage was constructed on the northeast corner of Valentine Street and South Fifth Avenue, large enough to house all the borough street and water department equipment, to serve as a workshop for the water department, and provide fireproof storage for borough records. It had office space and showers, lavatories, and lockers for employees. It was completed in 1949.

Mayor Cole also encouraged the expansion of the recreation program. He wanted to light the high school ball field so that night games could be played. Along with Donaldson and Johnson Park, there was sufficient land for summer programs. On Thursday evening August 4, 1949, a new recreation facility at the high school was dedicated. Hyman Katz sponsored a huge party attended by 400 children. Continuing the good relationship between the town and its first church, the Highland Park Reformed Church provided two large rooms for a Community Center. One room was used for basketball and a gymnasium, and the other was used for reading and games, including shuffleboard and ping-pong. There was a rifle and pistol range under the supervision of police captain Scheidig. Volunteers provided all the labor and many of the materials and additional funds were donated. According to Mayor Cole, there was "not one cent of cost to the taxpayers." The Community Center was open to all residents of Highland Park year round, "regardless of color, race or creed."

The New Brunswick Exchange Club awarded the Recreation Commission a plaque in recognition of the Highland Park recreation program's role in combating juvenile delinquency.

The adoption of the Van Nest's Master Plan resulted in a zoning change that allowed the construction of garden apartments on the old Abraham Schenck estate. There was opposition to this change from Councilman Joseph J. DeCoster, the lone Democrat. In 1949, Raritan Gardens, Inc. proposed to build 200-unit garden apartments on the former estate property on South Adelaide Avenue, once the site of the Redcliffe Manor House. This was Highland Park's first large, postwar apartment complex and was completed by 1951. Located at South Adelaide and Redcliffe Avenues, the Colonial Revival style buildings designed by architect Emil A. Schmidlin were situated on eleven acres overlooking the Raritan River. The apartments ranged from $65 to $85 to rent. Other complexes followed. The former seven-and-a-half acre Bissett tract on the north side of Raritan Avenue across from First Avenue became the site of a garden apartment complex of four large buildings, the Montgomery Street Apartments. A fifteen-foot-high retaining wall paralleled Raritan Avenue. The radically sloping terrain, a small stream once used for the brewery's drainage, and the remains of a former pond, caused building problems that needed to be addressed.

Mayor Cole proclaimed September 17, 1949 a General Holiday in honor of the 50th Anniversary Celebration of the Highland Park Fire Department. Fireworks held at Donaldson Park followed a grand parade.

The 1950s began with Alvah Cole's inauguration to a second two-year term. Returning veterans married, started families, and built homes. Family values were an important part of the 1950s and Highland Park, a strong residential community, embraced those values. No longer needed for the war-time work, most wives and mothers remained home, tended children, and joined numerous civic organizations. The 1950s were a decade of change for Highland Park. Big business challenged the existing zoning ordinances. The municipal center of town moved from Raritan Avenue to Fifth Avenue. The state and the borough clashed over the development of Route 27, Raritan Avenue. There was political change and Democrats usurped Republicans, in power since the 1920s. Highland Park was run in a more business-like manner and outside consultants helped determine the borough's future. The last in a long line of Republican mayors, Alvah H. Cole's administration continued until 1952. Among Cole's appointments was Carl C. Pisciotta as building inspector.

Both residential and commercial building continued in the 1950s. The majority of residential buildings erected in the early 1950s were single-family tract houses. In 1951, Style Homes, Inc., representing builder Louis Torok, planned construction of forty ranch-type dwellings in various locations throughout the borough. The cost per home was under $18,000. Edgar Tafel, an apprentice under Frank Lloyd Wright, also designed three individual houses located on Cliff Court, Elbert Court, and Harrison Avenue. The continuing foreclosure of tax liens strengthened the borough's financial position and many lots were immediately sold to house builders. There was not a great deal of borough-owned land still available except for the "Peach Orchard" tract, but by mid-decade it was evident that sales were not progressing. In 1956, a zoning change opened the area between South Ninth Avenue and the most easterly borough boundary line for development. As a result, the Peach Orchard Tract was put up for sale for garden apartments. Buyers were required to install all utilities and paving. Council cited surveys demonstrating that the school population from apartments was one-fifth less than single-family houses. Also, apartments required fewer municipal services. Apartment developments were viewed as very desirable tax ratables and an ordinance was introduced to restrict construction of new multi-unit dwellings to a minimum of eight units.

By 1950, the increased population in higher density housing created greater traffic. A study conducted in 1952 discovered that the number of cars had increased from 800 to 1,100 per hour along Raritan Avenue. The Municipal Court, in its first year of operation, had collected $6,735 in motor fines. Temporary public parking lots were on North Sixth and North Second Avenues, but there was need for more parking. The Planning Board wanted an ingress and egress to the side streets from the rear of business lots on Raritan Avenue. The Chamber of Commerce wanted parking with entrances and exits on Denison Street. Parking lots behind stores, in general, were not well received. The revised Zoning Map created a new parking district.

In 1951, a conflict arose over the boundary between residential and commercial zones when the First National Bank created an exit driveway from Raritan Avenue to Denison Street, between North Third and Fourth Avenues. It was also at this time that the Acme Market constructed a parking lot between North Fourth and Fifth Avenues with an exit onto Denison Street. Drivers used the driveways as shortcuts. The situation worsened and developed into a major confrontation lasting for several years. Eventually, Denison Street residents took the matter to court. In 1953, a series of court decisions favored the borough and declared that the First National Bank and Acme Market were in violation of the law. The rights of the grocery stores, Food Fair and A&P, were also in question. The Appellate Court upheld the decision of the Superior Court. The bank requested a rehearing and continued to use the driveway, hoping for a zoning change. In 1954, the Board of Adjustment granted a variance to the First National Bank for the construction of an eighteen-foot exit driveway to North Third Avenue.

Highland Park has always been a family-orientated community and numerous events and organizations supported this image. In the early 1950s, the Exchange Club established the first Park Town Outing to provide entertainment for those remaining home on Labor Day. The event began with a parade made up of sixteen civic organizations and clubs, including the Police, the American Legion color guard, the First Aid Squad, the Fire Department, Democratic and Republican clubs, and various lodges. From noon until 6:00 p.m., nearly 5,000 people gathered in Donaldson Park for the festivities. People had to be turned away because of a lack of space. Television sets and bicycles were awarded as prizes. Leaflets with lucky numbers were dropped from an airplane, guaranteeing another prize. Approximately 350 children engaged in potato sack races, balloon races, and various other events. Prizes were even awarded to the oldest person and the largest family.

The granite Doughboy paid tribute to the veterans of World War I, but Highland Park had no permanent memorial to the soldiers of World War II. During the 1940s, an Honor Roll had been erected on land at the corner of Raritan and Fourth Avenues and remained there until 1950. On Memorial Day, 1950, a parade of 2,000 honored those who had given their lives for their country. A bronze plaque engraved with the names of Highland Park residents killed in World War II and affixed to a granite block was dedicated. The memorial was placed in front of American Legion Post 88 at 808 Raritan Avenue and remained there until that building was sold in 2002. The memorial was relocated to the small park at the intersection of Route 27 and Woodbridge Avenue.

In 1952, Councilman Grover reported that the borough-owned tract of land between Hilton and Karsey Streets had been examined for park and recreation use. Grover said the area could be cleared and made into a "highly desirable small park where mothers could take small children for play in a protected area." Benches were provided and efforts to obtain recreational equipment for small children were successful. There was only a nominal expenditure of borough funds. The Recreation Committee was authorized to make the park usable. By October, slides, swings, and other equipment were being installed.

In 1953, the New Brunswick and the Highland Park Leagues of Women Voters jointly wrote and published the handbook *Our Towns*. The League conducted candidates' meetings prior to both the general and school elections and published other *Know Your Town* booklets throughout the years. Also in the 1950s, there was a very active Highland Park Woman's Club. A Republican support group, it was organized and federated in 1951. The meeting place was the Highland Park Reformed Church. This was a decade when the PTAs were very active. Attendance reports show that over 200 parents were present at each meeting, which usually featured speakers and refreshments.

On January 1, 1952, WCTC broadcast the inauguration of Joseph C. DeCoster, Highland Park's first Democratic mayor since George Leonard, who had served in 1924 and 1925. In his mayoral address, DeCoster stated:

> As many of you know, in any growing community zoning problems are continually arising. The Planning Board acts as a sounding board and must keep alert to the needs of any changes necessary to our zoning ordinances in order that we may be kept up-to-date. I am opposed to changes in our present ordinances that would reduce our residential areas until such time as the need is definitely proven.

DeCoster's administration became a period of local political conflict. The Republican controlled council, determined not to give the Democrat any power, denied DeCoster's appointments, making its own. The same thing happened the following year. Despite political infighting, Mayor DeCoster's administration did accomplish the development of municipal facilities and the dedication of the new Borough Hall on South Fourth Avenue. Paving and sewers were completed in various sections of the borough. There was a new water supply from Elizabethtown Water Company. Work had begun on the new firehouse and bids were in for a new police headquarters.

Up until these years, Highland Park had relied on surrounding communities for some of its basic needs. New Brunswick supplied water and Highland Park's garbage dump was located in Raritan Township, now Edison. During the 1950s, Highland Park became more independent. The town's water supply contract expired on January 1, 1952. New Brunswick's increased rates forced the borough to look to other sources. Highland Park signed a five-year contract with the Elizabethtown Water Company, which obtained its water from the Millstone River and the Delaware and Raritan Canal. Approximately $125,000 of new water mains were required. The borough still maintained a standby system with New Brunswick for emergency use. A twenty-year agreement was made with the Elizabethtown Water Company to begin on December 22, 1959.

For years, residents in Raritan Township had been complaining about the smoke and odor from burning garbage from the Highland Park dump at the end of North Eighth Avenue. In 1952, the dump was abandoned and a sanitary landfill in an isolated section of the Meadows at the foot of Crowells Road was established. Later, a four, rather than a six day, garbage collection was instituted. Low loaders, a closed type of garbage truck, were put into use.

Due to the explosive postwar growth, the municipal office space at the Masonic Temple became insufficient. Highland Park had long anticipated its own borough hall, but it was not until 1950 that the dream was realized. In August 1950, Council unanimously approved the purchase of Samuel Juston's property at 21 South Fourth Avenue. The New Brunswick–based dress manufacturer sold his land to the borough for $20,000. The former Barnwell House, a nine-room brick structure located on the 24,000-foot property, was slated for municipal offices. The acquisition allowed for additional parking, thus helping to alleviate the town's parking problem. In 1951, architect Alexander Merchant Jr. was in charge of the alterations to the new municipal building and on March 3, 1952, the Council held its first meeting in the new Borough Hall.

In 1949, Arthur and Helen McCallum had presented a fully equipped ambulance to the newly organized First Aid Squad of Highland Park. The town leased land to the squad, without cost, for as long as the site was used for the purpose of the organization. A ceremony on June 14, 1952 dedicated its new one-story brick building on South Eleventh Avenue. In 1954, Arcadia Avenue was changed to McCallum Place to honor Arthur McCallum in recognition of his many contributions to the borough. The First Aid Squad held its Annual Fund Week May 7 to 12, 1955. In April, the squad requested that the title to the land it occupied under a lease from the borough be conveyed to the squad. Borough Attorney Hoffman said it could not be done under the present status. A state organization required the state legislature to amend the status.

The Fire Department Building Committee presented designs by the architectural firm of Alexander Merchant & Son for a new headquarters to be placed on the borough-owned lot adjoining the old firehouse in 1953. However, a later decision relocated the new building to South Fifth Avenue near Mansfield Street. Restrictions were set for selling the old firehouse lots. There could be no gasoline station or garage, no public poolroom, bowling alley, or place of amusement other than a theater. If the old building were left standing, the bell tower had to be demolished to the height of the firehouse. Construction contracts were awarded to Canonico-Nora Builders. The new Public Safety Center, housing the Police and Fire Departments, was completed in April 1954. Highland Park became the second community in the world to plan and execute the new telephone emergency system. In 1959, Chief of Police Smalley was elected president of the International Association of Chiefs of Police and Mrs. Henry Shapanka donated the fifteen-foot fir tree planted in front of the headquarters.

Democrats gained greater control in 1954 when Mayor William C. Campbell and Councilmen Ward E. Ehrenfeld and Samuel J. Kronman, all Democrats, subscribed to the oath of office. The tide had changed and now there were only two Republicans in office. Mayor Campbell wanted to prepare and establish an adequate zoning code, stating, " in this Community, wherein more than half the homes are owner-occupied, zoning laws are the vital concern of all." The mayor had a three-point program to meet tax obligations: equalization of assessments, attraction of new ratables, and the strict economy of administration. There was an ordinance for the creation of a Planning Board to define the duties and responsibilities of the board to conform to the new state zoning laws. The Democrats made a clean sweep in 1955. Mayor Campbell began his second year in office and newly elected Councilmen Henry Hugly and Edward V. McGrath made up the all-Democrat administration, completing the political battle that had begun in 1952.

The Borough of Highland Park was fifty years old in 1955. A golden jubilee celebration was held on May 14, 1955 and it featured a parade and a party with the keynote address by Robert Wood Johnson Jr. By mid-decade, visages of the war years were disappearing. The veterans housing, in poor condition, was demolished and Camp Kilmer was closed. Numerous Highland Park residents were employed at the camp and Council feared the town would lose the purchasing power it derived from the facility. Borough Council urged the Department of the Army to reconsider the closing, but to no avail.

In an effort to relieve the homeowners from their tax burden, in 1955, the Borough Council voted on a Mercantile Licensing Ordinance to insure that businesses paid their fair share of taxes. The Chamber of Commerce opposed it. Food Fair questioned its legality and Acme Market protested. Robert Hall Clothes, located in the one-story commercial building at the gateway to town on Raritan Avenue near North Adelaide Avenue, questioned its fairness and expressed a fear that the ordinance would retard business growth in the community.

Mayor Luther H. Martin ushered in another Democratic administration in 1956. As it had been for the past few years, the adjourned and organization meetings were held in the Lafayette School. Mayor Martin, the registrar at Rutgers University, enjoyed two terms in office and served until 1960. There was the problem of an increased tax rate. The schools needed more funding, new equipment was needed for the Street and Fire Departments and the landfill operation, and more funds were needed for departmental operations and salary increases for borough employees. The new administration's first legislation was giving its members a salary. Early in 1957, it was determined that there would be an increase in taxes. The 1957 budget included $4,000 as a first installment of the total cost of $20,000 to have an outside appraisal firm. The balance of $16,000 was financed by notes maturing annually over the next four years. The reason was "so every taxpayer will bear his just share of the costs of government."

By 1955, renters were being heard. A petition of 200 requested to continue rent control under the local authorities after the State Rent Control Act expired on June 30. Bernard Hortz was appointed municipal rent control director under the ordinance providing for municipal rent control. The Highland Park Housing Authority was created in 1956 to undertake slum clearance programs and housing projects for low-income families. A grant was obtained from the Federal Housing Administration for a twenty-four-unit, low-rent housing project between South Sixth and Seventh Avenues near Benner Street. Its dedication was held on Sunday, October 22, 1961.

At the urging of the Ministerial Association, a committee to investigate the sale of indecent literature was formed in 1956. Reverend Lee R. Van Sickle was appointed chairman. There was an attitude favoring the old blue laws. Despite the growing Jewish population, the borough supported the "Newton Bill," which enforced the closing of mercantile business on Sundays throughout the state of New Jersey.

The footpath to Johnson Park was created in 1958 through the cooperation of the Middlesex County Sewerage Authority and the Pennsylvania Railroad Company. Their agreement stipulated that Highland Park could use the trunk sewer right of way for a footpath from Hubeli Street, a paper street, north into Johnson Park for a pedestrian entrance to eliminate the hazard to pedestrians who were using the River Road underpass.

On May 25, 1958, a fire at the Ten Broeck Motors sales and service building on Woodbridge Avenue, claimed the lives of two volunteer firemen, Frank R. Molimock, Jr., a member of the Recreational Commission and the Civil Rights Commission; and William C. Graff. There was an emergency appropriation for the payment of pensions to the widows. A memorial tablet and flagpole are on the site at the Harley-Davidson motorcycle dealership on Woodbridge Avenue.

Highland Park finally built a brand new library in the late 1950s. The new building, designed by Ernest Levine and financed by a fund drive, was constructed on the Lucas property situated between North Fifth and North Sixth Avenues. The old Lucas home, now recognized as Highland Park's last extant colonial-era house, was demolished, the land was cleaned up, and a path across the premises was constructed by the Street Department. The dedication ceremony was held on July 4, 1959. The library has remained in this location since 1959. A major renovation in the 1990s enlarged Levine's modern building and changed its exterior to brick, in essence giving the building a Colonial Revival appearance for the postmodern borough.

In 1959, Douglas S. Powell, planning director for the Regional Plan Association of New York, prepared a planning survey. The report recommended that a Citizens Advisory Committee be established for several reasons. It would help officials formulate long range development goals and policies; it would help arouse citizen interest and understanding in the borough's basic problems; and it would help focus thinking on the social and human qualities, values and characteristics that should be preserved and enhanced. Finally, it would express the opinions and constructive advice on those specific action programs as recommended by the technical studies of the planning program. Martin hoped to establish this committee in early 1959.

As the 1950s neared their end, the A&P Super Market at South Fourth and Raritan Avenues asked permission for an addition to its building. A New Brunswick synagogue purchased land at 220 Denison Street and a variance was given to the Trinity Methodist Church for an addition at Montgomery Street. Hurricane Connie hit Highland Park early Saturday morning, August 13, 1955, causing considerable damage. There were fallen trees and flooded cellars. Electrical power was out for some time. The original sewage treatment plant that had begun operating in December 1936 was abandoned on January 23, 1958, upon the town's connection to the Middlesex County trunk sewer. The old treatment plant was put to use storing the Recreation Commission's equipment. The Committee on Health and Welfare set up a definite system of handling health complaints. The processing of a food handler's license was facilitated and classes were conducted on the proper procedures for cleaning utensils. A new forty-nine-star flag displayed in Council Chambers was presented by Highland Park Post 88 of the American Legion. The borough's street lighting modernization program, which installed tall cobra-headed street lights, was being instituted from the Albany Street Bridge to the monument at the crossroads of Raritan and Woodbridge Avenues. Miniature golf, once popular in the 1930s, became popular again. Applications were received for a course at the southeast corner of Raritan Avenue and Columbia Street by Robert Fuller and for a course at 416 Raritan Avenue by Walter R. Rittrenhouse. Chanticleer Broadcasting Company requested to buy additional land around its radio transmitter. A polio benefit basketball game was held at the high school and St. Paul's Church announced the opening of a new recreation center. The New Brunswick postmaster said there would be house to house mail delivery on South Sixth between Benner and Mansfield Streets and on Madison Avenue north of Harrison Avenue. House delivery would also be extended to Hilton Street and Crowells Road. An ordinance was introduced to change the name of a part of Mill Road to Madison Avenue. A new police patrol station wagon equipped with a fire extinguisher and oxygen apparatus was brought into service. Fluoridation of the water supply became an issue in 1958. The Chamber of

Commerce voted to approve fluoridation and the Highland Park Board of Education and the Hamilton School PTA endorsed it in principle. That May, ninety-four members of the Lafayette School PTA came out for fluoridation as did the Highland Park Board of Health. Mr. William F. Ducca was appointed to the office of borough clerk, effective June 30, 1959. He continues to serve the community in the twenty-first century as one of two borough historians.

On January 1, 1960, an organizational meeting took place at the Lafayette School. The new mayor-elect, Democrat Samuel J. Kronman, and Councilmen-elect Kenneth F. Hungrige and Edward R. Isaacs, also Democrats, subscribed to the oath of office. The administration consisted of Mayor Kronman and Councilmen Hungrige, Isaacs, McGrath, Raspa, Tanzman, and Voorhees. Herman B. Hoffman was appointed borough attorney. Joseph J. Schultz was electrical inspector. Kronman wanted to improve the two commercial areas on Raritan and Woodbridge. A Citizens Advisory Committee for Redevelopment and Improvement, established the previous year as an advisory board to the mayor, would continue. Mayor Kronman hoped "appropriate steps might be taken to increase our ratables by attracting desirable business and professional activities." The borough was faced with the rising cost of education and government, and "one of the prime objectives" was to seek additional sources of income. He wanted to use the borough-owned land to get the best possible sale price. Mayor Kronman said fluoridation equipment would be installed and put in operation. Recreation would be expanded. He wanted more books for the library and an ice rink. The sanitary inspector, through the Board of Health, would pursue the enforcement of a lot-cleaning program and the Shade Tree Commission would be enlarged to five. The Finance Committee and tax assessors would complete the study of a personal property tax and the last remaining streets would be paved.

Kronman thought the term of mayor should be three or four years, not two. He wanted the question on the ballot for public approval the following year. Evidently, the voters rejected the plan because Kronman served two-year terms from 1960 through 1965. Democrat Herbert M. Tanzman finished out the decade, serving as mayor from 1966 through 1969, two two-year terms. Mayor Kronman returned in 1970 to serve through 1971, again a two-year term.

The decade of the 1960s was one of great change, both nationally and locally. There were great highs and great lows. Alan Sheppard became the first U.S. astronaut in sub-orbital flight. President John F. Kennedy was assassinated. The Civil Rights Movement gained momentum and protests against our involvement in Vietnam increased. The Raritan Arsenal, Central New Jersey's contribution to two world wars, closed at the same time bomb shelters were being constructed in Highland Park and throughout the country.

The Cold War affected Highland Park as it did the rest of the country. In the fast changing nuclear age no one could predict the future. The borough had adopted a program of planned progress for the future. There were numerous inquiries about the erection of bomb shelters. The mayor reported that the president of the United States had expressed the desire that bomb shelters should be erected wherever possible. The Highland Park Planning Board was asked to conduct a study and make recommendation for their construction.

Locals were also butting heads with the State Highway Department over the speed limit on Raritan Avenue. The state road on Raritan Avenue had a thirty-mile-per-hour limit from New Brunswick to Eighth Avenue. From that point to Metuchen, the limit was set at forty-five miles per hour. Council opposed the higher speeds in the section still in Highland Park. In 1959, a petition was presented against the increased speed limit near Irving School. The state would not allow a traffic signal at the hazardous site and the borough wanted the limit reduced. Mrs. Victoria Calantoni was appointed the first woman marshal in Highland Park and employed as a school crossing guard. It took civil action brought against the state to finally get the limit reduced. Early in January 1960, Borough Attorney Hoffman reported that he had filed a complaint in the Superior Court against the State Highway Department to have the speed limit on Raritan Avenue reduced to thirty miles per hour. In August, it was reported that a semi-actuated traffic signal would be installed at the intersection of Route 27 and South Eleventh Avenue. The borough would pay fifteen percent and the state would pay eighty-five percent. It took one-and-a-half years for the state to do something. A child had been struck by a car. The state agreed to install a light as a compromise if the borough would drop the suit. Council stated the suit would continue until the light was installed. In early September, Herbert Weiss, of 36 Highland Avenue, addressed Council on the subject of the traffic signal at Eleventh and Raritan Avenues. It was his son who had been hit by a car two years earlier. He thanked Council and said it was a wise thing "in selecting Mrs. Victoria Calantoni as crossing guard because she has performed her duties in such a manner as to alleviate all the fears of parents whose children use that crossing."

It was at this time that a local landmark came to an end. In December, Mayor Kronman wrote to the Trenton–New Brunswick Theatre Company of New York, owner of the Park Theatre, which had been abandoned for several years, requesting that action be taken to clean it up. Company executives decided to demolish the structure rather than invest in its upkeep. In February

1961, it was announced that the owners of the Park Theatre had started to raze the building. The mayor, saying it had been an eyesore for a number of years, hoped the property would be converted into a good ratable. Several years later, a three-story apartment building was constructed at this corner.

The Park Theatre and the Highland Park Hotel faded from view at the same time. In April 1961, a variance was granted to the Sibarco Corporation permitting the owners to construct a larger gas station at the triangle formed by the intersection of Woodbridge and Raritan Avenues. In May, Bela, Julia, and Bert Kovacs, owners of the Highland Park Hotel, applied for its liquor license to be transferred to the Highland Inn, not yet constructed. The Kovacs intended to erect a structure costing approximately $75,000 in front of the old dwelling at 85 Raritan Avenue. In November, the construction had been completed and the license was transferred.

By the 1960s, the town's growth had reached the point where six council members were responsible for forty-two individual phases of the borough government. Highland Park had fifty-three full time employees. There were three part-time advisors. There were fourteen voluntary committees and boards with 150 volunteers. The Fire Department, First Aid Squad, and Police Reserve were all volunteers. The borough tax rate was to be reduced by four points to $2.19 per $100 assessed valuation. However, with the proposed budget of the Board of Education and county taxes, the overall rate would be $9.31, an increase of seventy-one points over the 1959 rate of $8.60. A survey showed ninety-two percent were opposed to the proposed school budget for 1960.

In 1961, two million dollars worth of building permits were issued. Approximately $1,400,000 were for commercial buildings and apartment houses that contained one and two bedrooms. The Board of Adjustment granted Dr. Frank W. Pisciotta permission to erect a gasoline station at Raritan and Tenth Avenues. The high-rise on South Adelaide Avenue and Valley Place was approved and another high-rise apartment project on Raritan Avenue near the Albany Street Bridge at Lincoln Avenue would soon be erected. The Orchard Gardens project prompted the name change of Spring Street to Aurora and to become part of that street.

The library, built in 1959, was enlarged in 1967. Another developer oversaw the transformation of the Acme Market next to the Masonic Hall. Dr. Nathaniel Frankel purchased the old building and parking lot on Raritan Avenue formerly owned by the Acme Food Stores. The purchaser would erect a modern professional building and Councilman Tanzman helped convince the Metropolitan Insurance Company to locate here. It was a new ratable. The most shocking change, however, was the destruction of the Masonic Temple. Still a vibrant entertainment and commercial center, the building was greatly damaged in March 1965, when raging flames destroyed the upper story of the imposing structure. The lower floor remains today as a one-story commercial building.

In the 1960s, the Jewish population continued to increase. The Board of Adjustment recommended a variance to be granted to Highland Park Conservative Temple for an extension to its building on the corner of South Third Avenue and Benner Street. The Sephardic congregation Etz Ahaim's new temple at 230 Denison Street was dedicated.

Herbert and Carolyn Schwartz stated there was a desire to erect a building to be used as a U.S. Post Office on Raritan Avenue near South Fourth Avenue. The land abutted property owned by the borough, and South Fourth Avenue could be used as an access point to its driveway. Mayor Kronman was pleased that Highland Park would get a modern post office.

Despite commercial successes along Raritan Avenue, Highland Park was having problems with its industries. Herman Aschenback, a resident at 61 Cleveland Avenue, complained of the smoke and air pollution coming from the John Waldron Company. There were also problems with the behavior of some employees from the Ross Industries plant who worked late at night. In September 1961, Jack Turner, president of Turner Tubes Corporation, announced the removal of his plant due to the limited space in downtown Highland Park. He thanked Council for its cooperation over the years. The factory had three additions in the last twenty-five years, the most recent only one-and-a-half years before. Turner Tubes had been in Highland Park for sixty-three years. Jack Turner's grandfather started the company in 1898, but 1962 saw it leave for South Brunswick.

The population growth that had begun in the post-war years continued into the 1960s. The increase in residential dwellings and the birth of the baby boomers strained the educational system and it was soon evident that the school facilities were insufficient. In the 1960s, Highland Park had three elementary schools: Lafayette, Hamilton, and Irving. The high school had a new wing of classrooms named the "English wing" and a new middle school was built in 1967. Bartle School, located on Grove and Mansfield Streets near Fifth, conformed to an earlier plan of locating public buildings along the Fifth Avenue corridor. Named after Chrissie Bartle, the first teacher in the school system, the building served as a middle school in its early years and was later converted to an elementary school. The school population increased and in 1968 major renovations were made to Irving School and the high school, which received what is called the "science wing." Renovations were also completed at the Hamilton and Lafayette Schools.

In the 1970s, the country was involved in the unpopular Vietnam War, resulting in much social unrest. The borough's population had reached 14,458 and it has remained around this number since then. Yet Highland Park was still developing and growing. The library expanded again in 1977. A new modern Borough Hall was completed in 1979 on South Fifth Avenue. On Cedar Lane, off River Road, 350 apartment units were under construction. A business development and employment counselor, paid by a Community Development Block Grant from the U.S. Department of Housing and Urban Development, was hired in 1979 to encourage business development in the borough and to act as an employment counselor to businesses and individuals. In 1978, Raritan Avenue, the responsibility of the New Jersey Department of Transportation, was resurfaced and the discarded granite Belgian blocks became coveted elements in many borough residents' gardens. Also in 1978, Highland Park resident Arno A. Penzias received a Nobel Prize in Physics. Penzias was an astrophysicist at Bell Labs. The Highland Park Historical Commission got its start in the 1970s and was the active agent collecting historical photographs, documents, and oral histories of long-time residents. This book owes a great deal to the earliest stewards of Highland Park's historical documents and the passing of their collective knowledge to the next group.

The other mayors during this decade were all Democrats. G. Paul Beck, the first mayor elected for a four year term, served from 1972 to 1975. Harold Berman served his first four-year term from 1976 through 1979. Berman was beaten in the June primary by Charles W. Muhollen, who served from 1980 through 1983. Berman returned in 1984 to serve until 1987. Highland Park's political system continues to generate races of Democrat against Democrat and elections are determined in the June primaries. The Republican party has become a very small minority in town. Elected in 1973, the first woman to serve on Borough Council was Helen Hurd.

Highland Park showed innovative governmental practices when, in 1978, the Commission on the Handicapped was formed. The purpose of this commission was to asses the needs of handicapped residents and advise them of available programs and services. At the time of its formation, this group was the second local commission of its kind in the United States. The Human Rights Commission, an advisory body to reduce discrimination in housing, employment, or public services based on race, creed, sex, color, national origin, ancestry, age, or marital status, was also established. The 1970s saw a growing diversity of ages, incomes, ethnic origins, and religion among Highland Park residents. There were three synagogues: Congregation Etz Ahaim, Congregation Ohav Emeth at 415 Raritan Avenue, and the Highland Park Conservative

Temple. The Greek Orthodox Church relocated to larger facilities in Piscataway and sold its church on River Road to the congregation of Saint Mary of Zyrovicy Byelorussian Autocephalic, a Russian Orthodox group.

The Jewish population had become so important that in 1978, Highland Park became the site of New Jersey's first eruv, which extended from the U.S. 1 Highway Bridge west to the railroad span on River Road. This boundary circling the borough symbolically extends biblical space outside an individual's house and, in essence, allows actions interpreted as work, such as pushing a baby carriage or carrying keys, to take place in the larger public areas on Saturdays. The eruv installation was the result of the influx of strictly observant Jews interested in following the laws of the Sabbath.

In May 1978, the Office of Educational Opportunities of the State Department of Education directed the Board of Education to desegregate the schools by correcting an imbalance of minority enrollment in two of the three elementary schools. Irving had thirty-eight percent minority students, Hamilton had nine percent, and Lafayette had eighteen percent. The State Office of Equal Educational Opportunity ordered the board to correct the situation. Plans were developed to close one school and a "pairing system" for elementary grades was discussed. In 1979, Hamilton School was closed. Highland Park did not have school bussing until the fall of 1979, except for students with special needs. Beginning in the 1979–1980 school year, children who lived more than seven-tenths of a mile from the primary schools and one mile from the intermediate school were transported.

Economic revitalization and downtown redevelopment were proposed. In 1982, High School Athletics Director Jay Dakelman was named National Athletic Director of the Year. In 1984, Charles Figg, a Democrat, became the first African American elected to Council. The *Highland Park Herald* published by Forbes Newspapers was established as the weekly newspaper covering local events. Harold Berman won back his seat as mayor and served again from 1984 through 1987. Jeffrey Orbach became the first Republican mayor since 1955, and served from 1988 to 1991.

In the early 1980s, Highland Park experienced the concurrent problems of declining school enrollment, inflation, decreasing economic resources, and the order to desegregate the neighborhood schools. After closing Hamilton as a school, the Board of Education moved its offices into the newly renovated quarters at Hamilton Center, 319 North Third Avenue. The board's desire was to reuse Hamilton School as a community center and the room on the basement floor was made available for community activities. In 1984, newspapers ads attempted to lure out-of-district students to bring tuition money to the borough. The need to integrate all students resulted in the contested plan of Irving School becoming the school for all kindergarteners, first, second, and third graders; the middle school serving all the fourth through seventh graders; and the older students going to the high school. Lafayette School closed after June 30, 1983. The Lafayette Redevelopment Project commenced and Lafayette School was advertised for sale and development. The proceeds were to be used to renovate the remaining facilities, which included providing a new all-weather track and a federally mandated (under Title X) girls' locker room. Lafayette School was sold to developer Michael Kaplan for $195,000. The company converted classrooms into bedrooms and living rooms, and several former students actually reside in the converted school.

In 1985, a new public works building was built on Valentine Street near Donaldson Park. It was completed in December and would be formally dedicated. Highland Park's motto became *locus bonus* meaning "good place." There were proposals for development on unimproved borough-owned property between the banks of the Raritan and River Road, but no construction took place, and after years of negotiating, the land was set aside as a native plant reserve. In 1986, the Planning Board approved a 108-unit condominium development, L'Ambiance, on lands next to the Mill Brook formerly owned by the Sisters of the Cenacle, the Johnson family before them, and earliest of all in 1683, Henry and Mary Greenland. A luxury highrise would soon be constructed on South Adelaide Avenue next to the YW-YMHA. In 1987, Council finalized plans for a second Senior Citizens Apartment complex. A sixty-five unit, low to moderate income, senior citizen housing complex was approved for property on South Sixth Avenue. Mandatory recycling began in 1988.

Approximately 4,000 people lined Raritan Avenue from New Brunswick to Edison in the Hands Across America event on May 25, 1986. It was a national fundraising program to support the hungry and homeless. In 1987, tragedy struck the community when popular high school principal Bill Donahue was stabbed to death in his home by his daughter's former boyfriend. Repairs on the Albany Street Bridge were completed June 15, 1988 with each of the four lanes widened. On March 2, 1987, the town held a forum on AIDS.

By 1987, the borough was at a crossroads. As one of highest taxed communities in the state, there was a move for economic redevelopment. Of the borough's 1.8 square miles of land, most was fully developed. One third was non-taxable property—the county parks, Rutgers's land, public buildings, schools, and houses of worship. With little industrial development and a small commercial district, the property tax burden fell on homeowners. There were plans to create a gateway area of economic development on Raritan Avenue from Second Avenue down to Adelaide Avenue.

The recent past is difficult to analyze and we would like to leave it up to the next generation to decide what is important from all that is occurring now. Highland Park entered the last decade of the twentieth century under the leadership of Republican Mayor Jeff Orbach, who served until 1991 along with an all Democratic Council. He was defeated by Democrat and former Councilman H. James Polos, who served from 1992 through 1999. Highland Park returned to its strong and total Democratic party rule, which it has maintained since then.

By the 1990s, high school enrollment dropped to 550 from a high of 900 in the late 1960s. There were ideas to bring the seventh and eighth graders to the high school. In 1993 and 1994, plans were developed to construct a new middle school next to the high school in an effort to have the students in adjacent, but separate, buildings. The first referendum was defeated. On February 15, 1994, after months of campaigning guided by the Parent Teacher Organization (PTO), the voters approved a $15 million plan to fund renovations and improvements at the high school, Irving School, and Bartle School. Although always receiving smaller turn-outs, school budget votes and School Board elections received the same level of campaigning by activist parents as the governmental elections.

The new millennium began with a political coup when Democrat and former School Board member Meryl Frank defeated Mayor Polos in the June primary. She was assisted by a group of supporters who came to be known as the "PTO Moms" to become Highland Park's first female mayor. Mayor Frank printed the image of the first mayor, James Archer, and council taken in 1905 on tee-shirts along with her campaign slogan "a glorious past and an inspired future." (*See p. 79.*) As conformist as those all-male councils of the past were, the opposite is true today. As we hope has been well documented, complaints over high taxes and the lack of municipal services are not new. However, what is new is that they are joined by discussions about issues of tolerance, diversity, equality, accessibility, and inclusion in today's Highland Park.

BIBLIOGRAPHY

A Directory of the City of New Brunswick for 1855. New Brunswick: J. Terhune, 1855.

Atlas of Middlesex County. Philadelphia: Everts & Stewart, 1876.

Benedict, William H. *New Brunswick in History.* New Brunswick: privately printed, 1925.

Clayton, W. Woodford. *History of Union and Middlesex Counties, New Jersey.* Philadelphia: Everts & Peck, 1882.

First Baptist Church of Highland Park, NJ. "The Complete Hostess." Whatsoever Class: Privately printed, 1929.

Gordon, Thomas F. *A Gazetteer of the State of New Jersey Comprehending a General View of Its Physical and Moral Condition, Together with a Topographical and Statistical Account of its Counties, Towns, Villages, Canals, Rail Roads, &c.* Trenton, NJ: Daniel Fenton, Publisher, 1834.

Gunn, Alexander. *Memoirs of the Rev. John H. Livingston, D.D.S.T.P. Prepared in Compliance with a Request of the General Synod of the Dutch Reformed Church in North America.* New York: Rutgers Press, 1829.

Kolva, Jeanne. National Register nomination for the Livingston Manor Historic District. Washington, D.C.: National Park Service, 2004.

Kolva, Jeanne and Wayne T. McCabe. *A Penny A View . . . An Album of Postcard Views . . . Highland Park, NJ.* Newton, NJ: Historic Preservation Alternatives, 2005.

Kolva, Jeanne and Joanne Pisciotta. *Images of America: Highland Park, New Jersey.* Charleston, SC: Arcadia Publishing, 1999.

Kraft, Herbert C. *The Lenape-Delaware Indian Heritage: 10,000 B.C. to 2000 A.D.* Lenape Books, 2001.

Lee, Francis Bazley. *New Jersey as a Colony and as a State: One of the Original Thirteen.* New York: Publishing Society of New Jersey, 1902.

McCormick, Richard P. *New Jersey From Colony to State, 1609–1789.* Revised edition. Newark, NJ: New Jersey Historical Society, 1981.

Meeker, Edwin R. *New Jersey: A Historical, Commercial, and Industrial Review.* Elizabeth, NJ: Commonwealth Publishing Co., 1906.

National Park Service. *Lincoln Highway: Special Resource Study—Environmental Assessment.* Washington, D.C.: U.S. Department of the Interior, 2004.

Moore, S.S. and T.W. Jones. *Traveller's Directory: The Main Road from Philadelphia to Washington.* Philadelphia: Printed for Mathew Carey, 1802.

New Brunswick and Its Industries. New Brunswick: A.E. Gordon, Times Printing House, 1873.

New Jersey Historical Commission. "Steal Away, Steal Away:" A Guide to the Underground Railroad in New Jersey. Trenton, NJ: 2002.

Porter, Richard L. "A Chronological History of the Mercer/Bray/Snyder Mill Property, Borough of Highland Park, Middlesex County, New Jersey." New Brunswick: Center for Public Archaeology, 1992.

Saunders, Agnes Glen and Louis Du Bois. "Notes on the History of Piscatawaytown, Raritan Township, Middlesex County, New Jersey." Raritan Township: Privately printed, 1937.

Schultise, Samuel J. "The Public Schools of Highland Park: 1885–1940." Highland Park: Privately printed, 1940.

Segoine, H. Richard. "Remarks regarding the Livingston Property in Livingston Manor, Highland Park." New Brunswick Historical Club papers, 1951. Special Collections and University Archives, Rutgers University.

Siebert, Wilbur H. *The Underground Railroad: From Slavery to Freedom.* Reprint edition. New York: Arno Press, 1968.

Spies, Stacy E. National Register nomination for the Livingston Homestead. Washington, D.C.: National Park Service, 2001.

Vermuele, C.C. "With Coming of Henry Greenland, Raritan Landing Came into Existence." *The Sunday Times.* New Brunswick: November 30, 1930.

Wall, John P. *History of Middlesex County, New Jersey, 1664–1920.* New York: Lewis Historical Publishing Co., 1921.

———. "New Brunswick in the Critical Period of the Revolution." New Brunswick: Privately printed, 1908.

Watkins, J. Elfreth. *The Camden and Amboy Railroad: Origin and Early History.* Washington, D.C.: Gedney & Roberts, 1892.

INDEX